HIKING GREAT SMOKY MOUNTAINS NATIONAL PARK

D1166402

Contact

Help Us Keep This Guide Up to Date

Every effort has been made by the author and editors to make this guide as accurate and useful as possible. However, many things can change after a guide is published—trails are rerouted, regulations change, techniques evolve, facilities come under new management, etc.

We would love to hear from you concerning your experiences with this guide and how you feel it could be improved and kept up to date. While we may not be able to respond to all comments and suggestions, we'll take them to heart and we'll also make certain to share them with the author. Please send your comments and suggestions to the following address:

> The Globe Pequot Press
> Reader Response/Editorial Department
> P.O. Box 480
> Guilford, CT 06437

Or you may e-mail us at:

> editorial@GlobePequot.com

Thanks for your input, and happy travels!

Hiking
GREAT SMOKY MOUNTAINS NATIONAL PARK

Kevin Adams

FALCONGUIDES ®

GUILFORD, CONNECTICUT
HELENA, MONTANA

AN IMPRINT OF THE GLOBE PEQUOT PRESS

FALCONGUIDES®

Maps created by Jim Miller/Fennana Design © Morris Book Publishing, LLC.
All photos by Kevin Adams unless otherwise noted.

ISSN 1542-0477
ISBN 978-0-7627-1110-9

Manufactured in the United States of America
First Edition/Eighth Printing

*For Alecia, Laurie,
and Steve*

To buy books in quantity for corporate use
or incentives, call **(800) 962–0973**
or e-mail **premiums@GlobePequot.com**.

The author and The Globe Pequot Press assume no liability for accidents happening to, or injuries sustained by, readers who engage in the activities described in this book.

Contents

Locator Map

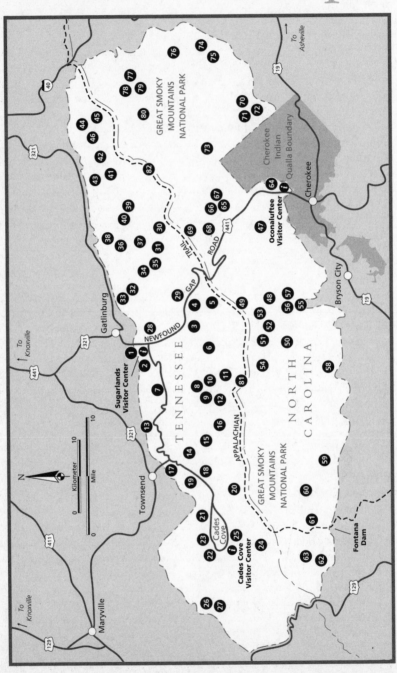

Northeast Section

Southwest Section

Southeast Section

Appalachian Trail

Acknowledgments

It seems that I must have asked at least a million questions of park rangers, interpretive volunteers, resource administrators, biologists, and even park trash collectors in preparing this book. And you know what? It seems that I received about a million answers. Although the Smokies continue to operate on a shoestring budget like most other parks—they have to keep doing more and more with fewer people and less money—the park rangers and other employees are always there with a smile and a helping hand. It is impossible to produce a book like this without them. I wish I could name every park employee, whether I spoke with them or not. Thanks to every single one of you for what you do and for the help you've given me.

Two people deserve special thanks. Thanks to Jill Gill for helping take care of so many of the little tasks and errands that always take a backseat when the "serious" writing begins. And thanks to Janet Johnson for her thorough and professional review of the manuscript—a Herculean task given the absurdly short time frame I gave her. And for being in the right place at the right time, thank you Austin and Jearleen Adams.

Thanks also to my brother, Steve, for performing his usual editorial mastery with my sometimes incoherent wording, and to all the people at Falcon and Globe Pequot who helped put this book in your hands, especially Scott Adams and Paulette Baker.

Finally, there is one person I can never thank enough. No matter how many days I spend in the field or how many hours I spend in front of the computer, she is always there for me. A special thanks to my wife, Patricia.

Regional Divisions

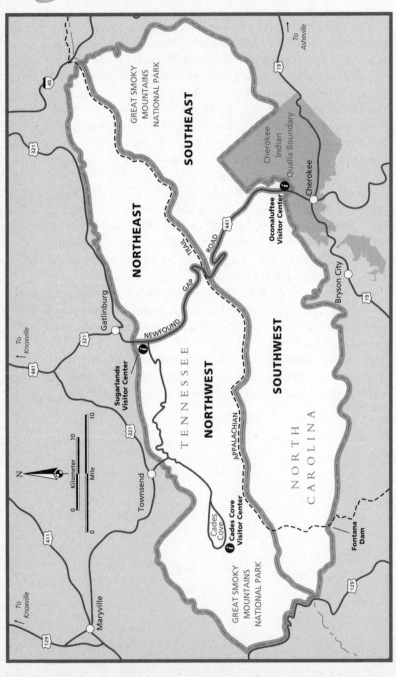

USGS Quads

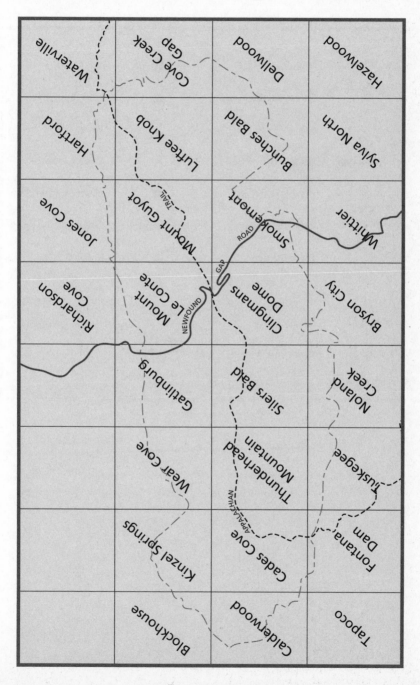

Map Legend

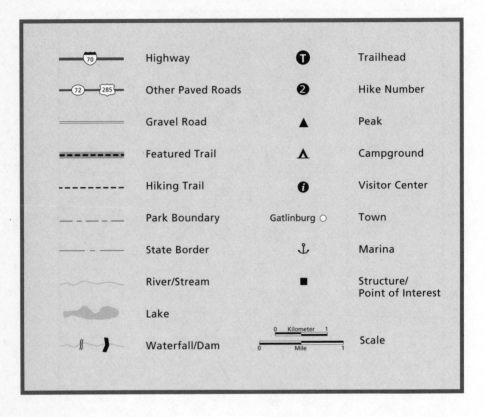

Highway		Trailhead	
Other Paved Roads		Hike Number	
Gravel Road		Peak	
Featured Trail		Campground	
Hiking Trail		Visitor Center	
Park Boundary	Gatlinburg	Town	
State Border		Marina	
River/Stream		Structure/Point of Interest	
Lake			
Waterfall/Dam		Scale	

Preface: The Great Smokies

We've always known that the Smokies are special. The Native Americans who took game here knew it. The early settlers who used the hollows to conceal their moonshine stills knew it. Even the loggers who raped the mountainsides of their trees knew it. Today, millions of people discover, or rediscover, this special place every year.

You won't find the country's highest peaks here nor its biggest waterfalls, widest rivers, or deepest canyons. No lakes, seashores, glaciers, volcanoes, or geysers exist in the Smokies. They aren't needed here.

"The trees." That's the answer you often hear when asking first-time visitors what impresses them the most about the Smokies. Except for a few mountaintop balds and a few fields in lowland valleys, trees cover nearly all the park. Living beneath all these trees is an amazing variety of flora and fauna. Flowing underneath the trees are hundreds of miles of cascading streams, from tiny branchlets to small rivers.

An experience here is different from that in many other national parks. It is more intimate, more down-to-earth.

It is Great.

LeConte Lodge.

Introduction: What It's Really Like

Here are a few things you might want to know about hiking in Great Smoky Mountains National Park.

Prime season: Different seasons offer different experiences. In spring the park's famous wildflowers bloom, with mid-April being about peak time. Mid-October is usually peak for autumn leaf color, but expect heavy visitation during the entire month of October. Winter is delightfully free of traffic jams and provides the clearest long-range views. Summer has traffic jams, and smog can severely restrict the views.

Weather: Snow is common in the higher elevations from November through March, and you should expect it in October and April. Spring is fickle, with warm, sunny days changing to cold, snowy ones in a heartbeat. Summer is hot and hazy, and afternoon thunderstorms are common. Autumn has wonderful weather, with a good number of warm, blue-sky days and clear, crisp nights.

Black bears: The Great Smokies have many black bears, and seeing one is always a possibility—and a thrill. Keep that encounter safe by reading Be Bear Aware, preceding the hikes.

Bugs: Mosquitoes are typically not a problem in the Smokies, since there is little standing water for them to breed. What *is* irritating here are no-see-ums and blackflies.

Finding solitude: Some trails are overcrowded; others receive little use yet offer a hiking experience just as good as the crowded trails. The Trail Finder lists some of the most popular trails. Avoiding hordes of people is simple: Don't hike the most popular trails except on winter weekdays, when your experience will range from seeing a few people to having the hike to yourself.

Thieves: Thieves prowl the remote parking areas looking for vehicles left overnight or during the day. Even vehicles parked within plain sight of major roads have been broken into and vandalized. The hike descriptions alert you to places that have had recurring problems, but you should be careful no matter where you leave your vehicle. Don't leave anything in sight, and don't leave a note on the dashboard saying how long you're going to be out. Using a blanket or jacket to cover up stuff is like displaying a sign for thieves that you're hiding something valuable.

Large furry things on the road: When hurrying to get to the trailhead in the early morning hours, or when feeling anxious while driving home in the evening, be especially watchful for white-tailed deer and other wildlife on the roadways. Hitting a deer will ruin your day—it's even harder on the animal.

Small flat things on the road: It's sad to see all the roadkill in a place as beautiful as the Smokies. Avoid adding to the flattened fauna by slowing down and watching the road. Box turtles and frogs like to come out after a rain in warm weather, and on a warm, wet night, the frogs are very active.

Water, water, everywhere: Water is everywhere in the Smokies, and nearly every drop of it started out as either rain or condensation. You're likely to have to hike in rain no matter when you visit the park. In winter it can rain solid for days. Summer can bring a thunderstorm every afternoon for weeks. The moral: Always carry rain gear with you, regardless of the weather conditions when you set out.

Planning Your Trip

Your hiking trip to Great Smoky Mountains National Park can be pleasant and stress-free when you plan it well. The following information will help you plan your adventure.

Getting to Great Smoky Mountains National Park

It's estimated that two-thirds of the people in the United States are within a day's drive of the Smokies. The park is located on the North Carolina–Tennessee border, near the northern border of Georgia. The major interstate accesses are I–40 from the east and west, I–81 from the north, and I–75 from the north and south. Both I–40 and I–75 pass through Knoxville, Tennessee, just northwest of the park and the nearest major city. I–81 joins I–40 east of Knoxville. A major access highway from the south is U.S. 23 from Atlanta, which joins U.S. 441 northeast of Atlanta. U.S. 441 is the only transmountain highway in the Smokies, and a large network of smaller roads provides access from all directions. Study a road map to determine the best route from your location.

On your first Smokies trip, you'll likely enter the park at one of two main entrances: Cherokee, North Carolina, or Gatlinburg, Tennessee. Newfound Gap Road (U.S. 441) connects the two towns, crossing over the Smokies' crest at Newfound Gap in the process and essentially splitting the park in half. The main park visitor centers are located a short distance from each town: Oconaluftee Visitor Center for Cherokee and Sugarlands Visitor Center for Gatlinburg. Only one other true visitor center lies within park boundaries: a small center located at the Cable Mill area in Cades Cove. Numerous ranger stations and campgrounds provide additional sources of information throughout the park.

If you are flying to the park and renting a car, you will fly into either Knoxville, Tennessee, or Asheville, North Carolina. Knoxville is a little closer and has a larger airport. If heading to the park's Gatlinburg entrance from the Knoxville airport, you will take U.S. 129 (Alcoa Highway) north to I–40 in the heart of Knoxville. Take I–40 east to Tennessee 66 at exit 407 (you will see the signs for the park); follow TN 66 south to Sevierville, where you'll pick up U.S. 441 and follow it south through Pigeon Forge and into Gatlinburg. If heading to the park's Townsend entrance in the western end of the park, take U.S. 129 south from the Knoxville airport and pick up U.S. 321/Tennessee 73 in Maryville. Follow U.S. 321 north to Townsend and continue straight where U.S. 321 turns left (you will see the signs for the park). The Townsend entrance is becoming increasingly popular; it is the closest access to Cades Cove, one of the most popular features of the park.

From the Asheville airport you will take I–26 north to I–40 and go west on I–40 to U.S. 23/74 at exit 27. U.S. 23/74 is called the Great Smoky Mountains Expressway and offers numerous approaches to the park. Most visitors will follow one of the two main routes from the expressway: U.S. 19 through Maggie Valley and into Cherokee or U.S. 441 into Cherokee. All routes are well signed.

The 469-mile-long Blue Ridge Parkway terminates at Newfound Gap Road between Cherokee and Oconaluftee Visitor Center. The Parkway is the nation's most visited unit of the national park system, with around twenty million visitors per year. Great Smoky Mountains National Park is second, with around ten million visitors.

If you don't already know something about the park, one of these four accesses is likely to be your entry point. There are many additional vehicle entrances to the park, but a first-time visitor will want to drive the main roads initially to get a handle on the park before branching out.

Finally, a word of warning. First-time park visitors are often startled by the juxtaposition of the park and ultra-touristy Gatlinburg and Pigeon Forge, 5 miles north of Gatlinburg and home to Dollywood. Although not exactly a wilderness experience, these towns provide valuable services, including accommodations for those who aren't into camping or backpacking.

Supplies and Services

Unlike many other national parks, Great Smoky Mountains National Park does not have any public lodging, food, or fuel services within its borders. (LeConte Lodge on Mt. LeConte is the only exception, but you have to hike 5 miles to get there.) The surrounding towns offer everything you need, but the services are seasonal at many places. The following immediate surrounding towns have basic year-round services: Cherokee, Maggie Valley, and Bryson City, North Carolina; Gatlinburg and Townsend, Tennessee. Other small communities have gas stations and small stores that are open year-round, but most other services close for the winter. Many businesses close for the season even in some of the larger towns, like Bryson City and Cherokee.

Park frontcountry (vehicle) campgrounds offer minimal services, such as ice, telephones, and snack machines. The Cades Cove frontcountry campground has a camp store with basic food and camping supplies, but it closes in winter.

Getting Backcountry Permits

In Great Smoky Mountains National Park, you must have a permit for any overnight stay in the backcountry. The Backcountry Camping Permit system is designed to protect the park's natural and cultural resources, as well as to provide the best backcountry experience for hikers.

You can get your permit from Oconaluftee or Sugarlands Visitor Center, ranger stations, most frontcountry campgrounds, and at some trail information boards. The permit is free and is obtained through a self-registration process. In the Smokies you must camp at a designated backcountry campsite unless you obtain a special cross-country permit, available only from designated park rangers. Many campsites are rationed due to heavy use, and these sites require reservations. If the site where you wish to camp is not rationed, simply read the instructions on the permit, fill it out, and place one copy in the permit box. If you choose a rationed site, you have to call the Backcountry Reservation Office to obtain a reservation. (Be prepared with alternative dates if you call at the last minute.) The Reservation Office will give you a number to write on your permit. The office is open seven days a week, from 8:00 A.M. to 6:00 P.M. EST. Call (865) 436–1231 for reservations. The general backcountry information number is (865) 436–1297.

Backcountry Campsites

All backcountry campsites in the Smokies are numbered, and all shelters are named. The sites have names, too, but only the numbers are referred to on trail maps and when obtaining permits. All locations that provide backcountry permits have a map showing the location of sites and a listing of rationed sites. While the list of rationed sites remains fairly constant, it can change in response to use patterns.

All sites and shelters have a water source nearby, either a spring or a stream. Springs are not always dependable, and it's a good idea to check ahead before beginning an overnight trip in dry conditions. Rangers may not know whether a particular spring is dry, but they can give you a general idea of conditions.

Another consideration is that the park closes campsites occasionally due to bear activity or other reasons. The park posts these closings where permits are obtained, but you don't want to find out at the last minute that the site you've planned on is closed. Call the permit office at (865) 436–1231 to make sure your site is open before you head out.

The following backcountry campsites are rationed and require a reservation:

	All shelters	38	Mount Sterling
9	Anthony Creek	47	Enloe Creek
10	Ledbetter Ridge	50	Lower Chasteen Creek
13	Sheep Pen Gap	55	Pole Road
23	Camp Rock	57	Bryson Place
24	Rough Creek	61	Bald Creek
29	Otter Creek	71	CCC Camp
36	Upper Walnut Bottom	83	Bone Valley
37	Lower Walnut Bottom	113	Birch Spring Gap

Backcountry Use Regulations

In the Great Smokies, do:

- Have a permit to camp in the backcountry.
- Follow all instructions on the permit, and keep the permit in your possession while hiking.
- Camp only at designated campsites and shelters.
- Build fires only in established fire rings at designated campsites or shelters.
- Use only wood that is dead and down to build fires. Backpacking stoves are encouraged.
- Suspend your food and odorous items from the provided suspension cables.
- Carry out all trash. If you can pack it in, you can pack it out.
- Have a valid state fishing permit from either North Carolina or Tennessee if you fish in the park.

In the Great Smokies, do *not*:

- Carry firearms.
- Feed, harass, or intentionally disturb wildlife.
- Cut, carve, or deface trees or buildings.
- Take pets into the backcountry.
- Make campsite "improvements," such as fire rings, rock walls, or drainage trenches.
- Use a wheeled vehicle or cart on most hiking trails. The exceptions for bicycles are Gatlinburg and Oconaluftee River Trails and the lower portions of Deep Creek and Indian Creek Trails. The exceptions for wheeled carts are the lower portions of Hazel Creek, Forney Creek, and Noland Creek.
- Cut switchbacks.
- Wash dishes or bathe (with soap) in park streams.
- Pitch a tent at backcountry shelters.
- Dispose of human waste within 100 feet of a campsite or water source or within sight of a trail. Bury feces in a 6-inch-deep hole.
- Gather ramps. The park no longer allows picking these onionlike plants.
- Stay more than one night in a row at a shelter or more than three consecutive nights at a campsite.

For More Information

For a great summary of basic facts on visiting Great Smoky Mountains National Park, call the main park number and ask for a copy of the *Smokies Guide*, a free newspaper published by the Great Smoky Mountains Natural History Association. You can also get a copy at park visitor centers. The publication contains information about visitor services, trip planning, updates on road and campground closures, emergency numbers, ranger-led activities, and general park features, plus lots more useful information.

You might consider becoming a member of the association. Membership entitles you to a 15 percent discount on books and other items at park visitor centers; a subscription to the *Smokies Guide*; the association's newsletter, *The Bearpaw*; the park science bulletin, *Sightline*; and other benefits. Memberships start at only $25 per year. To join call (865) 436–7318.

To contact the park, call or write:
Superintendent
Great Smoky Mountains National Park
107 Park Headquarters Road
Gatlinburg, TN 37738
www.nps.gov/grsm
Main park number: (865) 436–1200
General backcountry information: (865) 436–1297
Backcountry campsite reservations: (865) 436–1231

Commercial shuttle services:
Gatlinburg/Greenbrier/Cosby Area
A Walk in the Woods: (865) 436–8283
Laurel Springs: (423) 487–5081 or 487–5706
C&O Taxi: (865) 436–5893

Bryson City Area
Smoky Mountain Shuttles: (828) 488–2133

Fontana Area
Fontana Village (boat shuttles and land shuttles only between village
    and dam): (828) 498–2211
Charlie Watts: (828) 479–2504
The Hike Inn: (828) 479–3677

Using This Guidebook

The following sections will help you use this book effectively.

Types of Trips

Hikes have been split into the following categories.

Loop: The hike starts and finishes at the same trailhead, with no (or very little) retracing of your steps. Sometimes the definition of loop is stretched to included "lollipops" and trips that involve a short walk at the end of the road to get back to your vehicle.

Shuttle: A point-to-point trip that requires two vehicles (one left at each end of the trail) or a prearranged pickup. One good way to manage the logistical problems of shuttles is to arrange for another party to start at the other end of the trail. Trade keys when you meet that party on the trail, and each of you drive the other's vehicle home. Some shuttle trips are noted as being good "split-party" hikes. This is where your group drops you off and you hike back to meet them at the town or frontcountry campground where you're staying.

Out-and-back: Travel to a specific destination, then retrace your steps back to the trailhead.

Hike Ratings

To help you plan your trip, hikes are rated by difficulty. However, difficulty ratings serve only as a general rule, not the final word. What is difficult to one hiker may be easy to another. In this guidebook, difficulty ratings take into account both how long and how strenuous a route is. Following are general definitions of the ratings.

Easy: Suitable for any hiker, including children and elderly people; without serious elevation gain or hazardous sections.

Moderate: Suitable for hikers who have some experience and at least an average fitness level. Probably not suitable for children or the elderly unless they have above-average fitness. The hike usually includes some hills.

Difficult: Suitable for experienced hikers with an above-average fitness level; sometimes with serious elevation gain and possibly some hazardous conditions.

The Trails

In the Smokies, unlike at some other parks, you can't just strike out and hike wherever you want. The rugged landscape and dense vegetation are not conducive to much off-trail hiking. Besides, doing so can harm the ecosystem, and with more than 800 miles of maintained trails in the park, it's just not necessary. You can have an intimate experience and see everything you'd want to see, right from an official trail. Therefore, every hike in this guidebook uses only officially maintained trails. Some of the routes follow one trail only; others use a combination of several trails. One advantage to this is that you don't have to worry too much about getting lost—*as long as you stay on the trail*. Every trail junction is signed, and the park does a good job of keeping the signs up. (Bears sometimes chew them up, and some of the older ones are rotting away.)

This guidebook includes all the self-guiding nature trails in the park, but it does not include any of the "Quiet Walkways." You see signs indicating these walkways along the main park roads. They have small parking areas so that only a few persons can use the trails at a time. All of them are short and lead to some feature, such as a stream or an old homesite. Part of the charm of these paths is not knowing what's in store until you hike them. So, no clues here. Discover them yourself.

Distances

The distances used in this book come from Park Service information that is accurate and up to date as of this writing. The distances listed on the trail signs and maps, however, are sometimes incorrect. Distances in this book are rounded off to the nearest 0.1 mile.

Maps

The maps in this book serve as general guides only. They do not have sufficient detail and do not cover enough territory to use on their own in the field. You definitely should carry a more-detailed map with you on any hike.

A variety of maps are available for the Great Smokies, but in preparing this book I used the Trails Illustrated map exclusively for planning routes and getting an overall perspective of the hikes. Earthwalk Press also publishes a good map. For checking on detailed features like stream and ridge names, I used the U.S. Geological Survey (USGS) topographical maps. These maps show incredible detail with landscape features, but some are horribly outdated regarding trail routes. The best bet is to carry the USGS topo maps and either the Trails Illustrated or the Earthwalk Press map. All are available from park visitor centers or from the Great Smoky Mountains Natural History Association by calling (865) 436–0120.

Elevation Profiles

Elevation profiles are included with hike descriptions. These charts don't provide a detailed picture of elevation gain or loss on a hike, but they give you a general idea of how much climbing or descending you face on a hike.

Great Smokies Trail Finder

	Easy	Moderate	Difficult
Stream Hikes	5 Road Prong	9 Cucumber Gap and Little River	16 Lynn Camp Prong and Appalachian Trail
	10 Little River	11 Goshen Prong	34 Rainbow Falls
	59 Hazel Creek and Bone Valley	15 Indian Flats Falls	54 Silers Bald and Forney Creek
	68 Kephart Prong	22 Abrams Falls	60 Eagle Creek, Spence Field,
	78 Big Creek	29 Alum Cave Bluffs	and Hazel Creek
		39 Porters Creek	79 Big Creek and Mt. Sterling
		41 Ramsay Cascades	
		67 Bradley Fork and Chasteen Creek	
		74 Boogerman	
		75 Rough Fork and Caldwell Fork	
Hikes with Good Views		21 Rich Mountain Loop	24 Gregory Bald via Cades Cove
		29 Alum Cave Bluffs	31 Mt. LeConte via The Boulevard
		30 Charlies Bunion	35 Mt. LeConte via Rainbow Falls
		40 Brushy Mountain	and Bull Head
			45 Mt. Cammerer
			51 Clingmans Dome
			52 Andrews Bald
			54 Silers Bald and Forney Creek
			61 Shuckstack
			69 Charlies Bunion and Bradley Fork
			77 Mt. Sterling
			79 Big Creek and Mt. Sterling
			80 Big Creek Perimeter Loop
			81 Appalachian Trail West
			82 Appalachian Trail East

Hikes with Big Trees

3 Cove Hardwoods Nature Trail
32 Noah "Bud" Ogle Nature Trail
68 Kephart Prong

7 Laurel Falls and Cove Mountain
39 Porters Creek
41 Ramsay Cascades
42 Albright Grove
67 Bradley Fork and Chasteen Creek
70 Hemphill Bald
74 Boogerman
75 Rough Fork and Caldwell Fork

20 Spence Field via Cades Cove
24 Gregory Bald via Cades Cove
34 Rainbow Falls
35 Mt. LeConte via Rainbow Falls and Bull Head
46 Maddron Bald and Hen Wallow Falls
69 Charlies Bunion and Bradley Fork
79 Big Creek and Mt. Sterling
80 Big Creek Perimeter Loop

Wildflower Hikes

15 Indian Flats Falls
17 Chestnut Top Wildflowers,
22 Abrams Falls
39 Porters Creek
41 Ramsay Cascades
42 Albright Grove
46 Maddron Bald and Hen Wallow Falls
50 Noland Divide
67 Bradley Fork and Chasteen Creek,
73 Hyatt Ridge
74 Boogerman
75 Rough Fork and Caldwell Fork

16 Lynn Camp Prong and Appalachian Trail
24 Gregory Bald via Cades Cove
35 Mt. LeConte via Rainbow Falls and Bull Head
37 Mt. LeConte via Trillium Gap
46 Maddron Bald and Hen Wallow Falls
52 Andrews Bald
53 Forney Ridge and Noland Divide
61 Shuckstack
69 Charlies Bunion and Bradley Fork
79 Big Creek and Mt. Sterling
81 Appalachian Trail West

Hikes to Avoid if You Don't Want to See Lots of People

7 Laurel Falls and Cove Mountain
22 Abrams Falls
29 Alum Cave Bluffs
30 Charlies Bunion
36 Grotto Falls
41 Ramsay Cascades

4 Chimney Tops
34 Rainbow Falls
51 Clingmans Dome
52 Andrews Bald

	Easy	Moderate	Difficult
Hikes to Avoid if You Don't Like Crossing Unbridged Streams	59 Hazel Creek and Bone Valley	23 Cooper Road and Rabbit Creek 26 Pine Mountain and Abrams Falls	53 Forney Ridge and Noland Divide 54 Silers Bald and Forney Creek 60 Eagle Creek, Spence Field, and Hazel Creek 61 Shuckstack
Hikes for People Training to Be Navy Seals			4 Chimney Tops 53 Forney Ridge and Noland Divide 54 Silers Bald and Forney Creek 60 Eagle Creek, Spence Field, and Hazel Creek 61 Shuckstack 69 Charlies Bunion and Bradley Fork 77 Mt. Sterling 81 Appalachian Trail West
Hikes for People Training to Be Couch Potatoes	1 Gatlinburg Trail 10 Little River 28 Sugarlands Valley Nature Trail 33 Twin Creeks 56 Deep Creek Loop 64 Oconaluftee River		
Hikes for People Who Like Cultural History	2 Fighting Creek Nature Trail 8 Elkmont Nature Trail 10 Little River 28 Sugarlands Valley Nature Trail 59 Hazel Creek and Bone Valley 68 Kephart Prong	13 Walker Sisters Home 21 Rich Mountain Loop 43 Old Settlers Trail 75 Rough Fork and Caldwell Fork 76 Little Cataloochee	

Waterfall Hikes		
56 Deep Creek Loop	7 Laurel Falls and Cove Mountain	14 Spruce Flats Falls
78 Big Creek	15 Indian Flats Falls	34 Rainbow Falls
	22 Abrams Falls	38 Baskins Creek Falls
	36 Grotto Falls,	
	41 Ramsay Cascades	
	55 Juney Whank Falls	

Geology Hikes		
78 Big Creek	29 Alum Cave Bluffs	4 Chimney Tops
	30 Charlies Bunion	31 Mt. LeConte via The Boulevard
		35 Mt. LeConte via Rainbow Falls and Bull Head
		81 Appalachian Trail West
		82 Appalachian Trail East

The Author's Favorites		
3 Cove Hardwoods Nature Trail	29 Alum Cave Bluffs	24 Gregory Bald via Cades Cove
5 Road Prong	39 Porters Creek	31 Mt. LeConte via The Boulevard
17 Chestnut Top Wildflowers,	41 Ramsay Cascades	35 Mt. LeConte via Rainbow Falls and Bull Head
32 Noah "Bud" Ogle Nature Trail	73 Hyatt Ridge	46 Maddron Bald and Hen Wallow Falls
68 Kephart Prong		69 Charlies Bunion and Bradley Fork
78 Big Creek		79 Big Creek and Mt. Sterling

Zero Impact

Going into a national park such as Great Smoky Mountains National Park is like visiting a famous museum. You obviously do not want to leave your mark on an art treasure. If everybody going through the museum leaves one little mark, the piece of art will quickly be destroyed—and of what value is a big building full of trashed art? The same goes for a pristine wilderness such as the Smokies, which is as magnificent as any masterpiece by any artist. If we all leave just one little mark on the landscape, the wilderness will soon be despoiled.

A wilderness can accommodate human use as long as everybody behaves responsibly, but a few thoughtless or uninformed visitors can ruin it for everybody who follows. All wilderness users have a responsibility to know and follow the rules of no-trace camping. An important source of these guidelines, including the most updated research, can be found in the book *Leave No Trace*.

Today most wilderness users want to walk softly, but some aren't aware that they have poor manners. Often their actions are dictated by the outdated habits of a previous generation of campers who cut green boughs for evening shelters, built campfires with fire rings, and dug trenches around tents. In the 1950s these "camping rules" may have been acceptable, but they leave long-lasting scars, and today such behavior is absolutely unacceptable. The wilderness is shrinking, and the number of users is mushrooming. More and more camping areas show unsightly signs of heavy use.

Consequently, a new code of ethics is growing out of the necessity of coping with the unending waves of people who want a perfect wilderness experience. Today we all must leave no clues that we have gone before. Canoeists can look behind the canoe and see no trace of their passing. Hikers should have the same goal: Enjoy the wilderness, but leave no trace of your visit.

THREE FALCON PRINCIPLES OF ZERO IMPACT

Leave with everything you brought in.
Leave no sign of your visit.
Leave the landscape as you found it.

Leave nothing, regardless of how small it is, along the trail or at the campsite. Pack out everything, including orange peels, flip tops, cigarette butts, and gum wrappers. Also, pick up any trash that others leave behind.

Follow the main trail. Avoid cutting switchbacks and walking on vegetation beside the trail.

Make It a Safe Trip

The Boy Scouts of America have been guided for decades by what is perhaps the best single piece of safety advice: "Be Prepared!" For starters, this means carrying survival and first-aid materials, proper clothing, compass, and topographic map—and knowing how to use them.

Perhaps the second-best piece of safety advice is to tell somebody where you're going and when you plan to return. Pilots must file flight plans before every trip, and anybody venturing into a blank spot on the map should do the same. File your "flight plan" with a friend or relative—or at the hotel desk—before taking off.

Close behind your flight plan and being prepared with proper equipment is physical conditioning. Being fit not only makes wilderness travel more fun, but it also makes it safer. To whet your appetite for more knowledge of wilderness safety and preparedness, following are a few more tips:

- Check the weather forecast. You don't want to get caught at high altitude by a bad storm or along a stream in a flash flood. Watch cloud formations closely so that you don't get stranded on a ridgeline during a lightning storm. Avoid traveling during prolonged periods of cold weather.
- Keep your party together.
- Study basic survival and first aid before leaving home.
- Don't eat wild plants unless you have positively identified them.
- Before you leave for the trailhead, find out as much as you can about the route, especially the potential hazards.
- Don't exhaust yourself or other members of your party by traveling too far or too fast. Let the slowest person set the pace.
- Don't wait until you're confused to look at your maps. Follow them as you go along, from the moment you start moving up the trail, so that you have a continual fix on your location.
- If you get lost, try not to panic. Sit down and relax for a few minutes while you carefully check your topo map and take a compass reading. Most important, *do not leave the trail.* You are never truly lost while on a trail. Many tragedies have occurred in the Smokies because hikers became twisted around and thought they would be better off by leaving the trail. If you stay on the trail, the chances of meeting another hiker who can help you are much greater (probably impossible if you're off-trail). Also, if you don't make it back when you're supposed to and a search party is sent out, they will scan the trails first.
- Stay clear of all wild animals.
- Take a first-aid kit that includes, at a minimum, the following items: sewing needle, aspirin, antibacterial ointment, two antiseptic swabs, two

butterfly bandages, adhesive tape, four adhesive strips, four gauze pads, two triangular bandages, prescription codeine tablets, two inflatable splints, moleskin or Second Skin for blisters, one roll of 3-inch gauze, a CPR shield, rubber gloves, and lightweight first-aid instructions.

- Take a survival kit that includes, at a minimum, the following items: compass, whistle, matches in a waterproof container, cigarette lighter, candle, signal mirror, flashlight, fire starter, aluminum foil, water purification tablets, space blanket, and flare.
- Last but not least, don't forget that the best defense against unexpected hazards is knowledge. Read up on the latest in wilderness safety information with Falcon's books on the subject—*Wilderness First Aid, Wilderness Survival, Reading Weather,* and *Wild Country Companion.* (Check out the Falcon Web site at www.falcon.com.)

Lightning: You Might Never Know What Hit You

Although the Smoky Mountains aren't high compared with their western counterparts, they're still prone to sudden thunderstorms, especially in July and August. If you get caught by a lightning storm, take special precautions. Remember the following:

- Lightning can travel far ahead of a storm, so be sure to take cover before the storm hits.
- Don't try to make it back to your vehicle. It isn't worth the risk. Instead, seek shelter even if it's only a short way back to the trailhead. Lightning storms usually don't last long, and from a safe vantage point, you might even enjoy the sights and sounds.
- Be especially careful not to get caught on a mountaintop or exposed ridge; under large, solitary trees; in the open; or near standing water.
- Seek shelter in a low-lying area, ideally in a dense stand of small, uniformly sized trees.
- Stay away from anything that might attract lightning, such as metal tent poles, graphite fishing rods, or pack frames.
- Get in a crouch position, and place both feet firmly on the ground.
- Don't walk or huddle together. Instead, stay 50 feet apart so that if somebody gets hit by lightning, others in your party can give first aid.
- If you're in a tent, stay there, in your sleeping bag on your sleeping pad.

Hypothermia: The Silent Killer

Be aware of the dangers of hypothermia—a condition in which the body's internal temperature drops below normal. It can lead to mental and physical collapse—even death.

Hypothermia is caused by exposure to cold and is aggravated by wetness, wind, and exhaustion. The moment you begin to lose heat faster than your body produces it, you're suffering from exposure. Your body starts involuntary exercise, such as shivering, to stay warm and makes involuntary adjustments to preserve normal temperature in vital organs, restricting blood flow to the extremities. Both responses drain your energy reserves. The only way to stop the drain is to reduce the degree of exposure.

With full-blown hypothermia, as energy reserves are exhausted cold reaches the brain, depriving you of good judgment and reasoning power. You won't be aware that this is happening. You lose control of your hands. Your internal temperature slides downward. Without treatment, this slide leads to stupor, collapse, and death.

To defend against hypothermia, stay dry. When clothes get wet, they lose about 90 percent of their insulating value. Wool loses relatively less heat; cotton, down, and some synthetics lose more. Choose rain clothes that cover the head, neck, body, and legs and provide good protection against wind-driven rain. Most hypothermia cases develop in air temperatures between 30 and 50 degrees Fahrenheit, but hypothermia can develop in warmer temperatures.

If your party is exposed to wind, cold, and wet, think hypothermia. Watch yourself and others for these symptoms: uncontrollable fits of shivering; vague, slow, slurred speech; memory lapses; incoherence; immobile or fumbling hands; frequent stumbling or a lurching gait; drowsiness (to sleep is to die); apparent exhaustion; and inability to get up after a rest. When a member of your party has hypothermia, he or she may deny any problem. Believe the symptoms, not the victim. Even mild symptoms demand treatment, as follows:

- Get the victim out of the wind and rain.
- Strip off all wet clothes.
- If the victim is only mildly impaired, give him or her warm drinks. Then get the victim in warm clothes and a warm sleeping bag. Place well-wrapped water bottles filled with heated water close to the victim.
- If the victim is badly impaired, attempt to keep him or her awake. Put the victim in a sleeping bag with another person—both naked. If you have a double bag, put two warm people in with the victim.

Don't Drink the Water

Regardless of how "crystal clear" a stream or spring might appear, there is no guarantee that the water in the Smokies is safe to drink. You don't know what animal might have left its mark five minutes before you got there. All sorts of bacteria, viruses, and parasites could be in the water, including *Giardia lamblia*, a nasty little protozoan that causes severe abdominal cramps and diarrhea.

The best defense against illness is to bring all drinking water to a roiling boil for one minute. It is not necessary to boil the water for five or ten minutes. Boiling water is impractical on many trips, however, so many people (myself included) use pump-style water filters. Most of these types of filters will remove *Giardia* and bacteria, but most viruses are too small to filter. Iodine treatments are often impractical with the cold water temperatures of mountain springs. With very cold water, the time required for iodine to purify the water could be several hours, depending upon the concentration.

Crossing Streams

If you do much hiking in the Smokies, sooner or later you're going to have to ford a stream. In winter and early spring, with water levels at their highest, many streams are too large to rock-hop and must be waded. In summer, when streams are typically at their lowest levels, most creek crossings in the Smokies are rock-hoppable, but the conditions could change quickly if a thunderstorm moves through. During any time of year, prolonged or heavy rains can swell streams to unsafe levels.

Stream crossings in the Smokies are different from those at some other national parks. The creeks here are all steep and rocky mountain streams. When the water is up, they can become raging torrents. If you fall in, the accepted practice of lying on your back and going downstream feet first until you can right yourself still applies, but it may be impossible to do before you crash into a few dozen rocks and fallen trees. These aren't wide glacial or valley rivers we're talking about here. The best advice, of course, is *not* to fall in.

A good idea is to practice. Most creek crossings have bridges or foot logs. Try fording the stream on the upstream side of the foot log, using it to keep your balance. You'll quickly learn how to read currents. Before attempting any ford, consider the following:

- Don't attempt a crossing if you feel unsafe. Never feel embarrassed by being cautious.
- Don't automatically cross at the trail. Search upstream and downstream for a better crossing.
- Loosen the belt straps on your backpack. It will help you maintain your balance as you cross and allow you to quickly get out of the pack if you fall.
- Streams in the Smokies are very cold. Don't attempt a long crossing in bare feet, even in summer, unless you have experience doing so. Your legs can numb, and you can injure your feet on sharp rocks or sticks.
- Many hikers carry lightweight sandals, which work well as creek-crossing shoes and camp shoes.
- In winter, even a short crossing can be dangerous. A good idea is to take off your socks and cross wearing just your boots. Once across, immediately dry your feet and put your socks and boots back on. You can dry your boots by the campfire that night.
- Stay sideways to the current. Turning upstream or downstream greatly increases the force of the current against your body.
- A walking stick can help you keep your balance, but rocky creek bottoms make it difficult to get a good purchase with one. Be sure to plant the stick firmly before taking your next step.

Be Bear Aware

Something happened on May 21, 2000, that had never before happened in the Smokies: A person was killed by a black bear. It is not known whether the victim did anything to provoke the attack. While such incidents are extremely rare—and there's no reason to panic about man-eating bears prowling the park—the case does underscore the need for all hikers to educate themselves about proper conduct in bear country.

The majority of bear maulings occur when a hiker surprises a bear. Therefore, it's vital to do everything possible to avoid these surprise meetings. Be alert at all times, keeping a watchful eye on the surroundings, not just the trail ahead of you. Stay on the trail, where there's less chance of a sudden encounter. Be especially watchful in summer when hiking near berry patches or black cherry trees. That clump of blueberries ahead might have a black bear in it. Make noise when you hike to alert the bears to your presence.

If you see a bear on the trail, freeze. Chances are, the bear doesn't give a hoot about you and will carry on with its business. Let it. A bear that snorts or paws the ground is just telling you that you are too close. Listen up. Don't get any closer, and if the bear is not moving away, slowly separate yourself from the bear. A bear that feels threatened might make a bluff charge. Stand your ground; *don't* run. It's tough to stand your ground against a charging bear, but that is exactly what you should do. No human can outrun a bear.

A bear that follows you but does not exhibit aggressive behavior, such as snorting, pawing, or bluff charging, may consider you a food source. Continue retreating and change directions. If the bear continues to follow, arm yourself with whatever you can, such as a knife or stick, and stand your ground. If you're with a group, huddle together to appear larger. Raise and spread your arms slightly, but not over your head. You don't want the bear to think you're a whitetail buck with a nice rack. Start yelling and throwing rocks. Don't throw food, as this will only encourage more aggressive behavior. As an absolute last resort, try throwing your entire pack at the bear. The time the bear spends investigating its contents may be just enough time for you to get away. If the bear ignores your pack, particularly if it has food in it, you might be in serious jeopardy. Hold tight to your knife or stick, and if the bear makes contact and continues attacking, fight back as aggressively as you can. *Don't* play dead; that seems only to work with grizzlies. Black bears usually bluff charge, but if they do make contact, they might consider you as food.

Bears are attracted to campsites by the smell of food. Minimize those odors and you minimize bear encounters. Store all food and toiletry items in plastic bags when not in use, and don't cook in your tent. I have one stuff sack that is

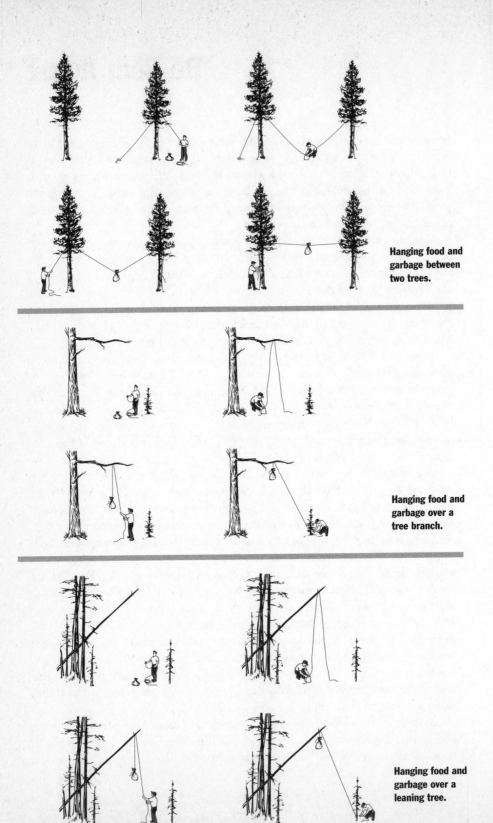

Hanging food and garbage between two trees.

Hanging food and garbage over a tree branch.

Hanging food and garbage over a leaning tree.

for food only. All food goes in plastic bags first, then in the stuff sack. All trash goes in plastic bags that also go in the stuff sack. This way, I keep odors to a minimum, and I have only one bag in the pack that makes contact with odors. Additionally, I wash the stuff sack after every trip.

Most shelters and campsites in the Smokies now have cable-hanging systems for suspending food. The safest approach is to suspend your entire pack, but if you are very careful with food odors, you can suspend just the food in a separate bag. All food, trash, toiletry items, lip balm, tobacco, etc., must be suspended. (See accompanying illustrations for proper technique.) The use of these cable systems has greatly reduced bear encounters in the Smokies.

Northwest
SECTION

1

Gatlinburg Trail

Highlights: *Easy hike, old homesteads, Cataract Falls*

Type of hike: Shuttle; day hike; a great split-party hike
Total distance: 2.0 miles one-way

Difficulty: Easy
Maps: Trails Illustrated; USGS Gatlinburg

Special considerations: This is a popular trail for joggers and bicyclists, and it passes near roads and under power lines. If you're looking for a "wilderness" experience, this trail is not for you.

Finding the trailhead: The hike begins at the Sugarlands Visitor Center.

Parking and trailhead facilities: Sugarlands Visitor Center has a large parking area, rest rooms, snack machines, and interpretive facilities.

Key points:
0.1 Junction with Fighting Creek Nature Trail.
0.3 Side trail to Cataract Falls.

The hike: This walk between Sugarlands Visitor Center and Gatlinburg is not for people who want to experience solitude in the Smokies. As a shuttle or out-and-back hike, there are better short hikes than this. It is, however, a great split-party hike, especially for those staying in Gatlinburg. Have your party drop you off at the visitor center and meet them back in town, or head out early in the morning and meet your party at the visitor center.

Begin the hike by walking between the rest rooms and main visitor center building to find the paved footpath. The Fighting Creek Self-guiding Nature Trail forks to the left; stay to the right and pass in front of the park headquarters building. Walk completely around the building on the right to reach Park Headquarters Road. Don't worry about getting lost; just keep walking and you'll eventually come

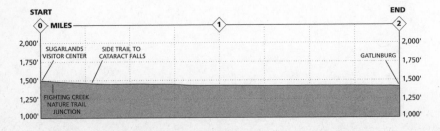

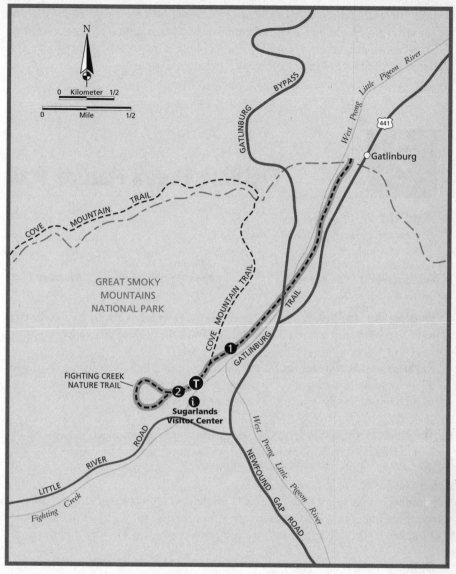

out on the paved road. Once on the road, go left and follow it to where it ends at the park maintenance yard. The Gatlinburg Trail leaves the road and bypasses the maintenance area on the right side.

Upon leaving the maintenance area you are finally on a real trail, but this is no wilderness walk. On your way to Gatlinburg you pass under the Gatlinburg Bypass road and parallel Newfound Gap Road. A few old homesites and the crossing of West Prong Little Pigeon River will keep your mind off asphalt for part of this hike.

Options: A short side path leads to a nice waterfall on Cataract Branch. From the paved road behind the park headquarters building, look for a road to the left that quickly crosses Fighting Creek. Take this road and turn right on the path immediately beyond the bridge. This path leads a short distance to Cataract Falls. The routes to Cataract Falls and Gatlinburg Trail are well signed.

2

Fighting Creek Nature Trail

Highlights: *Cultural history, waterfall option*
(See map for Hike 1: Gatlinburg Trail.)

Type of hike: "Lollipop" loop; day hike
Total distance: 1.0 mile round-trip

Difficulty: Easy
Maps: Trails Illustrated; USGS Gatlinburg

Finding the trailhead: The trail begins at the Sugarlands Visitor Center. It starts right in front of the rest rooms and heads toward the back of the complex.

Parking and trailhead facilities: Sugarlands has a huge parking lot, but it does fill up on summer weekends. The visitor center has telephones, rest rooms, a bookstore, interpretive displays, and a great movie presentation.

The hike: Fighting Creek Nature Trail provides a good introduction to the Smokies for families. It's short, easy, and crosses over streams and past a cabin. Pick up the self-guiding leaflet at the trailhead for 50 cents and read about the way of life here before the park was established.

Just behind the visitor center, the trail turns left (west); continuing straight takes you to park headquarters. If you visit in early spring, look to the right of this junction for Virginia bluebells. This is one of the few places to see this wildflower in the park.

Options: Hike 1: Gatlinburg Trail describes a side trail to Cataract Falls that is easily accessible from the visitor center and is a recommended side trip for this hike.

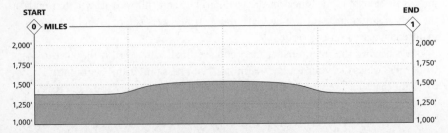

3

Cove Hardwoods Nature Trail

Highlights: *Spring wildflowers, old-growth forest, short trail*

Type of hike: "Lollipop" loop; day hike   **Best time of year:** April
Total distance: 1.0 mile round-trip   **Maps:** Trails Illustrated; USGS Mt. LeConte
Difficulty: Easy

Finding the trailhead: Drive south on Newfound Gap Road 4.5 miles from Sugarlands Visitor Center and turn right (east) into Chimneys Picnic Area. If coming from Newfound Gap, drive north (toward Gatlinburg) 12.8 miles and turn left into the picnic area. The trailhead parking is a few hundred yards up on the right, just across from the rest rooms. The picnic area is closed and gated from sunset to sunrise. If you want to do early-morning photography, you have to park at the gate and walk the extra distance.

Parking and trailhead facilities: Parking is at the first paved lot on the right, with room for several vehicles. This is a large picnic area, with rest rooms, garbage disposal, and telephone. The trail starts on the west end of the parking lot.

The hike: If you like wildflowers and scenic cove forests, it doesn't get much better than this. From early April until early May, the ground is carpeted with just about every spring ephemeral species you can think of. You don't even have to hike the trail; the picnic area itself is a good viewing spot. During the peak bloom of fringed phacelia, the flowers literally cover the ground. Indeed, more than one visitor has driven quickly by and thought he or she was seeing a late snow.

This is a self-guiding nature trail, so you might want to pick up a trail guide from the box at the trailhead. Return the guide after the hike, or drop 50 cents in the slot if you want to keep it. The trail goes by an open area on the left, which used to be an amphitheater, and soon forks. Take the right fork if you're following the trail guide. It's an easy hike, mostly, over packed ground and through a few small

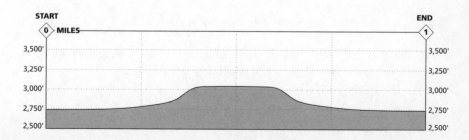

27

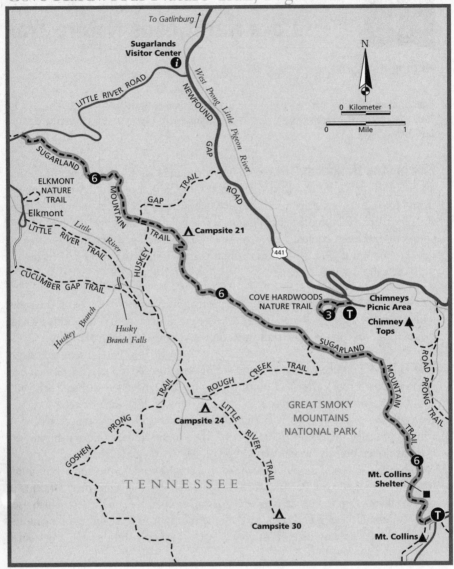

streams, but there are a few steep grades, some covered in asphalt to prevent erosion.

Resist the urge to leave the trail. Trampling is a concern here, and it's unnecessary since you can see every species of wildflower from the trail.

4

Chimney Tops

Highlights: *Scenic cascades, superb vistas, geology*

Type of hike: Out-and-back; day hike
Total distance: 4.0 miles round-trip
Difficulty: Difficult

Best time of year: Winter and spring
Maps: Trails Illustrated; USGS Mt. LeConte

Special considerations: Hike to the Chimney Tops on a weekend or during the summer or fall season and you can expect plenty of company. The steep trail seems to deter no one, even those who shouldn't attempt such a difficult and potentially dangerous trek. Scrambling up the peaks requires using both hands and feet, so make sure everything you carry can be strapped to your back or waist. Once on the summit, pay particular attention to where you step. The slightest distraction can cause disastrous results. Do not let the kids run free on this hike.

Finding the trailhead: The Chimney Tops parking area is located on Newfound Gap Road, 5.9 miles north of Newfound Gap and 6.8 miles south of Sugarlands Visitor Center. Don't confuse the Chimney Tops with the Chimneys Picnic Area, which is located 2.4 miles north of the trailhead.

Parking and trailhead facilities: The two parking lots can handle several vehicles, but they often fill up on weekends or on any day of the week during July, August, and October. Rest rooms are available 2.4 miles north of the trailhead at Chimneys Picnic Area or 5.9 miles south at Newfound Gap.

Key points:

0.1 Bridge over Walker Camp Prong.
0.2 First bridge over Road Prong.
0.4 Second bridge over Road Prong.
0.8 Third bridge over Road Prong.
0.9 Junction with Road Prong Trail at Beech Flats.

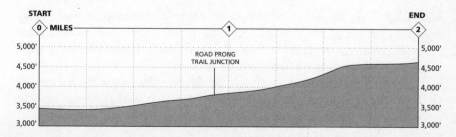

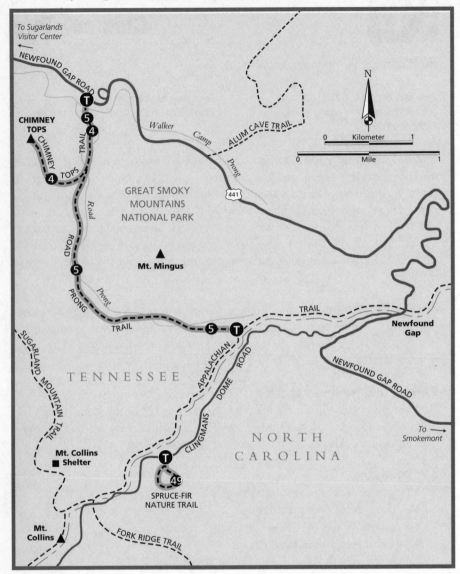

The hike: This hike offers cascading streams, wildflowers, scenic forest views, rugged rock outcrops, and unparalleled vistas. Access to the trailhead is easy, and the hike is relatively short. What it doesn't offer, though, is solitude. You're going to have company, so prepare your mind for it.

Begin from the main parking area at the sign and descend to the bridge over Walker Camp Prong. Cascades, pools, and huge boulders (many good for sunning) make this spot extremely popular. Look downstream to see the confluence with

Road Prong. You'll cross that stream very shortly. Where the two creeks join, the waterway becomes the West Prong Little Pigeon River. After the first crossing of Road Prong, the trail swings around to the left. (The old manway to the right is closed to the public because several people have been injured on this strenuous route.)

The trail now climbs noticeably, crosses Road Prong for a second time, and continues ascending to the third and final crossing. Just beyond that crossing, the trail swings around to the right; Road Prong Trail continues following the creek upstream (see Hike 5). Go right here, remaining on the wide and well-graded Chimney Tops Trail. A moderate ascent leads to a metal culvert across the trail. Stop here and rest; you'll need it. The next several hundred yards climb extremely steeply up the drainage, with no switchbacks to lessen the grade. You do make one switchback later on, but by that time you'll have put most of the steep part behind you. After that switchback, the grade moderates and even descends a short distance before leveling out somewhat on a narrow ridge. A short walk (scramble is a better term, what with all the roots and rocks) along this ridge leads to the base of the Chimneys. Now comes the difficult part of the hike—yep, worse than that steep climb you just made up the ravine.

A sign here warns GO NO FARTHER; consider it a "you've been warned" sign, and take heed. You now have two choices: You can scramble up the rocky ridge directly in front of you or continue around toward the right a little ways before climbing up. Considering the treacherous view up the ridge, you'll likely opt for the second route. Either way, you'll need to use both hands and feet to make it to the top.

Your reward at the summit is one of the finest panoramic views in the park. To the northeast, in bold relief, stands the imposing massif of Mt. LeConte. To the right of LeConte extends the narrow ridgeline called The Boulevard. To the southeast towers Mt. Mingus, which you may have noticed from a clearing back down the trail, and to the right of Mingus is the Road Prong drainage. If you follow the ridge leading down the left side of Mt. Mingus, you'll see "The Loop" on Newfound Gap Road, although vegetation hides most of it in summer. Toward the west are the steep slopes of Sugarland Mountain, of which the ridgeline forming the Chimney Tops is a spur. To the northwest lies the West Prong Little Pigeon River drainage leading into Sugarlands, with Cove Mountain in the distance.

At your feet is the jagged, slatelike Anakeesta Formation. The rock is difficult and dangerous to walk on, so be careful. The red squirrels don't have a problem with it, though, and you're sure to get a scolding from one if you spend much time reflecting up here. Their constant chatter seems to say, "Why don't you feed me? Don't you see how cute I am?" You can tell them that the park strictly forbids you to feed any wildlife. Those little gray birds flitting around the rocks are juncos.

The best time for this hike is in winter or spring, when the people traffic is lowest. Winter also has the best air quality, an important consideration with hikes to vistas. In summer, moisture and smog severely restrict the views. Just be careful if hiking in winter. Snow and ice makes the Chimney Tops summit too dangerous to attempt.

View of Mt. LeConte and The Loop from the Chimneys.

5

Road Prong

Highlights: *Waterfalls, wildflowers, lush forest, historical route*

(See map for Hike 4: Chimney Tops.)

Type of hike: Shuttle; day hike
Total distance: 3.3 miles one-way
Difficulty: Easy

Maps: Trails Illustrated; USGS Clingmans Dome and Mt. LeConte

Special considerations: One unbridged crossing of Road Prong is potentially dangerous in high water.

Finding the trailhead: At Newfound Gap, turn west on Clingmans Dome Road and drive 1.2 miles to the Indian Gap Parking Area on the north side. Clingmans Dome Road is closed to vehicles from December 1 to March 31. During this time, you could hike along the road or take the Appalachian Trail. The AT roughly parallels the road from Newfound Gap and passes through Indian Gap. You need to leave a second vehicle (or your own, if using a shuttle service) at the Chimney Tops trailhead on Newfound Gap Road, 5.9 miles north of Newfound Gap or 6.8 miles south of Sugarlands Visitor Center.

Parking and trailhead facilities: Rest room facilities are available at Newfound Gap.

Key points:
- **0.8** Landslide.
- **2.0** Unbridged creek crossing at Standing Rock.
- **2.4** Junction with Chimney Tops Trail at Beech Flats.
- **3.3** Chimney Tops trailhead on Newfound Gap Road.

The hike: The easy hike along Road Prong of West Prong Little Pigeon River offers a little something of everything the Smokies is famous for except grand vis-

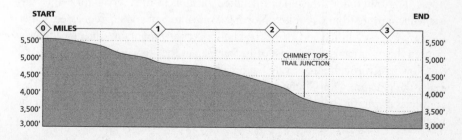

tas, and if you take the side trip to the Chimneys, you get that, too. The best part is that you'll have most of this hike to yourself, since few people hike the 2.4-mile section from Indian Gap to Chimney Tops Trail. The topo map shows Indian Gap being located about 0.75 mile to the east; the gap at the parking area is unnamed (the Trails Illustrated map calls it Little Indian Gap). All Smokies publications list the gap at the trailhead as Indian Gap.

The hike begins from the middle of the parking area, immediately crosses the Appalachian Trail, and then heads down the Road Prong drainage. The first section is steep and rocky; you'll think you're walking through a creek during heavy rains. There are a few more short stretches like this, but mostly this is an easy downhill stroll. Spruce, fir (near the beginning), buckeye, and birch trees anchor the lush forest.

You soon come to the first creek crossing—no problem at this stage. Look for coneflower and jewelweed in summer. Now the trail and the creek are the same for a few yards, and you pass a massive landslide. Watch the trout swimming in the pool above the debris dam. They're lucky to be where they are. When you cross the creek just below the huge debris pile, notice that the stream is orange from the iron leachate released from the slide. That's the same nasty stuff that creates acid rainwater, and it makes the creek below inhospitable to aquatic creatures. Notice also the heavy siltation in the creek.

After a few more yards through the creek channel, an up-and-down stretch takes you away from the stream. As you begin descending again to the creek, notice the forest to the right. You'd think you were in a Pacific Northwest rain forest, with thick moss and ferns covering every inch of ground. The trail descends steeply to the creek near the top of a small and beautiful waterfall, sometimes called "Talking Falls." Continue down the trail a bit to a short scramble path leading to the base of the falls. In summer it's difficult to resist jumping in the large, deep pool at the base of the falls; you might want to pack a swimsuit. Below the falls, the creek continues as a series of small falls and cascades, but there is no good way to view any of them.

Just before crossing the creek again, pass by a large, narrow, sharp-pointed rock on the left that looks like an ax head stuck in the ground. This is Standing Rock, and the crossing just below it is Standing Rock Ford. Most of the time this ford is a great rock-hop, with large rocks that don't wobble when jumped on, but after heavy rains it could be a wade. In flood conditions you can't cross safely. Downstream is a small cascading waterfall informally called "Trickling Falls," but like the cascades above the ford, there's no way to access the creek for a good view.

Below the ford, the trail looks as though it might have been a road at one time; it was. This trail follows the old Oconaluftee Turnpike, which served for many years as the main route from Cherokee, North Carolina, to Sevierville, Tennessee. When the park was established and a new road built over the mountains, the new highway crossed the mountains a mile east of Indian Gap at the "new found" gap.

Now pass through a relatively flat area known as Beech Flats, and at 2.4 miles reach the junction with Chimney Tops Trail. Straight ahead, Chimney Tops Trail continues down the Road Prong drainage, and to the left it ascends 1.1 miles to the Chimney Tops. If going left to the Chimneys, which is highly recommended, turn to Hike 4. If continuing straight, descend and quickly cross Road Prong again, this time on a wide, sturdy footbridge. Chimney Tops Trail is one of the most popular hikes in the park, so expect company any time of year. Continue descending along the creek and make two more crossings, both on footbridges. The bridges make perfect platforms for composing photographs of the cascading stream.

Shortly after the third footbridge over Road Prong, the trail crosses Walker Camp Prong on a long footbridge. Just downstream from the crossing, Walker Camp Prong joins Road Prong to form West Prong Little Pigeon River. The picturesque setting, with cascades and large rocks, and the proximity to the parking area make this spot extremely popular on sunny weekends. The Chimney Tops trailhead parking area is a few yards farther up the bank.

Options: You can do this hike in the opposite direction, but it would be uphill all the way. Hike it in the direction outlined and you'll have enough energy to take the side trip to the Chimney Tops and experience its grand views.

6 Sugarland Mountain

Highlights: *Solitude, views, changing forest, wildflowers*
(See map for Hike 3: Cove Hardwoods Nature Trail.)

Type of hike: Shuttle; day hike or overnighter; a good split-party hike
Total distance: 12.3 miles one-way

Difficulty: Moderate
Maps: Trails Illustrated; USGS Clingmans Dome, Mt. LeConte, and Gatlinburg

Special considerations: The trailhead is not accessible during winter due to the closing of Clingmans Dome Road from December 1 to March 31. The only dependable water source on this hike is a tiny spring near the start.

Finding the trailhead: From Newfound Gap drive 3.5 miles west on Clingmans Dome Road. Park on the left (south) side of the road at the Fork Ridge trailhead. The hike begins on the opposite side of the road. (You need to leave a vehicle at the lower trailhead. From Sugarlands Visitor Center, drive 3.7 miles west on Little River Road to the trailhead at Fighting Creek Gap.)

Parking and trailhead facilities: There's room for only a few vehicles, but that's usually not a problem. Rest rooms are available at Newfound Gap and at the end of Clingmans Dome Road, 3.4 miles farther west.

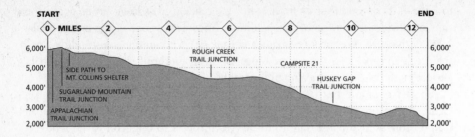

Key points:

0.1 Junction with Appalachian Trail.

0.4 Sugarland Mountain Trail starts at the Appalachian Trail junction.

0.7 Side path to Mt. Collins Shelter.

5.2 Junction with Rough Creek Trail.

8.3 Campsite 21.

9.3 Huskey Gap and junction with Huskey Gap Trail.

The hike: It's almost unheard of that you can hike more than 12 miles in the Smokies without having to do much climbing, but that's exactly the situation here. By starting on the main Smokies crest, it's pretty much downhill all the way, except for a moderate stretch toward the end. Along the way you drop more than 3,500 feet in elevation and pass through several forest types—spruce-fir at the highest elevation, then high-elevation birch, hemlock, northern hardwood, and pine. Some of the trees at the upper end are quite impressive.

Begin by crossing Clingmans Dome Road and taking the connector path that leads a few hundred feet to the Appalachian Trail (AT). Turn left (west), and hike 0.3 mile to the junction with Sugarland Mountain Trail, on the right. Head north on Sugarland Mountain Trail, and at 0.3 mile from the AT pass a side path to the right leading to the Mt. Collins Shelter. This is the closest shelter to a road in the park and consequently receives a lot of use. A few hundred yards farther, the trail passes a tiny spring, water source for the shelter and the only dependable water along this entire hike. Along this stretch you pass several impressive birch trees, some with good-sized spruces growing out of limb crotches high above the ground.

The good views soon appear and continue intermittently all the way to the junction with Rough Creek Trail. Off to the right, toward the northeast and northwest, you can see Mt. LeConte, the Chimneys, Gatlinburg, and Pigeon Forge. Off to the left are Goshen Ridge and the Little River drainage. Beyond Rough Creek Trail, the best views end and the forest changes from old growth to second growth. You pass through two pine stands killed by native Southern pine beetles.

At 8.3 miles you find yourself standing in Campsite 21. You're probably a little surprised, since you're in the middle of the upper drainage of Big Medicine Branch surrounded by rocks—lots of rocks. There are a few ground spots for tents and it's usually dry, but it seems as though a heavy storm could wash you and your tent down the mountain. One huge boulder creates an overhang that would make an interesting campsite. You usually have to walk a good distance down the drainage to find water. Despite the negatives, this is a neat site, and if you decide to camp here, you might have it to yourself.

Cross over Huskey Gap Trail at 9.3 miles and about 0.5 mile farther, look toward the east for an overgrown view of Mt. LeConte. The trail passes through two more dead-pine stands—the last one quite large—and reaches Mids Gap at about 11.0 miles. An unmaintained side path to the left leads to Mids Branch.

Just past the gap, you begin the longest uphill stretch of the hike, at nearly 0.5 mile long. Next begin the descent to Fighting Creek Gap, the steepest grade of the hike. There's considerable tree blowdown along this stretch, evidence of the thin soil layer on these steep hillsides.

The hike ends at a large parking area on Little River Road. This is also the trailhead for the popular Laurel Falls Trail, so expect to reacquaint yourself with people when you finish the hike.

Options: There are two other possible endings for this hike. From Huskey Gap, at the 9.3-mile point, you can take the Huskey Gap Trail in either direction. A right (northeast) turn takes you to Newfound Gap Road in 2.0 miles, and a left (southwest) takes you to Little River Trail in 2.1 miles, where you would turn right and follow Little River downstream 2.7 miles to the trailhead near Elkmont Campground. Either of these routes might work better as a split-party plan.

You can hike this route in the opposite direction, but why would you want to? Save the uphill hiking for when you don't have a choice.

7 Laurel Falls and Cove Mountain

Highlights: *Easy trail, waterfall, old-growth forest*

Type of hike: Out-and-back with shuttle option; day hike
Total distance: 8.0 miles round-trip (2.6 miles round-trip if only hiking to falls)

Difficulty: Moderate
Best time of year: Winter or early spring
Maps: Trails Illustrated; USGS Gatlinburg

Special considerations: The first 1.3 miles to Laurel Falls is possibly the most popular hike in the park. The only way to avoid a billion people is to hike first thing in the morning or on a weekday during winter or early spring.

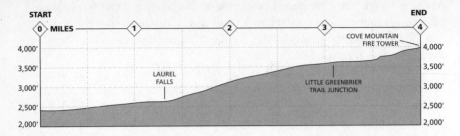

Finding the trailhead: From Sugarlands Visitor Center, drive 3.7 miles west on Little River Road to the trailhead at Fighting Creek Gap. Laurel Falls Trail begins on the north side of the road, opposite the Sugarland Mountain Trail on the south side.

Parking and trailhead facilities: Two large parking lots line each side of Fighting Creek Gap, but don't be surprised to find them both full on weekends or weekdays in summer and October. Rest rooms are available at Sugarlands Visitor Center.

Key points:

1.3   Laurel Falls.
3.1   Junction with Little Greenbrier Trail.
4.0   Cove Mountain Fire Tower.

The hike: This hike has two different personalities. The first 1.3 miles to Laurel Falls is a paved, relatively easy jaunt suitable for baby strollers. A hike on this stretch can be frustrating for those seeking solitude. If that's you, you might want to reconsider this hike altogether. The trail comes out at the flat area in the middle of the two-section Laurel Falls. Even if you don't see anyone on the trail (unlikely), there always seems to be people at the falls—wading, sitting, climbing (discouraged), picnicking, and photographing. An unsightly concrete bridge extends partly across the pool and presents a challenge to photographers not wanting any man-made elements in their images, but you can crop it out if you're careful.

The second personality of this hike shows itself the instant you leave the falls. Now you're hiking a legitimate trail (no pavement) and you're probably all alone, since few people venture beyond the falls. They don't know what they're missing. After a sharp switchback and a broad swing around a ridge, the trail passes through an old-growth forest of incredible beauty. Large trees of several species grow here—hemlock, basswood, buckeye—as well as some huge yellow-poplars (tulip trees). In early spring, wildflowers cover the forest floor; later in the season, mushrooms are abundant. The last time I made this hike, I watched a mother bear and two cubs foraging in the cove.

The trail leaves the big trees and ascends gradually to the junction with Little Greenbrier Trail on the left (west), which leads 4.3 miles to Wear Cove Gap. Our

Laurel Falls and Cove Mountain; Walker Sisters Home

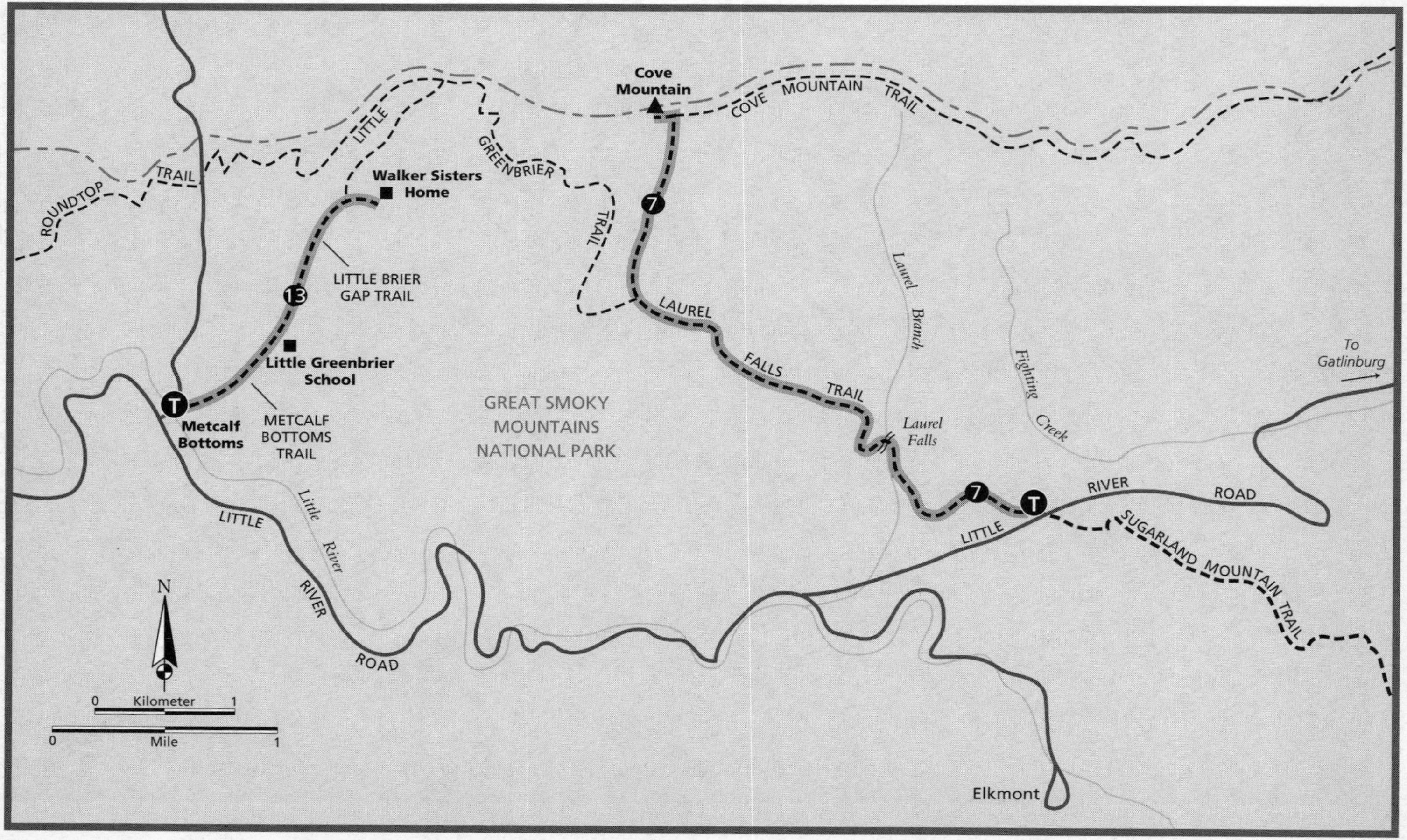

To Gatlinburg

Fighting Creek

Laurel Branch

Laurel Falls

SUGARLAND MOUNTAIN TRAIL

RIVER ROAD

LITTLE

Elkmont

COVE MOUNTAIN TRAIL

LAUREL FALLS TRAIL

Cove Mountain

7

7

GREAT SMOKY MOUNTAINS NATIONAL PARK

GREENBRIER TRAIL

Walker Sisters Home

LITTLE BRIER GAP TRAIL

13

Little Greenbrier School

METCALF BOTTOMS TRAIL

LITTLE

LITTLE RIVER ROAD

Little River

ROUNDTOP TRAIL

Metcalf Bottoms

N

Kilometer 1

0

Mile 1

0

Laurel Falls.

hike continues straight on Laurel Falls Trail, climbing moderately on the flanks of Cove Mountain to the junction with Cove Mountain Trail on a ridge. A service road for the fire tower is just ahead. To the right (east), the Cove Mountain Trail leads 8.4 miles to the park headquarters. To the left (west), a short walk leads to a small clearing on the summit of Cove Mountain and the fire tower.

No good views greet the hiker on the Cove Mountain summit, since an air-quality monitoring station now occupies the fire tower above the first few flights. The other side of the clearing affords a meager view toward Wear Cove. If you can ignore the fact that you're looking down a power line swath, I suppose this view is better than no view at all.

Options: With a second vehicle or prearranged shuttle service, you have two options that allow you to avoid backtracking. You could hike back down to the junction with Little Greenbrier Trail and follow it to Wear Gap, or you could hike along the ridge from Cove Mountain to the park headquarters near Gatlinburg. Before choosing this option, however, note that the Cove Mountain Trail rarely strays from the sight of the development surrounding Gatlinburg. There are better shuttle hikes in the park.

Elkmont Nature Trail

Highlights: *Easy trail, cultural history*

Type of hike: Loop; day hike
Total distance: 1.0 mile round-trip

Difficulty: Easy
Maps: Trails Illustrated; USGS Gatlinburg

Finding the trailhead: Drive 4.8 miles west on Little River Road from Sugarlands Visitor Center and turn south at the sign for Elkmont Campground. Drive 1.4 miles and turn left just before the campground entrance station. The parking area for the Elkmont Self-guiding Nature Trail is on the left at 0.3 mile.

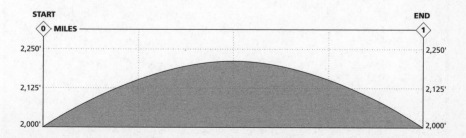

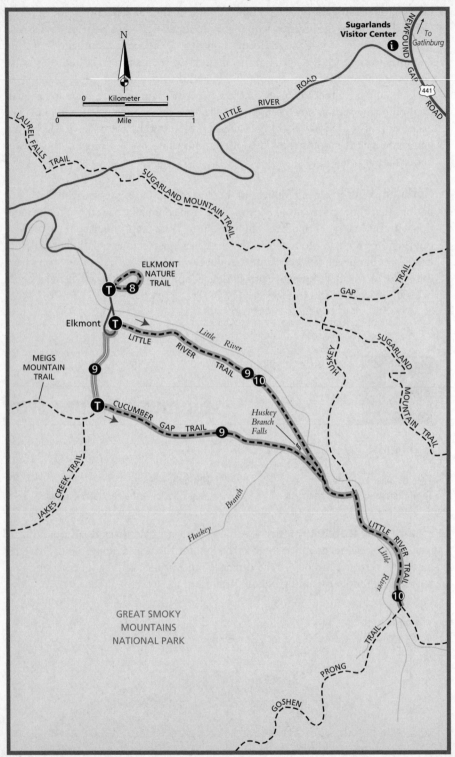

Parking and trailhead facilities: The parking lot is small but rarely fills. Rest rooms are available at Elkmont Campground.

The hike: This self-guiding nature trail begins at the south corner of the parking lot and winds its way up an old railroad line along Mids Branch before circling back to the parking area. Along the way you pass remnants of early settlement and through a neat rhododendron and mountain laurel tunnel. Grab a copy of the self-guiding brochure (50 cents to keep) before starting the hike, and use it to help interpret the features encountered along the way. This makes a great day hike for families staying at Elkmont Campground.

9 Cucumber Gap and Little River

Highlights: *Wildflowers, waterfall, Little River*
(See map for Hike 8: Elkmont Nature Trail.)

Type of hike: Loop; day hike
Total distance: 5.5 miles round-trip
Difficulty: Moderate

Best time of year: Early April or October
Maps: Trails Illustrated; USGS Gatlinburg

Finding the trailhead: The trailhead is located in the Elkmont section of the park, near the Elkmont Campground. Drive 4.8 miles west on Little River Road from Sugarlands Visitor Center and turn south at the sign for the campground. Drive 1.4 miles, turn left just before the campground entrance station, and go 1.1 miles farther to the gate. You pass through a section of dilapidated former vacation homes along the way.

Parking and trailhead facilities: Parking is limited on the side of the road, but space is usually available. If not, you have to park farther back from the trailhead and walk along the road. Rest rooms are available at the campground.

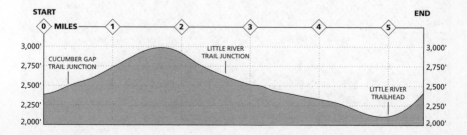

Little River Trail.

Key points:

0.3 Junction with Cucumber Gap Trail.
2.7 Junction with Little River Trail.
5.0 Junction with paved road at Little River Trailhead.

The hike: If you're looking for an easy, relatively short, and interesting loop, it doesn't get much better than this. It makes a wonderful day hike for parties staying at Elkmont Campground. They don't even have to drive to the trailhead, since the campground is so close. Two and three-tenths miles of this hike are along Little River on the Little River Trail. That trail is so popular, and its features and history so outstanding, that I've devoted a separate hike to it (See Hike 10). Read that hike description as well as this one for a better understanding of this section of the park.

Walk up the gravel road a few yards, take the left (southeast) fork, and walk by the gate. You're on Jakes Creek Trail, and you climb fairly steeply to the junction with Cucumber Gap Trail, cutting sharply back to the left (east). Take the Cucumber Gap Trail and make a long, gradual ascent through second-growth yellow-poplar and abundant spring wildflowers to Cucumber Gap. Beyond the gap the forest changes to hemlocks, with a dense rhododendron understory. It's darker and cooler here. After easily crossing Huskey Branch in a pleasant setting, you soon reach the junction with Little River Trail—a wide, gravel road on which you could drive a Winnebago most of the way.

Turn left (north) on Little River Trail; soon after first spotting the river, cross Huskey Branch once more, this time right over Huskey Branch Falls. (The portion of the falls above the trail is especially photogenic on overcast days with diffused lighting.) The water continues falling under the bridge and into a deep pool in Little River. Now follow closely along the Little River the remaining 2.0 miles to the road. Turn left onto the road and follow it 0.5 mile back to the trailhead.

10

Little River

Highlights: *Wildflowers, waterfall, Little River cascades, fly-fishing, cultural history*
(See map for Hike 8: Elkmont Nature Trail.)

Type of hike: Out-and-back; day hike, with a one-
or two-night backpack option
Total distance: 7.4 miles round-trip, or whatever
distance you choose

Difficulty: Easy
Best time of year: Early April or October
Maps: Trails Illustrated; USGS Gatlinburg

Finding the trailhead: The trailhead is located in the Elkmont section of the park, near the Elkmont Campground. Drive 4.8 miles west on Little River Road from Sugarlands Visitor Center and turn south at the sign for the campground. Drive 1.4 miles, turn left just before the campground entrance station, and go 0.6 mile to a fork in the road. The trail is a continuation of the left fork, beyond the gate.

Parking and trailhead facilities: Parking is limited on the side of the road, and on weekends during the busy season you might have to park some distance from the gate and walk. Rest rooms are available at the campground.

Key points:
- **0.1** Synchronous fireflies.
- **2.0** Huskey Branch Falls.
- **2.3** Junction with Cucumber Gap Trail.
- **2.7** Junction with Huskey Gap Trail.
- **3.7** Junction with Goshen Prong Trail.

The hike: On this hike you can devote half an hour, half a day, or half a week if you choose to camp. You can amble along the flat trail as far as you like, and when you've had enough, turn around and amble back. It's a creek walk, a forest walk, and a history lesson all in one. During early April you see dwarf irises, trilliums, and numerous other wildflowers. During October the Little River Trail becomes a riot

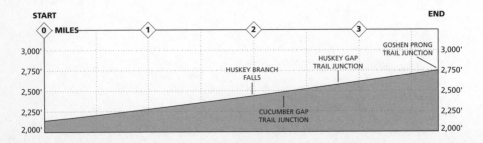

Little River.

of color and is one of the finer autumn forest walks. At any time of year you can dip a fly into the river and try your hand at the large brown and rainbow trout, though spring and fall are traditionally the better seasons.

The Little River Trail follows an old logging grade used by the Little River Lumber Company to extract the virgin timber before the park was established, and even afterward. The company agreed to sell their lands only if they could continue logging for an additional five years, which they did. All along the hike you see evidence of the logging operations—a railroad rail here, a steel cable over there. The forest has recovered nicely, but you see no old growth on this hike.

You begin the hike with a question: What's the deal with all the dilapidated houses? These are vacation cottages built in the early 1900s before the park was established. While most everyone else had to leave when the park began, the owners of these cabins successfully lobbied to retain use of their property. Many of these leases remained in effect until the early 1990s, but all have now expired. Currently the park is debating the future of these cabins with various groups. As of this writing, it appears that the park will preserve a small representative portion of the nearly eighty structures and remove the remainder to allow the area to regain its natural state.

As you walk the first mile or so by the old cabins, you pass through habitat for one of the Smokies' most interesting—and lately, most famous—inhabitants, *Photinus carolinus*. This is the scientific name for a species of firefly that flies all across the East. However, here in Elkmont you might see something very special. Groups of male fireflies of this species sometimes flash at the exact same time. Synchronous flashing of fireflies is extremely rare in the world; in fact, the Elkmont discovery in 1993 was the first authenticated existence in North America. Today park visitors from all over the country hike the short distance along Little River Trail the first few weeks of June to witness this event. One of the most popular field courses offered by the Smoky Mountains Field School is its annual "Light Show in the Smokies," led by the scientist who studies the Elkmont fireflies, Dr. Jonathan Copeland.

Once you leave the cabins behind, you enjoy an easy walk along Little River, sometimes kissing it, sometimes out of sight of it, but always close to it. After about 2.7 miles, the road crosses the river and becomes more trail-like. Another mile takes you to the junction with Goshen Prong Trail, the farthest point where most day hikers venture. You can continue on the Little River Trail an additional 2.5 miles if you like, passing the popular Rough Creek Backcountry Campsite 24 and proceeding to Three Forks Backcountry Campsite 30, at trail's end. If you choose to turn around at the Goshen Prong Trail junction, at least hike a few hundred yards on Goshen Prong Trail to the bridge over Little River. The bridge crosses at a point just downstream from where Split Branch enters the river and just upstream from where Fish Camp Prong enters it. Photographers, especially, will want to spend some time in this scenic setting.

Options: A couple of possibilities exist using Little River Trail as a base. See Hike 9: Cucumber Gap and Little River for a good day hike loop. A good overnight loop would be to hike Little River Trail to Campsite 24 or 30 and spend the first night. The next day, follow Rough Creek Trail up to Sugarland Mountain Trail; go north on it to Huskey Gap Trail and then back to Little River Trail. You could spend a second night at Campsite 21 on Sugarland Mountain Trail for a leisurely trip, or hike all the way back on the second day. Total round-trip mileage, if staying the first night at Campsite 24, is 16.2 miles.

11

Goshen Prong

Highlights: *Views, changing forest types, cascading stream, wildflowers*

Type of hike: Shuttle; day hike or overnighter; a great split-party hike
Total distance: 13.9 miles one-way

Difficulty: Moderate
Maps: Trails Illustrated; USGS Clingmans Dome, Silers Bald, and Gatlinburg

Special considerations: Clingmans Dome Road is closed from December 1 until March 31. After heavy rains, two crossings of Fish Camp Prong may be tricky.

Finding the trailhead: At Newfound Gap, turn west onto Clingmans Dome Road and follow it 7.0 miles to its end at the Forney Ridge Parking Area. The trail begins on the extreme western end of the parking lot, near the water fountain.

You need to leave a vehicle at the lower trailhead. Drive 4.8 miles west on Little River Road from Sugarlands Visitor Center and turn south at the sign for Elkmont Campground. Drive 1.4 miles, turn left just before the campground entrance station, and go 0.6 mile to a fork in the road. Park here, at the trailhead for Little River Trail.

Parking and trailhead facilities: The parking area is huge but still manages to fill up on summer and October weekends. Rest rooms are located near the start of the paved trail to the Clingmans Dome Tower. If the parking lot is full, you might want to wait and use the woods.

Key points:

0.2 Junction with Clingmans Dome Bypass Trail.
0.7 Junction with Appalachian Trail.
2.6 Junction with Goshen Prong Trail.
7.0 Campsite 23.
10.1 Bridge over Little River.
10.2 Junction with Little River Trail.

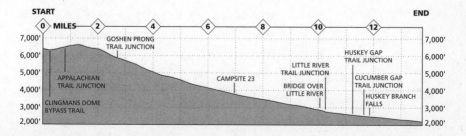

Goshen Prong

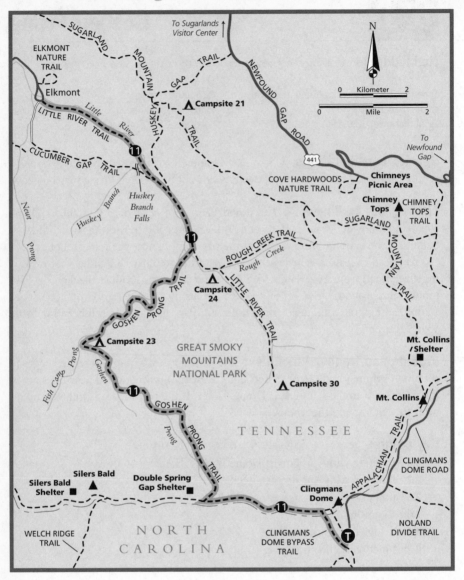

11.2 Junction with Huskey Gap Trail.

11.6 Junction with Cucumber Gap Trail.

11.9 Huskey Branch Falls.

The hike: You have a decision to make at the beginning of this hike. You can take the paved path to the Clingmans Dome Tower and pick up the Appalachian Trail (AT) from there, or bypass the tower (and the crowds) by taking the Clingmans Dome Bypass Trail. If you've never seen the view from the observation tower, by all means, go for that route. You need to see it at least once. But if you've "been there, done that," you might want to get away from the pavement—and the crowds—as quickly as possible.

For the tower route, see Hike 51: Clingmans Dome. For the "I'm sick of crowds route," turn left (west) off the paved tower path, just beyond the water fountain. The rocky Forney Ridge Trail leads about 0.2 mile to the junction with Clingmans Dome Bypass Trail, which takes off straight (north) from the junction. The 0.5-mile moderate climb from here to the AT is rocky and depressing. Here is the best (or worst) example in the park of the destruction caused by the balsam woolly adelgid and air pollution. (See Hike 51 for the gory details.)

Once at the AT, turn left (west), but take time to admire the view (if the smog allows) off the north side of the trail toward Mt. LeConte. The 1.9 miles on the AT to the Goshen Prong Trail are relatively easy and provide numerous open vistas. At a nondescript junction, the Goshen Prong Trail turns off to the right (north) and begins a rocky and steep course down the upper drainage of Goshen Prong. A birch forest, with scattered spruce, soon replaces the spruce forest of the ridgeline. Farther down you find beech trees, and hemlock replaces the spruce. The trail gradient has moderated considerably.

Look out to the right for a rock overhang with a small fissure cave. A few hundred yards farther, the trail crosses an unnamed side branch below a scenic cascade over mossy, stratified rock. Soon you cross another side stream (both easily rock-hopped) and begin a noisy parallel of the cascading Goshen Prong. Along a stretch where the trail swings away from the creek, look for old logging relics. The path you're on follows the old logging railroad line, so you might spot a railroad rail or a steel cable. Once back alongside the creek, you have to cross a small landslide on the bank. The park has installed steel cables to make it safer to negotiate the landslide when the rocks are wet or icy.

A few hundred yards farther, where Goshen Prong joins Fish Camp Prong, the trail passes Campsite 23, popular with fishers. (Fishing is prohibited in all waters upstream of the creek junction). The campsite sits a few hundred feet off the trail on the right. Fish Camp Prong, which you now follow, splits below the campsite and forms an island. You must cross the creek first to get onto the island and then again on the other end. Both crossings are a little tricky in high water, but usually they are an easy rock-hop.

Bridge over Little River on Goshen Prong Trail.

For the remainder of the hike on Goshen Prong Trail, you keep close company with Fish Camp Prong. The creek (more like a little river at this point) spills, churns, cascades, and slides all the way to its junction with Little River. Photographers will have a difficult time leaving this stretch. Near the end of Goshen Prong Trail, you swing away from the creek a bit and cross Little River on a long, steel footbridge, amusingly nicknamed the "Goshen Gate Bridge." Upstream, Split Branch joins Little River. Downstream is the mouth of Fish Camp Prong.

If you can pull yourself away from the views at the bridge, continue a few hundred yards to the junction with Little River Trail. To the right, it's 0.5 mile to Campsite 24. To the left, the Little River Trail follows Little River 3.7 miles to the trailhead near Elkmont Campground. See Hike 10: Little River for a description of this portion of the hike.

12 Jakes Creek and Lynn Camp Prong

Highlights: *Wildflowers, views, Indian Flats Falls*

Type of hike: A "lollipop" loop; long day hike, overnighter, or two-night backpack
Total distance: 16.9 miles round-trip

Difficulty: Difficult
Maps: Trails Illustrated; USGS Gatlinburg, Silers Bald, and Thunderhead Mountain

Special considerations: The Lynn Camp Prong crossing is rock-hoppable only after a prolonged dry spell. Expect to wade this one.

Finding the trailhead: The trailhead is located in the Elkmont section of the park, near Elkmont Campground. Drive 4.8 miles west on Little River Road from Sugarlands Visitor Center and turn south at the sign for campground. Drive 1.4 miles, turn left just before the campground entrance station, and go 1.1 miles farther to the gate. You pass through a section of dilapidated former vacation homes along the way.

Parking and trailhead facilities: Parking is limited on the side of the road, but space is usually available. Otherwise you have to park farther back from the trailhead and walk along the road. Rest rooms are available at the campground.

Key points:

0.3 Junction with Cucumber Gap Trail.
0.4 Junction with Meigs Mountain Trail.
2.6 Campsite 27.
3.3 Jakes Gap at junction with Miry Ridge and Panther Creek Trails.
5.2 Campsite 26.
5.8 Junction with Lynn Camp Prong Trail.
8.0 Campsite 28.
9.5 Junction with Middle Prong and Greenbrier Ridge Trails.
9.7 Side path to Indian Flats Falls.

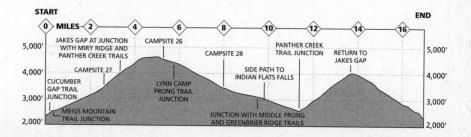

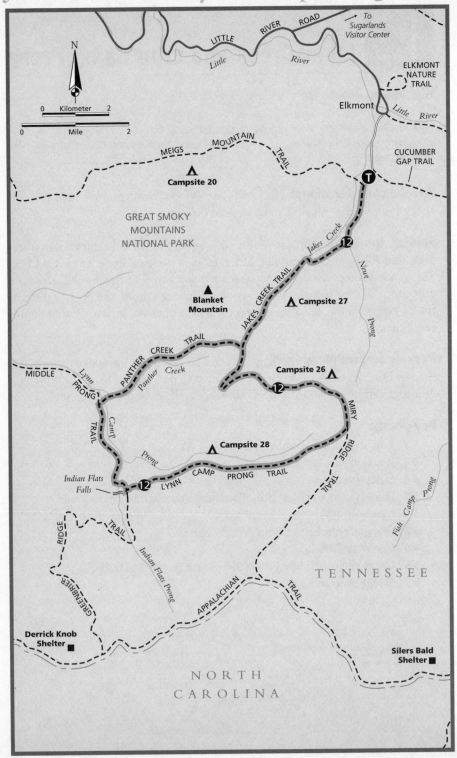

11.3 Junction with Panther Creek Trail.

13.6 Return to Jakes Gap.

The hike: Walk up the gravel road a few yards, take the left (southeast) fork, and walk by the gate. You're on Jakes Creek Trail, following an old logging grade. Climb somewhat steeply to the junction with Cucumber Gap Trail on the left, and then descend slightly a few hundred feet to the junction with Meigs Mountain Trail on the right. Stay on Jakes Creek Trail and hike through a characteristic second-growth yellow-poplar forest while making a steady ascent on a wide parallel of Jakes Creek. You meet up with the creek at an especially scenic cascade. Look for a steel cable sticking out of the side path leading down to the pool. That's a sign of old logging activity.

A short distance beyond the cascade, the graded roadbed ends at a crossing of Newt Prong. Look for an old railroad rail sticking out of the ground here, an even surer sign that logging occurred in these woods. Cross the creek on an asphalt-covered foot log and begin ascending alongside Jakes Creek. After a steep section, cross the creek on stepping stones (tricky in high water) and swing away from the creek on a level grade before climbing again after a switchback.

Pressing on, pass Campsite 27 on the left, right beside the trail. The forest here is pleasant, but the campsite is not one of the best. The ground is bare and rooty, and it looks as though it could become a miserable collection of muddy runnels during a hard rain. Maybe that's why campers at this site tend to spread out through the woods—not the most environmentally sound practice.

It's a rooty climb, though not too steep, from the campsite to Jakes Gap. Four trails intersect here. Straight ahead, the Panther Creek Trail descends to Lynn Camp Prong, which you climb from the stream later on in the hike. To the right, an unmaintained and overgrown manway leads to the summit of Blanket Mountain. As with all unmaintained trails in the park, hiking this one is not recommended.

Turn left (south) on Miry Ridge Trail, despite the unflattering name. As you climb moderately up the northwest slope of Dripping Spring Mountain, pay attention to the forest. When you swing around the ridge and begin skirting the southeast side, notice the difference in both the temperature and plant life. On the more south-facing slope, you pass through a long mountain laurel tunnel with a ground cover of galax, trailing arbutus, and wintergreen—all indicator plants of a dry environment. Soon you pass through another tunnel, this one created by rhododendron, and now you come out in a clearing just below the summit of Dripping Spring Mountain. There's a good view from here of Cold Spring Knob on the Smokies crest and of Mellinger Death Ridge straight ahead. A side path climbs to a higher vantage point on the summit of Dripping Spring Mountain, but the view from here is perfectly fine.

Now pass through another laurel tunnel and have a good walk along the contour line before descending easily through a scenic hemlock forest to a saddle. A signpost here indicates that Campsite 26 lies off to the left (northeast) side of the saddle. The obvious side path leads a few hundred yards to the site, situated pleasantly in a grove of hemlock, silverbell, and maple.

A gentle walk takes you from the saddle to the junction with Lynn Camp Prong Trail. Turn right (southwest) and follow the Lynn Camp Prong Trail down and away from the ridgeline. The next 2.2 miles are a cakewalk (in this direction)—not too steep, easy creek crossings, and downhill all the way. Watch for wildflowers along this stretch, but don't get so caught up that you overlook the stinging nettle that's everywhere. You don't want to brush against that stuff. The trail dumps out in a clearing on an old railroad bed. This is Campsite 28. Straight ahead is the horse-hitching rail, and to the right is the camping area on both sides of Buckeye Cove Branch.

To the left is the continuation of Lynn Camp Prong Trail, following the mostly level railroad bed 1.5 miles to the Greenbrier Ridge and Middle Prong Trails junction. Greenbrier Ridge Trail turns left at the junction, while Middle Prong Trail (our route) turns right as a continuation of the railroad grade. The trail descends moderately now, making a left switchback and then a right switchback. In the outside curve of this second switchback, an obvious side path leads a few hundred feet to Indian Flats Falls, a highly recommended side trip. Continuing down the trail, you make a few more switchbacks and cross Indian Flats Prong on a low bridge. From here it's an easy 1.2 miles on the gradually descending railroad grade to the obvious junction with Panther Creek Trail.

Panther Creek Trail crosses Lynn Camp Prong immediately from the start. There's no bridge, and it's a safe bet that you won't be able to rock-hop it. Come prepared with sandals or old sneakers. Once across, your reward is a long, rocky and rooty haul up the Panther Creek drainage. You cross the creek many times and finally pull away for a final steep grind to Jakes Gap. Take a breather at the gap—you deserve it.

From the gap retrace your steps on Jakes Creek Trail to complete the hike.

Options: The hike passes three backcountry campsites, providing numerous possibilities for backpacking trips. For an overnighter, I'd recommend staying at Campsite 26. This gives you a tough 11.7-mile hike the next day, so you might want to go ahead and push to 28 and spend the night there. For two-night trips, there are two good options. One is to stay both nights at 27, using the second day to make a day hike loop of the remainder of the hike. The other option is to stay the first night at 27 and the second night at 28.

13

Walker Sisters Home

Highlights: *Good family hike, cultural history*

(See map for Hike 7: Laurel Falls and Cove Mountain.)

Type of hike: Out-and-back with shuttle option; day hike
Total distance: 3.2 miles round-trip

Difficulty: Moderate
Maps: Trails Illustrated; USGS Wear Cove

Finding the trailhead: The trail begins from the Metcalf Bottoms Picnic Area, located roughly halfway between Sugarlands Visitor Center and the Townsend Y on Little River Road. Turn into the picnic area and cross the bridge over Little River. The trail starts on the right side, immediately beyond the bridge, heading upstream.

Parking and trailhead facilities: There's usually room for a few vehicles along the road. Otherwise you can park back at the picnic area. You pass rest room facilities as you drive through the picnic area.

Key points:
0.6 Little Greenbrier School.
1.6 Walker Sisters Home.

The hike: The first section of the hike is on the Metcalf Bottoms Trail, beginning as a gravel road heading upstream. The trail soon swings away from the river and climbs rather steeply. It passes a water tower on the right and an old homesite across from the tower. After the climb the trail descends through a rhododendron tunnel to Little Brier Branch and follows the branch upstream, crossing it twice on foot logs, to the old Little Greenbrier School and church building.

If you make this hike during the spring through fall season, you might find cars at the school. A narrow, winding, gravel road leads to the school from the paved road between Metcalf Bottoms and Wear Cove. You can drive here, too, but hiking the Metcalf Bottoms Trail is the better option; it's the only option during winter, when the road is closed.

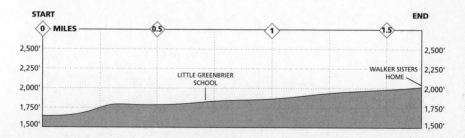

After exploring the old combination schoolhouse and church, continue your hike on the Little Brier Gap Trail. It begins beyond the gate on the gravel road above the cemetery. After about 1.0 mile of mostly easy walking, the Little Brier Gap Trail continues straight, while our hike swings around to the right and continues less than 0.25 mile to the Walker Sisters Home. Here you find a springhouse, corncrib, and the cabin where the five Walker sisters lived as spinsters. When the park was established, the sisters adamantly opposed leaving their home. They agreed to a compromise that allowed them to live out their lives on the land with a "lifetime lease." The last sister died in 1964.

Options: The Little Brier Gap Trail continues 0.4 mile to Little Brier Gap and the junction with Little Greenbrier Trail. With a second vehicle left as a shuttle, you could go west from the gap to Wear Cove Road, a little more than a mile above Metcalf Bottoms Picnic Area, or head east and pick up Laurel Falls Trail and take it back to the trailhead on Little River Road.

14

Spruce Flats Falls

Highlights: *Waterfall*

Type of hike: Out-and-back; day hike
Total distance: 2.0 miles round-trip

Difficulty: Difficult
Maps: Trails Illustrated; USGS Wear Cove

Special considerations: Watch the kids closely on the hike and especially near the falls.

Finding the trailhead: The trail leads from the Great Smoky Mountains Institute, an environmental education facility in the Tremont section of the park. To reach the institute, head southwest from the Townsend Y (junction of Little River Road and Tennessee 73) toward Cades Cove. At 0.2 mile from the Y, Tremont Road turns to the left. Follow this road 2.0 miles to the institute, on the left. Turn into the complex and park at the office, the first building on the left.

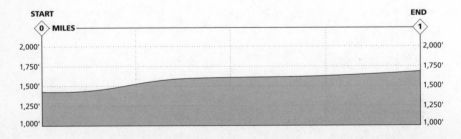

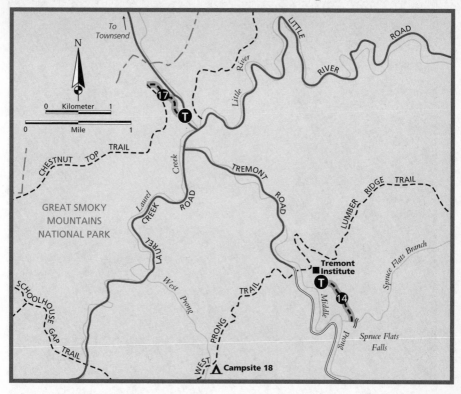

Parking and trailhead facilities: The office for the Great Smoky Mountains Institute has several paved parking spots, but they can fill up quickly during the summer and fall busy season. If the office is open, you can obtain information and purchase park literature. The office has rest rooms.

The hike: Follow the paved institute road away from the office to its end at the employee housing building parking area. The hiking trail leads from the far left (southwest) end at a small sign saying FALLS TRAIL. Switchbacks take you up the initial steep section, after which the trail levels out and becomes very rocky, rooty, and poorly graded. Here's a good place for the kids to skin a knee or their parents to twist an ankle. A final steep descent takes you to the falls.

You may not see a soul on the trail, but don't be surprised to find people at the falls. The hike is not as well known or publicized as many others in the park, but it's no secret either. If you're after photos and you don't want people in them, you need to be here early in the morning. The waterfall consists of four separate drops; however, only the lower sections are safe to view. That's okay—what you can see is one of the most scenic drops of water in the park and more than worth the difficult hike getting there.

Indian Flats Falls.

15

Indian Flats Falls

Highlights: *Classic stream walk, waterfalls, spring wildflowers*

Type of hike: Out-and-back; day hike
Total distance: 8.0 miles round-trip
Difficulty: Moderate

Best time of year: Early April
Maps: Trails Illustrated; USGS Thunderhead Mountain

Special considerations: The last 3.0 miles of Tremont Road close in winter. An excellent option is to bring a bicycle for the closed road section and make this a hike/bike combination trip. Bicycles are not allowed on the hiking trail.

Finding the trailhead: The trail begins at the end of Tremont Road. Head southwest from the Townsend Y (junction of Little River Road and Tennessee 73) toward Cades Cove, and at 0.2 mile turn left onto Tremont Road. The road passes the Great Smoky Mountains Institute on the left at 2.0 miles and then changes to gravel. Drive 3.0 miles on the gravel portion to the road's end at a traffic circle.

Parking and trailhead facilities: Ample parking is available at the road's end, but on busy weekends you may have to park a ways back from the gate. The closest rest rooms are back at the Great Smoky Mountains Institute office. If the institute is not open, the next closest facilities are at the Cades Cove Campground.

Key points:

0.5 Lynn Camp Prong Cascades.
2.3 Junction with Panther Creek Trail.
3.5 Bridge over Indian Flats Prong.
3.9 Side path to Indian Flats Falls.

The hike: The easy walk along Lynn Camp Prong is the quintessential Smokies stream hike. Many photographs taken along this stream show up on postcards or framed prints sold in area stores. The first couple weeks of April, the trail sides explode with trilliums, dwarf irises, jack-in-the pulpits, violets, anemones, and seemingly countless other wildflowers.

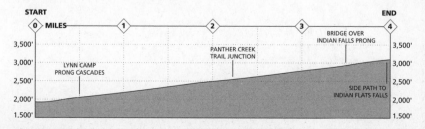

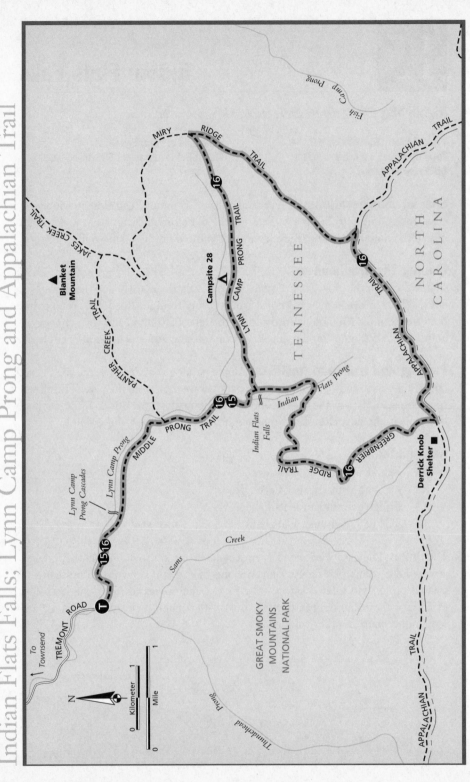

The trail is a continuation of the gravel road and follows an old railroad grade built by Little River Lumber Company in the early twentieth century. After crossing Lynn Camp Prong on a sturdy bridge, stay to the left on the main gravel road. Unless you don't mind stepping in horse pies, it's a good idea to keep an eye on your feet as well as the trail ahead. At about 0.5 mile the road makes a wide swing to the left at the largest set of cascades on Lynn Camp Prong. The trail continues alongside the creek and comes out near the top of the uppermost drop. Photographers enjoy this stretch of the creek.

The road continues alongside the creek another 3.0 miles to a bridge over Indian Flats Prong, just above where that creek joins Lynn Camp Prong. (Back at the trailhead, Thunderhead Prong joins Lynn Camp Prong to form Middle Prong Little River.) Beyond the bridge, the grade increases. You make a couple of broad left-hand switchbacks and then a sharp right-hand switchback. Then you come to the first sharp left-hand switchback. Look here for an obvious side path to the right leading toward the creek. The path leads a few hundred feet over rocks and roots to the base of the uppermost drop of Indian Flats Falls.

The waterfall consists of four separate drops, each of them scenic and worthy of a photograph. However, only the uppermost fall is easily accessible. If you want to see the lower drops, you have to scramble down the makeshift paths, over and under rhododendron thickets. Resist the urge to do this, for both safety and environmental reasons.

Options: Two other hikes in this book use portions of Middle Prong Trail and pass Indian Flats Falls. See Hike 16: Lynn Camp Prong and Appalachian Trail and Hike 12: Jakes Creek and Lynn Camp Prong.

16 Lynn Camp Prong and Appalachian Trail

Highlights: *Wildflowers, cascading creek, Indian Flats Falls, Smokies crestline*
(See map for Hike 15: Indian Flats Falls.)

Type of hike: A "lollipop" loop; tough over-nighter or easy two-night backpack
Total distance: 21.0 miles round-trip
Difficulty: Difficult

Best time of year: Early spring or mid-October
Maps: Trails Illustrated; USGS Thunderhead Mountain and Silers Bald

Special considerations: The last 3.0 miles of Tremont Road are closed in winter, so you probably want to hike this one only from spring to fall. There are better winter trips than this one with 6.0 additional miles of road walking.

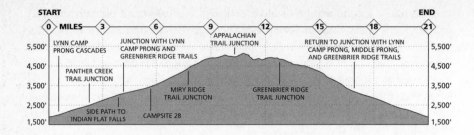

Finding the trailhead: The trail begins at the end of Tremont Road. Head southwest from the Townsend Y (junction of Little River Road and Tennessee 73) toward Cades Cove; at 0.2 mile turn left onto Tremont Road. The road passes the Great Smoky Mountains Institute on the left at 2.0 miles and then changes to gravel. Drive 3.0 miles on the gravel portion to the road's end at a traffic circle.

Parking and trailhead facilities: Ample parking is available at the road's end, but on busy weekends you may have to park a ways back from the gate. The closest rest rooms are back at the Great Smoky Mountains Institute office. If the institute is not open, the next closest facilities are at the Cades Cove Campground.

Key points:

0.5 Lynn Camp Prong Cascades.

2.3 Junction with Panther Creek Trail.

3.5 Bridge over Indian Flats Prong.

3.9 Side path to Indian Flats Falls.

4.1 Junction with Lynn Camp Prong and Greenbrier Ridge Trails.

5.6 Campsite 28.

7.8 Junction with Miry Ridge Trail.

10.3 Junction with Appalachian Trail.

12.7 Junction with Greenbrier Ridge Trail.

16.9 Return to junction of Lynn Camp Prong, Middle Prong, and Greenbrier Ridge Trails.

The hike: This hike provides a good opportunity to get deep into the Smokies without making an overly strenuous effort. You get to experience a few miles of the Smokies crest (without views, though), and after the first 4.0 miles, you have the hike pretty much to yourself. Try to make the trip around mid-April when the wildflowers peak or mid-October when the fall color peaks.

The first 7.8 miles are also covered in Hike 15: Indian Flats Falls and Hike 12: Jakes Creek and Lynn Camp Prong; refer to them for more details. The hike begins along Middle Prong Trail, following an old railroad bed upstream along Lynn Camp Prong past scenic cascades, waterfalls, and great spring wildflowers. At mile 3.5 the trail crosses Indian Flats Prong on a low bridge and begins climbing on switchbacks.

Lynn Camp Prong.

At the second sharp switchback an obvious side path (right) leads a few hundred feet to Indian Flats Falls. Plan to spend a little reflection time here.

Back on the Middle Prong Trail, it's a short climb to the junction with Lynn Camp Prong and Greenbrier Ridge Trails. You come back to this junction later in the hike. Now you want to go left (north) on Lynn Camp Prong Trail. After an easy 1.5 miles you arrive at Campsite 28, your first night's stay on a two-night backpack. Pressing on from the campsite, make a continuous climb of 2.2 miles to the junction with Miry Ridge Trail on the ridgeline.

Turn right (south) on the ridge and follow it 2.5 miles to the junction with the Appalachian Trail. Although you climb to the crest of the Smokies along this ridge, the grade is not as steep as you might expect. My favorite feature of this section is the gnarled trees covered in moss and lichens. Look for a large birch tree with a good-sized rhododendron growing from a crotch in the tree more than 15 feet above the ground. Who says you have to go to the tropics to find epiphytic plants?

At the junction with the Appalachian Trail (AT), turn right (west) and make the steepest climb of the hike up Cold Spring Knob. Now you get a real lesson in Smokies ridge walking. It's sort of like Smokies weather in the spring—if you don't like it right now, don't worry because it'll change real soon. Up and down you go until the final descent to the Greenbrier Ridge Trail junction. The Derrick Knob Shelter is 0.3 mile farther along the AT. The shelter is your second night's stay on a two-night backpack.

If skipping the shelter, turn sharply right (northeast) and head down the Greenbrier Ridge Trail. It's a nearly continuous descent of 4.2 miles back to the junction with Lynn Camp Prong and Middle Prong Trails. You pass through a variable second-growth forest along the way and make two uncertain stream crossings. The first, on a tributary to Indian Flats Prong, is the easier and isn't a problem except in very high water. The second crossing is over Indian Flats Prong and requires careful negotiation in high water. After prolonged rains, this crossing could be a wade. The creek here is very scenic, but try not to let that distract you on the crossing.

After the second creek crossing it's less than 0.5 mile back to Middle Prong Trail. Retrace your steps on Middle Prong Trail to the trailhead.

Options: While it's possible for experienced hikers to do this trip in a day, I don't recommend it. A better choice is to spend two nights, staying at Campsite 28 the first night and Derrick Knob Shelter on the second night. You could do the trip as an overnighter, staying the first night at site 28, but this leaves you with 15.4 miles on the second day with a heavy pack. If you spend the night at Derrick Knob Shelter, add 0.6 mile to the total round-trip mileage.

17 Chestnut Top Wildflowers

Highlights: *Wildflowers galore*

(See map for Hike 14: Spruce Flats Falls.)

Type of hike: Out-and-back; day hike with a shuttle option

Total distance: 1.0 mile round-trip

Difficulty: Moderate

Best time of year: Mid-April

Maps: Trails Illustrated; USGS Wear Cove

Finding the trailhead: The hike begins from Tennessee 73, near the junction with Little River Road and Laurel Creek Road, known locally as the Townsend Y. Look for a split-rail fence marking the trailhead on the south side, opposite Little River.

Parking and trailhead facilities: There's tons of parking available at the Townsend Y, but if you hike this trail in summer, you might not find an empty spot. The Y is an extremely popular swimming, sunning, and tubing spot. The nearest facilities are available in Townsend, a couple of miles north.

The hike: The first 0.5 mile of the Chestnut Top Trail provides the finest spring wildflower show of any trail in the Smokies of comparable distance. Considering that the Smokies have perhaps the greatest flowering display in the country, that's a bold statement. Hike the trail in the middle of April and see for yourself. There are trilliums, waterleaf, violets, dwarf iris, spring beauty, squawroot, anemone, toothwort, bloodroot, jack-in-the-pulpit, hepatica, false Solomon's seal, fire pink, cancer root, purple phacelia, wild ginger—I'm just warming up! See how many species you can count.

The flowering display continues somewhat throughout the spring and summer, but try to make this hike in April if possible. After about 0.5 mile the trail leaves the northeast-facing slope and swings around to a south-facing slope. Turn around here if you came for the wildflowers.

Options: With a second vehicle or a shuttle, you can hike all of Chestnut Top Trail to Schoolhouse Gap, 4.3 miles from the trailhead. At the gap you pick up the

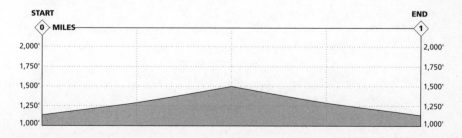

Schoolhouse Gap Trail and follow it 2.2 miles down to Laurel Creek Road, 3.6 miles from the Townsend Y. This is an OK hike, but if you're going to the trouble of taking two vehicles or arranging a commercial shuttle, there are better options in the park.

Lead Cove and Finley Cane

Type of hike: Loop; day hike
Total distance: 7.1 miles round-trip
Difficulty: Moderate

Maps: Trails Illustrated; USGS Thunderhead Mountain

Finding the trailhead: From the junction of Little River Road and Tennessee 73 (Townsend Y), head south on Laurel Creek Road toward Cades Cove. At 5.6 miles there's a narrow parking area on both sides of the road. The hike starts on the Lead Cove Trail, which begins on the south side of the road.

Parking and trailhead facilities: The combination of a popular trailhead and limited parking might mean you have to park alongside the road during busy weekends. Be careful; traffic on Laurel Creek Road can be terrible. Rest rooms and a camp store are available at the Cades Cove Campground, a few miles farther from the trailhead.

Key points:
   1.8 Junction with Bote Mountain Trail.
   4.3 Junction with Finley Cane Trail.

The hike: Both Finley Cane and Lead Cove Trails start from the south side of the road. Take Lead Cove Trail, on the right. You soon meet up with Sugar Cove Prong on the left, which you cross a short distance later. The trail ascends, steeply in places, through second-growth mixed hardwoods. You pass an old homesite on the

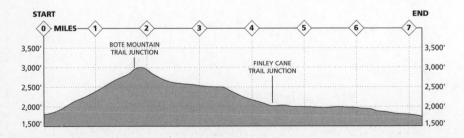

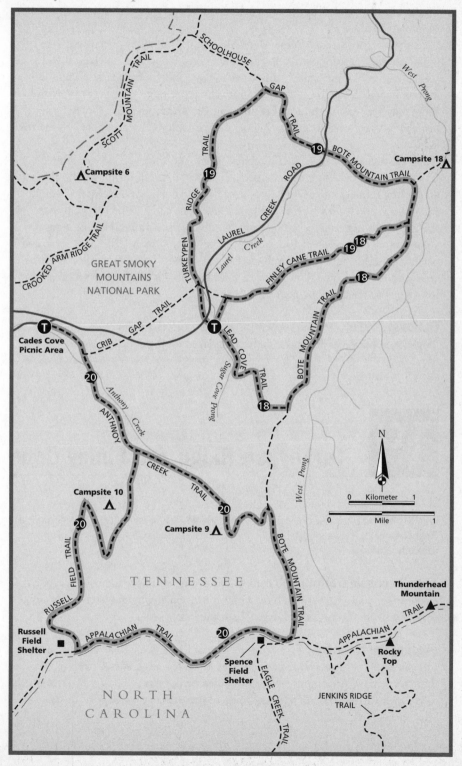

left, and at one point the forest opens up in a clearing with views of Turkeypen Ridge. Shortly beyond the clearing, the Lead Cove Trail ends on a ridge at Bote Mountain Trail.

Turn left (north) and follow Bote Mountain Trail along the ridge. The ridge walk is an easy descent, with a few steep sections. Good views of Defeat Ridge are off the east side of the trail. In a few places you can look back to see Thunderhead Mountain and Rocky Top. After 2.5 miles along the ridge the trail forks, with Bote Mountain Trail going right and continuing along the ridge and Finley Cane Trail heading left and away from the ridge. Take the Finley Cane Trail back to the trailhead.

As described in Hike 19: Turkeypen Ridge and Finley Cane, the Finley Cane Trail descends gradually through a scenic hardwood forest, spring wildflowers, rhododendron tunnels, and a patch of cane to the starting point on Laurel Creek Road. About 0.25 mile from the road you pass a limestone sinkhole on the right that looks like a filled-in mine shaft. Just beyond the sinkhole the trail forks. The right fork is a connector to Turkeypen Ridge Trail at its junction with Crib Gap Trail, and it passes through a tunnel under Laurel Creek Road. The tunnel allows horses to cross the road safely. Taking the left fork, ascend slightly and cross Sugar Cove Prong before reaching the parking area.

Options: See Hike 19: Turkeypen Ridge and Finley Cane for a description of two longer loop hikes involving the three trails hiked on this loop.

19 Turkeypen Ridge and Finley Cane

(See map for Hike 18: Lead Cove and Finley Cane.)

Type of hike: Loop; day hike
Total distance: 9.0 miles round-trip
Difficulty: Moderate

Maps: Trails Illustrated; USGS Wear Cove and Thunderhead Mountain

Special considerations: To complete the loop, you have to cross Laurel Creek Road twice. The road is often busy with vehicles (including monster motor homes) traveling to and from Cades Cove. Watch the kids.

Finding the trailhead: From the junction of Little River Road and Tennessee 73 (Townsend Y) head south on Laurel Creek Road toward Cades Cove. At 5.6 miles there's a narrow parking area on both sides of the road. The hike starts on the Turkeypen Ridge Trail, on the north side of the road.

Parking and trailhead facilities: The combination of a popular trailhead and limited parking might mean you have to park alongside the road during busy weekends. Be careful; traffic on Laurel Creek Road can be terrible. Rest rooms and camp store are available at the Cades Cove Campground, a few miles from the trailhead.

Key points:

0.2 Junction with Crib Gap Trail.

3.6 Junction with Schoolhouse Gap Trail.

4.7 Cross Laurel Creek Road at Schoolhouse Gap and Bote Mountain trailheads.

5.9 Junction with West Prong Trail.

6.2 Junction with Finley Cane Trail.

The hike: You pass large patches of squawroot to begin this hike on Turkeypen Ridge Trail. Squawroot is bear food in early spring, being one of the few edibles available at this time. After 0.2 mile the Crib Gap Trail turns left and an unnamed path goes right. Continue straight ahead on Turkeypen Ridge Trail. Soon you cross Laurel Creek at a small rock overhang and begin a moderate ascent to a small gap where a sawed-off stump makes a perfect resting seat. Look for an old piece of a stove lying here.

From the gap the trail continues on an easy, undulating course along the flanks of Turkeypen Ridge. You eventually cross over the ridge before descending to the Schoolhouse Gap Trail at Dosey Gap. Turn right (east) on Schoolhouse Gap Trail and follow this old roadbed 1.1 miles to Laurel Creek Road. Along the way you meet up with Spence Branch and follow it downstream. In late summer, look for cardinal flower, joe-pye weed, and ironweed growing along the creek.

At the road, turn left and walk 100 yards along the path, then cross over the road to the trailhead for Bote Mountain Trail. Hike this trail 1.2 miles up an unnamed creek drainage to a saddle and junction with West Prong Trail coming in from the left (north). Go right (south), continuing on Bote Mountain Trail, and follow the dry ridge about 0.3 mile to the junction with Finley Cane Trail. The river you hear on the east side of the ridge is West Prong Little River. Finley Cane Trail, which you want to take, turns sharply right (west) and descends gradually through a scenic hardwood forest, spring wildflowers, rhododendron tunnels, and, yes, a patch of cane to the starting point on Laurel Creek Road. About 0.25 mile from the road you

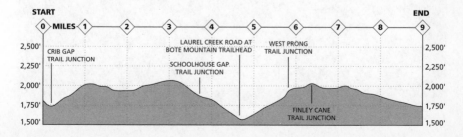

71

pass a limestone sinkhole on the right that looks like a filled-in mine shaft. Just beyond the sinkhole the trail forks. The right fork is a connector to Turkeypen Ridge Trail at its junction with Crib Gap Trail, and it passes through a tunnel under Laurel Creek Road. The tunnel allows horses to cross the road safely. Taking the left fork, ascend slightly and cross Sugar Cove Prong before reaching the parking area.

Don't forget to look both ways before crossing the road. It's a safe bet that the traffic on this road isn't looking out for you.

Options: Since this loop crosses the road twice, you can hike in four different directions. None is any better than the others, so you might as well hike it in the direction described above.

You can leave out the Finley Cane Trail from this hike and instead continue up Bote Mountain Trail and follow Lead Cove Trail back to the trailhead. This adds approximately 1.6 miles to the total distance. See Hike 18: Lead Cove and Finley Cane for a description of a shorter loop using the Lead Cove, Bote Mountain, and Finley Cane Trails.

View from Schoolhouse Gap Trail of auto bridge over Laurel Creek.

20

Spence Field via Cades Cove

Highlights: *Anthony Creek, Spence Field, big trees*

(See map for Hike 18: Lead Cove and Finley Cane.)

Type of hike: A "lollipop" loop; day hike, overnighter, or two-night backpack
Total distance: 13.2 miles round-trip

Difficulty: Difficult
Maps: Trails Illustrated; USGS Cades Cove and
Thunderhead Mountain

Special considerations: Spence Field Shelter is one of the most popular shelters in the park. Make reservations as early as possible if you plan to overnight there,
and be prepared with alternative dates. You might choose to stay at Russell Field
Shelter instead.

Finding the trailhead: The trail begins from the Cades Cove Picnic Area, but
there is no suitable hiker parking, and the picnic area is gated at night. Park just outside the picnic area at the start of the one-way loop road. To reach the parking area
drive 7.5 miles west on Laurel Creek Road from the Townsend Y (the junction of
Little River Road and Tennessee 73), and park in the large paved parking lot on the
left, just after passing the road to the campground and just before you begin the
loop road. To reach the trailhead, walk back to the road that leads to the campground. The picnic entrance is directly across from it. Walk to the far end of the
picnic area to a gated gravel road. A sign is here for Anthony Creek Trail.

The mileages given are from the trailhead. The distance from the parking area
to the trailhead is about 0.2 mile.

Parking and trailhead facilities: Parking is limited at the trailhead. If you can't
find a place there, don't park in a picnic space. Go back out to the large parking lot
at the start of the Cades Cove Loop Road. Rest rooms are at the picnic area. Basic
supplies are available at the nearby campground store.

Key points:
0.2 Junction with Crib Gap Trail.
1.7 Junction with Russell Field Trail.
2.9 Campsite 9.
3.6 Junction with Bote Mountain Trail.
5.3 Junction with Appalachian Trail at Spence Field.
5.4 Junction with Eagle Creek Trail. Spence Field Shelter is 0.2 mile on
Eagle Creek Trail.
8.0 Junction with Russell Field Trail at Russell Field Shelter.

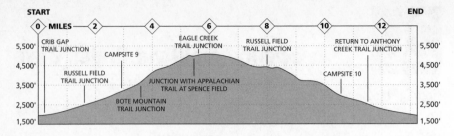

START   END

10.6 Campsite 10.

11.5 Return to junction of Anthony Creek and Russell Field Trails.

The hike: Spence Field is a favorite destination of backcountry hikers, so you can count on meeting lots of other hikers during the summer and on weekends any time of year.

The trail starts on a roadbed and soon passes Crib Gap Trail on the left. Remaining on the road, you pass a horse camp; a little later you cross Anthony Creek on a wide bridge. Stay to the left beyond the bridge (the road to the right leads to water tanks serving the campground). Shortly ahead you pass a bridle path on the right that leads around the campground. Stay to the left again. The forest through here is lovely, with big hemlocks and yellow-poplars and a lush understory of rhododendron.

Soon you cross Anthony Creek again—this time on a foot log—and the grade increases. Make one more crossing of Anthony Creek, then cross Left Prong Anthony Creek just before the junction with Russell Field Trail. You come down this trail later in the hike. Now you want to go left and remain on Anthony Creek Trail.

The trail passes through a scenic cove forest with several impressive trees. Cross Anthony Creek a final time, and climb alongside it to reach Campsite 9 on a slight slope. Beyond the campsite, the trail steepens on its approach to Bote Mountain Trail.

Reach Bote Mountain Trail on the ridgeline and turn right (south) onto it. The first 0.3 mile or so is along an old roadbed ending at a turnaround. In prepark days, herders drove livestock to the high grassy balds to graze during the summer, and Bote Mountain Trail was one of the routes they traveled. Countless grinding hooves created deep gullies in places beyond the turnaround, but the park rebuilt this section of the trail in 2001.

Bote Mountain Trail becomes very rocky on its approach to the Appalachian Trail (AT) at Spence Field. On reaching the AT, our hike goes right (west), but you might want to take a short side trip to the left and hike up to the grassy knoll. Off to the right on this knoll is a fine view into the Eagle Creek watershed. Actually, despite having read about the "spectacular" views from Spence Field, this is the only good view I have found. Spence Field itself is spectacular—an open, grassy bald with azaleas, mountain laurel, rhododendron, mountain ash, black cherry, and

Anthony Creek Trail in autumn.

numerous serviceberry trees growing with low, spreading branches. The views *of* the bald are wonderful, the views *from* the bald are lacking.

From the junction of Bote Mountain Trail and the AT, head west on the AT and in a few hundred feet come to the junction with Eagle Creek Trail on the left. A 0.2-mile walk down this trail takes you to the Spence Field Shelter, your home tonight if doing this trip as an overnighter. If continuing on the hike, keep heading west on the AT.

The 2.6-mile stretch from Spence Field to the Russell Field Shelter is easy compared with the hike up to Spence Field. You climb a little hump near the start and one toward the end, but mostly it's a pleasant downhill grade. Russell Field Shelter sits at the junction with the AT and Russell Field Trail. The setting is attractive, and the rustic shelter—as seen at my last visit—is charming. Hopefully, when you see it, it won't have ugly blue plastic tarps secured to the fencing as at some other park shelters.

Russell Field Trail leads directly in front of the shelter, heading north. On it you quickly pass a spring; at about 1.4 miles from the shelter you pass through the remaining vestiges of Russell Field. This open grassy area is scenic, but the bald is now mostly overgrown and the views obscured.

The hike between Russell Field and the junction with Anthony Creek Trail is a scenic forest walk marked by big trees and muddy quagmires. Reach Campsite 10 at 0.9 mile before the junction. It's an attractive site, situated in a grove of hemlock and rhododendron.

On returning to the junction with Anthony Creek Trail, turn left and retrace your steps to the trailhead.

Options: With two shelters on the AT and a campsite on the way up and down, you could do this hike as a lazy four-nighter. Most people opt for either a long day hike or an overnighter using Spence Field Shelter as the camp. A good number of people hike to Spence Field and return by the same route, but this shaves only 2.4 miles off the loop described here.

21

Rich Mountain Loop

Highlights: *John Oliver Cabin, views of Cades Cove*

Type of hike: Loop; day hike or overnighter
Total distance: 8.6 miles round-trip
Difficulty: Moderate

Best time of year: October
Maps: Trails Illustrated; USGS Cades Cove and Kinzel Springs

Finding the trailhead: Park in the large parking area at the entrance gate to Cades Cove. Reach the cove by driving 7.5 miles west on Laurel Creek Road from the Townsend Y (the junction of Little River Road and Tennessee 73). The trail begins opposite the parking lot, just beyond the gate.

Parking and trailhead facilities: The parking lot is huge, so you should have no problem finding a spot. Rest room facilities and basic supplies are available at the nearby campground store.

Key points:

0.5 Junction with Crooked Arm Ridge Trail.
1.4 John Oliver Cabin.
3.3 Junction with Indian Grave Gap Trail.
4.1 Junction with Rich Mountain Trail at Campsite 5.
5.9 Junction with Crooked Arm Ridge and Scott Mountain Trails.
8.1 Return to junction with Rich Mountain Loop Trail.

The hike: The best part about this hike is that you can experience some of the beauty of Cades Cove without having to encounter the crowds that sometimes appear on the 11-mile loop road through the cove. Except for a short stretch at John Oliver Cabin, you have this hike pretty much to yourself. The 1.4-mile stretch to the cabin is an easy, undulating course along the edge of cleared fields and in open forests with many standing dead trees. This is a great place to look for pileated and other woodpeckers. Even if you don't see a pileated, there's a good chance you'll

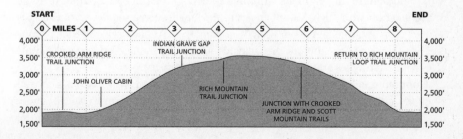

Rich Mountain Loop

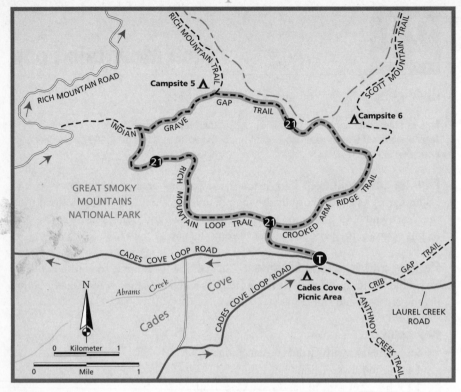

hear its junglelike call. About 0.5 mile into the hike you pass Crooked Arm Ridge Trail. This is where you come out after completing the loop.

Spend a little time exploring the John Oliver Cabin, built in the early 1820s, but not too much time. If you were interested in hordes of people, you'd have skipped this hike and driven the Cades Cove Loop Road. After leaving the cabin and crowds behind, the trail soon meets up with Marthas Branch and starts climbing in earnest. Pass an old crumbled chimney on the right, and cross over the branch several times before leaving the drainage to climb the flank of Cave Ridge. At mile 3.0, on the crest of the ridge, there is a great narrow-field view of Cades Cove. Below you is Sparks Lane, and far in the distance lie Spence Field, Russell Field, and Mollies Ridge.

From the overlook, it's 0.3 mile to the junction with Indian Grave Gap Trail, where you want to turn right and continue ascending the ridge for another 0.8 mile to the junction with Rich Mountain Trail in a small, scenic saddle. Campsite 5 is located a few hundred feet down Rich Mountain Trail. At one time, the Rich Mountain Shelter stood here, but all that remains now is the foundation. Water is available from a spring several hundred feet down the drainage.

Continuing along the ridge on Indian Grave Gap Trail, you reach a side trail about 0.3 mile from the Rich Mountain Trail junction. You're on Cerulean Knob, the highest point on Rich Mountain. The side path leads 100 steep yards to the summit and the foundation remains of the old Rich Mountain Fire Tower. Views are not good—you might catch a few winter glimpses into Dry Valley to the north. Back on the main trail, continue heading east. After a short distance you get a great winter view into Dry Valley, much better than the one from Cerulean Knob.

Continue along the Indian Grave Gap Trail until you come to a power line clearing that is right before the junction with Scott Mountain Trail, which goes left, and Crooked Arm Ridge Trail. Crooked Arm Ridge Trail is a continuation of Indian Grave Gap Trail. A couple hundred yards down the Scott Mountain Trail is Campsite 6 and a small spring. If doing this hike as an overnighter, you have the option of staying here or back at Campsite 5. I recommend Campsite 6.

From the trail junction, continue straight ahead on Crooked Arm Ridge Trail. The trail descends steeply to Rich Mountain Loop Trail, 0.5 mile from the parking area. Deep ruts and horse pies make this stretch an unpleasant hiking experience. However, several good leafy views into the cove make it bearable.

22 Abrams Falls

Highlights: *Abrams Creek and Abrams Falls, swimming hole, wildflowers*

Type of hike: Out-and-back; day hike
Total distance: 5.0 miles round-trip
Difficulty: Moderate

Best time of year: A rainy, winter weekday
Maps: Trails Illustrated; USGS Cades Cove and Calderwood

Special considerations: To make this hike, you have to drive the one-way, 11-mile loop road around Cades Cove. Cades Cove receives more visitors (more than two million annually) than all but ten of our national parks. To say it becomes crowded during the summer and fall is a gross understatement. Even in the off-season, the cove can become jammed on weekends. The Park Service is currently studying ways to lessen the crowding, including shuttle buses and trams.

Also consider that the trail to Abrams Falls is one of the most popular hikes in the park. Now you know I'm not kidding when I say it's best to make this hike on a

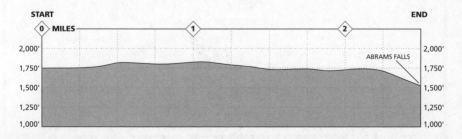

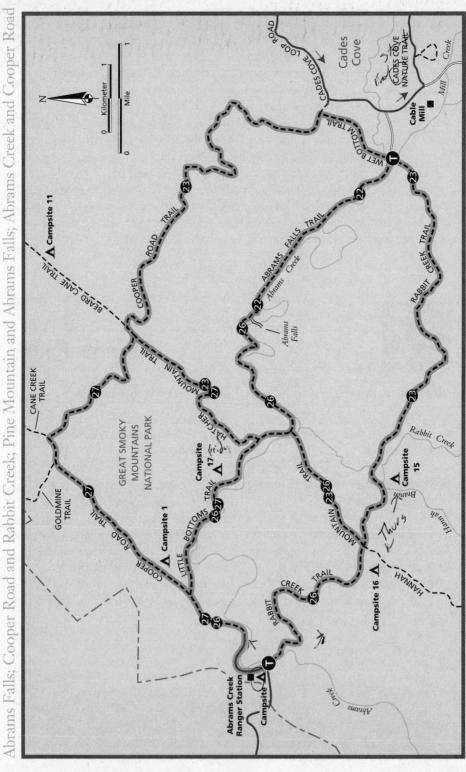

Abrams Falls; Cooper Road and Rabbit Creek; Pine Mountain and Abrams Falls; Abrams Creek and Cooper Road rainy, winter weekday. And, hey, if you want the best photos, this is the best time anyway.

Finding the trailhead: Reach Cades Cove by driving 7.5 miles west on Laurel Creek Road from the Townsend Y (the junction of Little River Road and Tennessee 73). From the start of the Cades Cove Loop Road, drive 4.9 miles and turn right onto the gravel side road. Continue 0.4 mile along this road to a large parking area. The trailhead for Abrams Falls is on the north end of the lot.

Parking and trailhead facilities: Even if the large gravel parking area is full, there is plenty of parking in the fields along the gravel road. Of course, if the parking area is so full that you have to park in a field, you might want to seriously reconsider this hike and choose a trail that offers more solitude. Rest rooms are available at Cades Cove Campground at the entrance to the cove and at the Cable Mill area 0.5 mile farther along the loop road. Keep in mind, though, that the loop road is one-way. You can't backtrack from Cable Mill.

Abrams Falls.

The hike: Cross the long footbridge over Abrams Creek and turn left on the other side, following the creek downstream. The trail is well graded and packed hard from thousands of footsteps. In several spots, you have close-up views of the creek; at other points the creek is out of sight. Although Abrams Creek loses only a little more than 200 feet in elevation along this hike, the trail is not level. It undulates in typical Smokies fashion. Look for wildflowers at any time from March until September. In spring you might spot the uncommon (in the Smokies) fringed polygala.

Abrams Falls is worthy of the attention it gets. It's not high (about 20 feet), but it has the greatest water volume of any major falls in the park—and also the largest plunge pool. On a hot summer day it's hard to resist a dip in the pool. The waterfall channels into the far side of the rock ledge extending across the river, and you can walk underneath the ledge right to the edge of the falls. Don't climb on the mossy rocks; many people have been hurt at this waterfall due to such carelessness.

Options: See Hike 26: Pine Mountain and Abrams Falls for a route to Abrams Falls that does not require driving the Cades Cove Loop Road.

23 Cooper Road and Rabbit Creek

Highlights: *Solitude, big trees*

(See map for Hike 22: Abrams Falls)

Type of hike: Loop; long summer day hike, overnighter, or two-night backpack
Total distance: 16.3 miles round-trip

Difficulty: Moderate
Maps: Trails Illustrated; USGS Cades Cove, Kinzel Springs, Blockhouse, and Calderwood

Special considerations: There are three significant creek crossings on this hike. The first one, over Abrams Creek, is a definite wade and may be too dangerous to attempt in high water. The next one, over Rabbit Creek, could be a wade in very high water, and the last one, over Mill Creek, is a sure wade except in very low flows.

See the other special considerations under Hike 22: Abrams Falls. The Abrams Falls hike has the same trailhead as this one.

Finding the trailhead: Reach Cades Cove by driving 7.5 miles west on Laurel Creek Road from the Townsend Y (the junction of Little River Road and Tennessee 73). From the start of the Cades Cove Loop Road, drive 4.9 miles and turn right onto the gravel side road. Continue 0.4 mile along this road to a large parking area. The trailhead for Abrams Falls Trail, which you start on, is on the north end of the lot.

Cooper Road Trail.

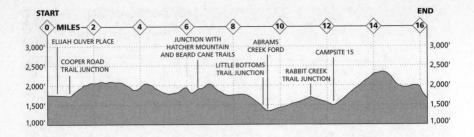

Parking and trailhead facilities: Even if the large gravel parking area is full, there is plenty of parking in the fields along the gravel road. Rest rooms are available at Cades Cove Campground at the entrance to the cove and at the Cable Mill area 0.5 mile farther along the loop road. Keep in mind, though, that the loop road is one-way. You can't backtrack from Cable Mill.

Key points:

0.5 Elijah Oliver Place.

1.0 Junction with Cooper Road Trail.

6.5 Junction with Hatcher Mountain and Beard Cane Trails.

9.2 Junction with Little Bottoms Trail.

9.3 Junction with Abrams Falls and Hannah Mountain Trails at Abrams Creek ford.

11.2 Junction with Rabbit Creek Trail at Scott Gap. Campsite 16 is nearby.

12.2 Campsite 15.

The hike: Although there really isn't a preferred time of year to make this hike, June is a good option. It's warm enough to make the creek wades bearable, and that's when the mountain laurel blooms. Winter has a special charm, but Abrams Creek can be impassable then.

Start on the Abrams Falls Trail like everyone else, but once you cross Abrams Creek on the footbridge, turn right at the sign for Elijah Oliver Place. An easy (and dry) walk takes you to the cabin in 0.5 mile. By going this route you bypass the first section of Wet Bottoms Trail, an appropriately named connector from the parking area to Cooper Road Trail that's used mainly for horses. After exploring the Elijah Oliver Cabin and outbuildings, continue on the dirt road leading from the cabin. Pass a barn on the left and cross a small creek. Just past the creek crossing, take the Wet Bottoms Trail to the left and go 0.25 mile to Cooper Road Trail.

A right turn on Cooper Road Trail leads back to the Cades Cove Loop Road in 0.2 mile. Our hike turns left (northwest) and follows the old road for 5.5 miles. It's typical Smokies hiking along this stretch, up over humps and ridges, down to cross small creeks and dry drainages. The road makes for good walking, with mostly moderate grades, though a few are a little steep. In summer look for cardinal flowers growing near the streams and yellow fringed orchids along the side of the road.

At a small gap, Hatcher Mountain Trail goes left, Beard Cane Trail goes right, and Cooper Road Trail continues straight ahead. If doing this hike as a two-night backpack, turn right (east) and hike 1.0 mile on the Beard Cane Trail to Campsite 11, a small, rarely used site. The next morning, backtrack to this junction. If continuing on the hike, go left (west) on the Hatcher Mountain Trail. After an easy climb, the trail descends to cross two streams and ascends again to a ridgeline. From here it's a long, easy ridgeline walk and descent to Abrams Creek. At 0.1 mile from the creek, the Little Bottoms Trail comes in sharply from the right; continue straight to reach the creek.

The ford at Abrams Creek marks the junction of three trails: Hatcher Mountain Trail, which brought you here; Hannah Mountain Trail, which you now take; and Abrams Falls Trail, which leads 1.7 miles upstream to Abrams Falls. Abrams Falls is a highly recommended side trip, but on this hike you probably won't have time unless you're doing a two-night backpack.

Now you must wade across Abrams Creek. In summer slip off your boots and enjoy the invigorating water. In winter, or after prolonged rains, be very careful. The creek (actually a small river) can become a raging torrent during these times, and crossing it might be extremely dangerous, even impossible. Don't hesitate to turn back if you feel uncomfortable. If you do turn back, you can salvage the trip by taking Abrams Creek Trail back to the trailhead so that you don't have to backtrack.

After the crossing, Hannah Mountain Trail climbs steeply a short distance then becomes a gentle ascent to a broad ridge. From the ridge to Scott Gap is easy walking along the contour line. At Scott Gap, Hannah Mountain Trail crosses Rabbit Creek Trail and continues 7.6 miles to Parson Branch Road. Rabbit Creek Trail goes right to the Abrams Creek Ranger Station; that leg and the section of Hannah Mountain Trail you just hiked are part of Hike 26: Pine Mountain and Abrams Falls. If doing an overnighter or two-night backpack, your home tonight is Campsite 16, a few hundred yards down the other side of the gap.

After admiring the large trees (one huge yellow-poplar) at the gap, turn left (east) on Rabbit Creek Trail and pass through a scenic forest with more large trees. About 0.75 mile from Scott Gap, steep banks squeeze the trail and you find yourself hiking in a small streambed through a narrow passage. Shortly beyond, you reach the crossing of Rabbit Creek, easily rock-hopped in low flows but a possible wade in higher water. Don't worry; the fact that you made it across Abrams Creek to get to this point means you won't have a problem here. Beyond the crossing, on the right in a hemlock grove, is Campsite 15. You could camp here on the second night of a two-night backpack if you don't mind adding an extra mile to your second day's hike.

Now comes the hardest part of the hike—a mile-long, nearly continuous uphill grind along a spur to Andy McCully Ridge. Once on the ridge, you have a few ups and downs typical of ridge hiking, and you might start to think this trail can't possibly go uphill anymore. The forest is an open mixture of pine and hardwoods, typical of the western end of the park.

Coon Butt marks the last of the climbing except for a few slight swells. From here the trail descends to cross More Licker Branch then climbs over a small ridge before joining Victory Branch and following it downstream to Mill Creek. In the summer and fall dry season, you might be able to cross Mill Creek in high-top boots without getting your feet wet, but don't count on it. Usually this is a wet wade, but it's an easy one. Don't worry about cold feet. The trailhead, and the heater in your car, is just a few feet on the other side of the crossing.

Options: The Abrams Creek area presents several possibilities for day hike loops, as well as short or extended backpacking trips. The six backcountry campsites in the area provide many overnight options; study a trail map for possibilities. All the possible routes will combine trails described in Hikes 22, 23, 26, and 27.

24

Gregory Bald via Cades Cove

Highlights: *Superb views, old-growth forest, brilliant display of azaleas*

Type of hike: Out-and-back; day hike or over-nighter, with loop option
Total distance: 11.4 miles round-trip

Difficulty: Difficult
Best time of year: Middle to late June
Maps: Trails Illustrated; USGS Cades Cove

Special considerations: If you don't like meeting other people on your trips, avoid this hike during the azalea bloom. Also, reaching the trailhead requires driving halfway around the insanely popular 11-mile Cades Cove Loop Road. If you wait more than a few hours after sunrise to drive the road, expect delays from slow or stopped traffic.

Finding the trailhead: Reach Cades Cove by driving 7.5 miles west on Laurel Creek Road from the Townsend Y (the junction of Little River Road and Tennessee 73). From the start of the one-way Cades Cove Loop Road, drive 5.4 miles and turn right on Forge Creek Road, just past the large parking area for Cable Mill. Follow the gravel road 2.2 miles to its end at a small traffic circle. Gregory Ridge Trail starts from the circle and is obvious.

Parking and trailhead facilities: Unless you get here early in the morning, expect to find the traffic circle full and cars lined up along the road. Rest room facilities are located at the Cable Mill area.

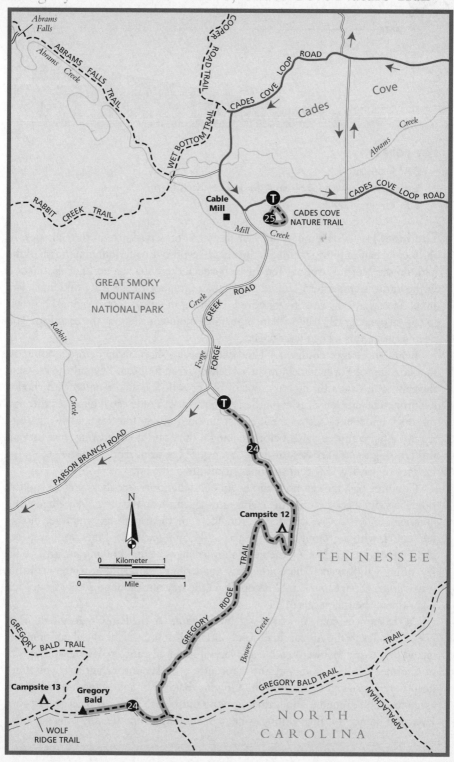

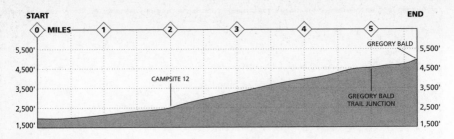

Key points:

2.0 Campsite 12.

5.0 Junction with Gregory Bald Trail at Rich Gap.

5.7 Gregory Bald.

The hike: For every time of the year there is a preferred hike in the Smokies. In the second half of June, this hike is the one. Excepting Roan Mountain (north of the park on the North Carolina–Tennessee border), there may be no finer destination in the entire southeastern United States than Gregory Bald during middle to late June. Azaleas are the reason—hundreds of them, in every color imaginable, growing on an open, grassy bald with incomparable mountain views as the backdrop. You need to make this hike at least once.

Begin on Gregory Ridge Trail and climb over a short hump before leveling off to a crossing of Forge Creek on an asphalt-covered foot log. Beyond the crossing the trail soon passes through a grove of old-growth forest, entangled with rhododendron. The creek is nearby on the left, but you can only catch glimpses through the thick understory. Cross the creek again on a mossy foot log and swing away from it a few hundred yards before making a third and final crossing. Just beyond this crossing the trail passes through Campsite 12, a wonderful campsite except for the lack of privacy. One tent site does sit off the trail a bit.

Continue past the campsite and begin climbing more steeply as you ascend the ridge on switchbacks. Notice the change in vegetation on the drier ridge. Below, the dominant understory was rhododendron. Here, on the drier ridge, you'll see mountain laurel, with a ground cover of galax and trailing arbutus. Pines are here, too, and blueberries. Farther up, the vegetation changes again; if hiking in April you'll see spring wildflowers. There are a few good views, especially in winter with the leaves gone. From Campsite 12 it's uphill all the way until about 0.2 mile from Rich Gap, where the trail levels off.

At the gap you come to a four-way intersection. To the left, Gregory Bald Trail goes 2.1 miles to the Appalachian Trail on Doe Knob. Straight ahead, an unmaintained (but easily followed) path leads several hundred yards to Moore Spring, site of a former herder's cabin and, more recently, a backcountry shelter. If you don't need water, turn right (west) on the Gregory Bald Trail and follow the ridgeline, ascending first around a knoll, then leveling out before the final push to Gregory Bald. Just before this final climb, a side path comes in from the left. This path also

Gregory Bald.

leads to Moore Spring, so if you take the manway from Rich Gap to the spring, you can continue on that path to the junction here. The final push to Gregory Bald is short, but rather steep.

Gregory Bald is a ten-acre clearing on the ridgeline. Thick mountain oat grass carpets the clearing, and scattered everywhere are hundreds of flame azalea shrubs. Every imaginable color—whites, reds, yellows, and oranges—is represented, including my personal favorite, the stark fuchsias that look almost electrified, like wet finger paint. As with many Southern Appalachian balds, nobody knows how Gregory formed or even whether it's man-made or natural, though there seems to be a consensus that this one is natural. We do know that the clearing is a small representation of a much larger meadow that existed in prepark days. Back then the bald served as prime grazing land for livestock. The Park Service is attempting to restore the bald to something resembling its prepark status. You see countless stubs where crews have cut back the blueberries, blackberries, and other shrubs that have invaded the bald.

If you can't make this hike when the azaleas bloom, don't fret. The views alone are more than worth the climb. Cades Cove sprawls out to the northeast, and to the southwest lies the Joyce Kilmer–Slickrock Wilderness in the Unicoi Mountains. Due south is Fontana Lake, and between the lake and you stands Shuckstack Tower. Trees obscure the view to the west.

Our hike ends on the bald, but if you're doing this trip as an overnighter, continue on the Gregory Bald Trail and descend 0.4 mile to Campsite 13, one of the finest in the Smokies. A large, grassy, and somewhat open clearing in a level swag provides several tent sites offering relative privacy. The site is rationed and usually full on weekends and on weekdays in June. If spending the night here, set your alarm clock and hike back up on the bald to watch the sunrise. You have the bald, and the show, to yourself at this hour. The last time I watched the sunrise from Gregory Bald, I also witnessed two fawns suckling from their mother not 20 feet away. One fawn mistook me for another mommy and followed me around the bald like a puppy.

Options: If you don't want to backtrack, you can take Gregory Bald Trail to the trailhead on Parson Branch Road and then walk along the road back to Forge Creek Road. The Gregory Bald section is 4.5 miles and the Parson Branch Road section about 5 miles. From Parson Branch Road to the traffic circle is only 0.1 mile. This makes for a loop hike of about 15.3 miles, which is doable as a long day hike. Or you could camp at Campsite 13 and finish the loop the next day. You can drive to the trailhead on Parson Branch Road, but the road is one-way from the cove and makes shuttling a hassle. Getting back to the cove requires a two- to three-hour drive from the Gregory Bald trailhead.

25

Cades Cove Nature Trail

(See map for Hike 24: Gregory Bald via Cades Cove.)

Type of hike: Loop; day hike

Total distance: 0.4 mile round-trip

Difficulty: Moderate

Maps: Trails Illustrated; USGS Cades Cove

Finding the trailhead: Reach Cades Cove by driving 7.5 miles west on Laurel Creek Road from the Townsend Y (the junction of Little River Road and Tennessee 73). The nature trail is located along the Cades Cove Loop Road, 5.8 miles from its start and 0.4 mile from the Cable Mill area.

Parking and trailhead facilities: Rest room facilities are available at the Cable Mill area or near the start of the loop road at the campground store. The store sells basic camping supplies. Bicycle rentals are also available.

The hike: This is a typical Smokies interpretive nature trail. It's great to kill a half hour or for a leisurely outing with the kids, but it's not a hike you plan your trip around. The interpretive brochure (50 cents to keep) for this nature trail emphasizes the early settlers' uses of forest products and is interesting reading. Don't look for the sourwood tree at marker #7, however, because it's no longer there.

From the parking area, hike 100 feet on an old roadbed and turn left to ascend a narrow rut. The sign calls this hike "a very easy walk," but the first half is a moderate ascent. At marker #10, turn right to complete the loop.

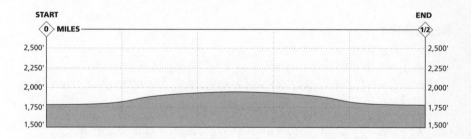

26 Pine Mountain and Abrams Falls

Highlights: *Abrams Creek, Abrams Falls, mountain laurel in June*

(See map for Hike 22: Abrams Falls.)

Type of hike: Loop (actually an upside-down "lollipop"); day hike or one- to two-night backpack
Total distance: 11.7 miles round-trip

Difficulty: Moderate
Best time of year: June
Maps: Trails Illustrated; USGS Calderwood

Special considerations: An unbridged crossing over Abrams Creek cannot be rock-hopped, and in high water it might be too dangerous to wade.

Finding the trailhead: Trailhead parking is in a field near the Abrams Creek Ranger Station at the western end of the park. From the junction of Foothills Parkway and U.S. 129 (approximately 22 miles south of Maryville, Tennessee, and 25 miles north of Fontana, North Carolina), go less than 0.1 mile south on U.S. 129 and turn left on Happy Valley Road. Drive 5.7 miles on this road through Happy Valley and turn right at the sign for the campground and ranger station. Pass the ranger station at 0.6 mile; the parking area is a short distance farther on both sides of the road.

Parking and trailhead facilities: The parking area is in a large field, so all possible parking places rarely fill up. However, on summer weekends you might not get an easy spot to pull into. There are no facilities available to noncampers anywhere near here.

Key points:

0.1 Cross Abrams Creek on a foot log.
2.7 Junction with Hannah Mountain Trail; Campsite 16 is nearby.
4.6 Abrams Creek Ford at junction with Hatcher Mountain and Abrams Falls Trails.
6.3 Abrams Falls.
8.0 Return to junction with Hatcher Mountain and Abrams Falls Trails.

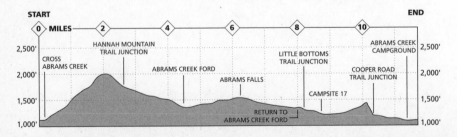

The hike: The pine-oak woods in the western end of the park receive little visitation compared with the park's other regions. You'll have most of this hike to yourself, but expect lots of company at Abrams Falls.

From the parking area walk back up the road 125 yards and turn left onto Rabbit Creek Trail, just beyond the ranger station. The trail leads a short distance to Abrams Creek and follows it downstream to a foot log below a ford. From the foot log you have a fine view of Abrams Creek. Study the creek carefully here. If you'd feel uncomfortable wading this ford (which you might have to do anyway if heavy flooding has washed away the foot log), you need to reconsider making this hike, since the crossing later on has no foot log. While that crossing is much farther upstream—with a lower water flow—the ford here still provides a good indication of what you can expect.

Shortly beyond the crossing, the trail passes through a clearing with wild roses, day lilies, and daffodils, revealing that this was once a homesite. Here the trail begins climbing Pine Mountain. You get a few level spurts along the way, but this is mostly a long, sometimes steep, haul up the mountain. A man-made flat pad in an outside bend marks the high point of the climb and the highest elevation of the entire hike at 2,064 feet. You can rest your lungs on the 0.5-mile descent to Scott Gap.

Scott Gap marks the intersection of Rabbit Creek and Hannah Mountain Trails. Rabbit Creek Trail continues straight and reaches Cades Cove in another 5.1 miles, while a right turn on Hannah Mountain Trail takes you to Parson Branch Road. A few hundred feet down the west side of the gap, Campsite 16 lies on a bed of pine needles. If you're making this hike as a leisurely two-night backpack, this will be your first night's stay. The small spring here may dry up during prolonged rainless periods, so consider the undependable water supply when planning your trip.

Before leaving the gap, take time to admire the large trees here, including the massive yellow-poplar. Now turn left (east) on the Hannah Mountain Trail and enjoy one of the easiest stretches of trail in the park as you follow the contour line on a long hike over cushiony pine needles. At a broad ridge, the trail begins a gradual descent to Abrams Creek, with only the last portion being steep. The creek must be waded. Don't hesitate to turn back if you feel uncomfortable.

Once on the far side, turn right on Abrams Falls Trail and follow it upstream 1.7 miles to Abrams Falls. (See Hike 22: Abrams Falls for a discussion of the waterfall.) After viewing the falls, backtrack to the trail junction and head downstream on the Hatcher Mountain Trail. Soon the trail forks, with the Hatcher Mountain Trail heading right and up the mountain, while the Little Bottoms Trail (our route) goes left and downhill. Little Bottoms Trail is poorly graded in places, looking more like a spot on the hillside with the leaves raked away than it does a hiking trail. You definitely need ankle-supporting shoes on this trail.

About 0.7 mile from the Hatcher Mountain Trail junction is Campsite 17, one of the most pleasant sites in the Smokies. It sits on a large level bench above Abrams Creek in a forest of hemlock and white pine. Pine needles cushion the tent pads, and the sites are far enough apart to provide reasonable privacy. This is your second night's stay on a two-night backpack, and if spending only one night this would be a better choice than Campsite 16. For one thing, you have most of the hike behind you, and you can laze your way back to the car the next day. The site is very popular but not rationed, so you take a chance on having a decent tent site on summer weekends.

Beyond the campsite, the trail continues to follow Abrams Creek downstream before eventually pulling away and climbing steeply to a ridge. An even steeper descent takes you to Cooper Road Trail at Campsite 1. At only 1.3 easy miles from the trailhead, this site is often crowded—particularly with youth groups. A left turn onto Cooper Road Trail takes you to Abrams Creek Campground in 0.9 mile. Walk through the campground and along the gravel road back to the trailhead.

This hike is rewarding in any season, but you may want to avoid winter and early spring because of the high water in Abrams Creek. The best time may be in June, when the abundant mountain laurel is in bloom.

Options: You can shave 3.4 miles off the total distance by passing up the side trip to Abrams Falls. For an all-day loop or a one- to two-night backpacking trip, you can combine this hike with Hike 27: Abrams Creek and Cooper Road. Camp the first or second night at Campsite 17, then backtrack to the junction with Hatcher Mountain Trail. Take Hatcher Mountain Trail to Cooper Road Trail, and follow Cooper Road Trail back to the trailhead. See Hike 27 for more details.

Abrams Creek and Cooper Road

Highlights: *Abrams Creek, mountain laurel in June*

(See map for Hike 22: Abrams Falls.)

Type of hike: Loop; day hike or overnighter
Total distance: 11.6 miles round-trip
Difficulty: Moderate

Best time of year: June
Maps: Trails Illustrated; USGS Calderwood and Blockhouse

Special considerations: Portions of this hike receive heavy horse traffic, so look out for horse pies. You might stop at a few and observe the dung beetles.

Finding the trailhead: Trailhead parking is in a field near the Abrams Creek Ranger Station at the western end of the park. From the junction of Foothills Parkway and U.S. 129 (approximately 22 miles south of Maryville, Tennessee, and 25 miles north of Fontana, North Carolina), go less than 0.1 mile south on U.S. 129 and turn left on Happy Valley Road. Drive 5.7 miles on this road through Happy Valley and turn right at the sign for the campground and ranger station. Pass by the ranger station at 0.6 mile; the parking area is a short distance farther on both sides of the road.

Parking and trailhead facilities: The parking area is in a large field, so all potential parking places rarely fill up. However, on summer weekends you might not get an easy spot to pull into. There are no facilities available to noncampers anywhere near here.

Key points:

0.4 Cooper Road trailhead at Abrams Creek Campground.

1.3 Junction with Little Bottoms Trail.

2.9 Campsite 17.

3.6 Junction with Hatcher Mountain Trail.

6.4 Junction with Cooper Road Trail.

8.1 Junction with Cane Creek Trail.

8.7 Junction with Goldmine Trail.

10.3 Return to junction with Little Bottoms Trail.

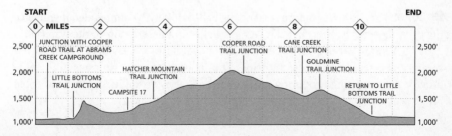

The hike: Walk along the gravel road to Abrams Creek Campground and take one of the forks through the campground to the other side. Cooper Road Trail begins here beyond the gate. Cooper Road was once a major access route to Cades Cove. Its wide and relatively gentle grade makes it a popular horse and hiking trail. After 0.9 mile and two quick fords of Kingfisher Creek, arrive at the junction with Little Bottoms Trail on the right, just before Campsite 1. Take Little Bottoms Trail on an extremely steep climb up and over a ridge, eventually leveling out at Abrams Creek. If making this hike in the summer, you immediately notice, and appreciate, the temperature difference between here and back up on the ridge.

Now follow the poorly graded trail upstream along scenic Abrams Creek, arriving at Campsite 17 on the left. Camp here if making this trip as an overnighter. The site sits at a former homesite a few feet above Abrams Creek. It's large, with good privacy and a soft pine needle ground cover. The site is especially popular among fishers.

Pressing on from Campsite 17, and watching your footing along the poor trail, you come to the junction with Hatcher Mountain Trail, cutting sharply left (northwest) and climbing the mountain. Continuing straight at this junction will take you in 1.8 miles to Abrams Falls, a highly recommended side trip. If skipping the falls, turn left onto Hatcher Mountain Trail (incorrectly labeled HANNAH MOUNTAIN TRAIL on the Calderwood USGS map) and begin a long, moderate ascent through a forest of pine, sassafras, oak, and huckleberry. The trail now descends gradually and crosses a couple of branches before ascending again and making the final descent to the junction with Cooper Road Trail in a small gap.

To the right on Cooper Road Trail, it's 5.7 miles to Cades Cove. Straight ahead, the Beard Cane Trail leads 4.2 miles to the Ace Gap Trail. Our hike goes left (north) on Cooper Road Trail and follows an easy, mostly downhill route to Cane Gap. Look for pink lady's slipper orchids growing along this stretch in May and June. At the gap the Cane Creek Trail goes straight ahead, while Cooper Road Trail swings around to the left. Continuing on Cooper Road Trail, hike along a short level section before making a steep climb to the junction with Goldmine Trail, forking off to the right. Stay left (south) and enjoy a 1.6-mile downhill run to the junction with Little Bottoms Trail. Along the way you cross Kingfisher Creek and some of its tributaries. The creek is appropriately named. On every visit I've made to the Abrams Creek Campground area, I've been rewarded with the sight of a belted kingfisher.

From the trail junction, retrace your steps back to the trailhead.

Options: The 3.6-mile side trip to Abrams Falls is highly recommended if you have the time and energy. See Hike 22: Abrams Falls for a description of the waterfall.

The Abrams Creek area presents several possibilities for day hike loops, as well as short or extended backpacking trips. The six backcountry campsites in the area provide many overnight options; study a trail map for possibilities. All the possible routes will combine trails described in Hikes 22, 23, 26, and 27.

Northeast
SECTION

Hiking to Mt. LeConte

The Cascades have Mt. Rainier, Yellowstone has Old Faithful, and Great Smoky Mountains National Park has Mt. LeConte. At 6,593 feet, LeConte is only the third-highest peak in the Smokies, but in many people's mind, it's bigger than Everest. In 1924, when the U.S. government sent a party to study the possibility of creating a national park in the region, a local group of park supporters took them to LeConte. Of all the places in the Smokies from which they could choose, they knew that Mt. LeConte would make the biggest impression. The mountain continues to impress.

Three hikes in this guidebook lead to the summit of LeConte: Mt. LeConte via The Boulevard (31); Mt. LeConte via Rainbow Falls and Bull head (35); and Mt. LeConte via Trillium Gap Trail (37). All three are doable as day hikes, and you have two options for staying overnight on the summit. The Mt. LeConte Shelter sits in an open field a few feet below High Top, the highest of LeConte's peaks. Its amenities are just like any other shelter in the park.

Not too far from the shelter, but still on LeConte's summit, is the LeConte Lodge. Hikers who don't know anything about LeConte's history are quite startled when they happen upon the lodge after making what they thought was a hike into the "wilderness." The lodge opened in the late 1920s and has been in operation ever since, albeit with many improvements along the way. There is no electricity or running water, but modern enhancements include flush toilets and gas heat.

Helicopters fly in supplies for the lodge at the start of the season. (The lodge closes in winter). During the operating season, llamas pack fresh food and laundry to the lodge. Passing the llama train on Trillium Gap Trail is a special treat for hikers.

The meals never change: stew beef, green beans, mashed potatoes (from a mix), stewed apples, biscuits, and a cookie for supper; pancakes, Canadian bacon, biscuits with jam and butter, grits, and scrambled eggs for breakfast. After supper, guests hike a short trail to Cliff Top to watch the sunset. Before breakfast, a few guests hike out to Myrtle Point to watch the sunrise. Cliff Top is also the site of a number of weddings. Yep, more than one bride and groom have hiked up here with a minister and wedding party and exchanged vows on the rocks of Cliff Top.

Reservations for the lodge are not only required but also nearly impossible to get. The number to call is (865) 429–5704. Appendix A lists a number of publications that make good reading before making a trip to the summit.

The four hikes detailed in this guidebook use every trail that leads to LeConte's summit and cover the most popular and practical hike combinations. A few other options exist if taking advantage of a shuttle service or second vehicle. Study a trail map for possibilities.

Finally, a word of caution. You might think that a winter hike to LeConte would allow you to experience the mountain without encountering hordes of other hikers. You'd be right, but before you embark on such a trek, consider your abilities honestly. That sunny 50-degree weather you leave in Gatlinburg can become a severe snowstorm in single-digit temperatures on LeConte's summit. Also, the north-facing sections of the rocky trails keep a near-constant glaze of ice throughout winter, making hiking dangerous even when the weather is pleasant. I'm not saying you should cancel the trip; just that you must prepare for it and not overestimate your abilities.

LeConte Lodge.

28 Sugarlands Valley Nature Trail

Highlights: *Handicapped-accessible trail*

Type of hike: Loop; day hike
Total distance: 0.5 mile round-trip

Difficulty: Easy
Maps: USGS Gatlinburg

Special considerations: This is the only trail in the park that is easy for persons in a wheelchair to traverse.

Finding the trailhead: Drive 0.4 mile south of Sugarlands Visitor Center on Newfound Gap Road. The paved parking area is on the left. The trail is signed and obvious.

Sugarlands Valley Nature Trail; Noah "Bud" Ogle Nature Trail; Twin Creeks

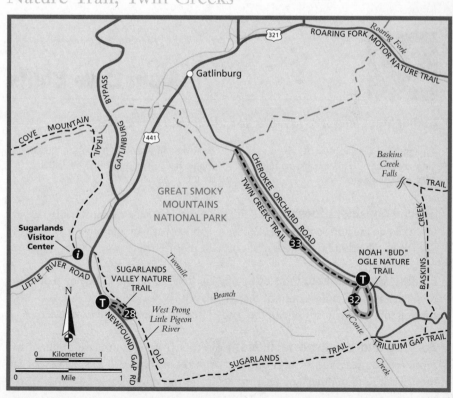

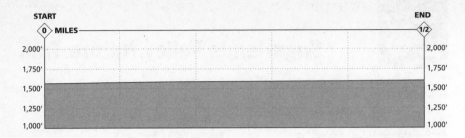

Parking and trailhead facilities: The parking lot is small but rarely full. Rest rooms are available at Sugarlands Visitor Center.

The hike: Physically challenged persons will enjoy this chance to explore the Smokies away from the roads. The entire path is paved and nearly level. As a self-guiding nature trail, it has numbered features along the way; an interpretive leaflet (50 cents to keep) is available at the trailhead. Additionally, features along this trail have been recorded on audiotape. A copy of the tape and a tape player are available at Sugarlands Visitor Center. While the paved path, easy access, and proximity to the main park road might detract from a "wilderness" experience, this hike is a wonderful opportunity for those wanting a short, easy hike.

29

Alum Cave Bluffs

Highlights: *Cascading creek, Arch Rock, Alum Cave Bluffs, views*

Type of hike: Out-and-back; day hike
Total distance: 4.6 miles round-trip
Difficulty: Moderate

Best time of year: Winter, to avoid the crowds
Maps: Trails Illustrated; USGS Mt. LeConte

Special considerations: If you don't make this hike on a winter weekday, expect lots of company. On summer weekends, or in October, you might as well walk the sidewalks in Gatlinburg. There won't be a lot of difference.

Finding the trailhead: On Newfound Gap Road, drive 4.2 miles north of Newfound Gap or 8.5 miles south of Sugarlands Visitor Center. There are two large parking lots on the north side of the road. The trail is signed and obvious.

Parking and trailhead facilities: Even though the Alum Cave trailhead has more parking places than most other trails in the park, it also fills up faster than most. Wait until midmorning on a weekend and you might not get a spot.

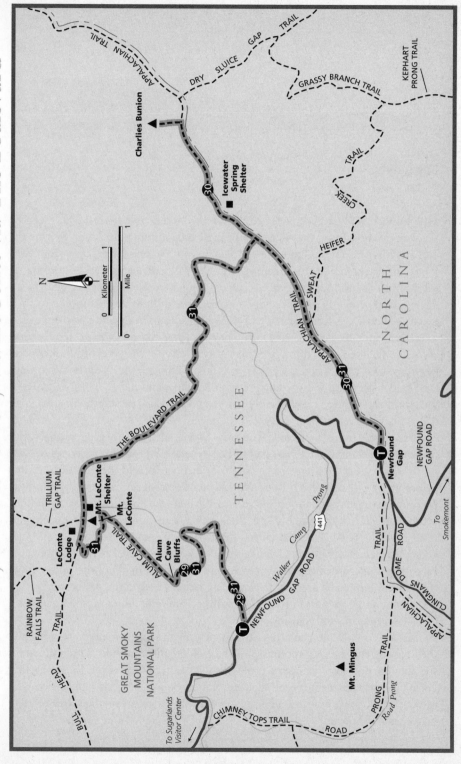

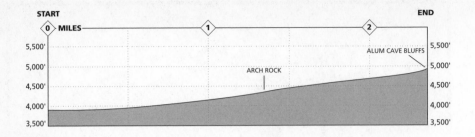

Key points:
1.4 Arch Rock.

The hike: It doesn't get much better than this. Every able person who visits the Smokies needs to make this hike at least once. If continuing the 2.7 miles from the bluffs to Mt. LeConte, I'd rate this the best hike in the park. Even if you stop at the bluffs and backtrack—as outlined in this hike—it's still hard to beat. Of course, there always seems to be a downside. On a summer weekend you can expect to see a few billion people along this hike—and that's just a slight exaggeration.

The Alum Cave Trail quickly crosses Walker Camp Prong and then Alum Cave Creek on sturdy bridges. For the next mile or so, you hike on a gentle uphill course alongside the creek and through an old-growth forest. The creekbed looks different from other creeks in the Smokies, and it is. The steep slopes of the Alum Cave Creek drainage make it especially prone to flooding, and the regular torrents keep the streambed scoured clean of moss, ferns, and the usual undergrowth seen along other Smoky Mountain waterways.

After a little more than a mile, you cross Styx Branch on a foot log, probably not realizing that Alum Cave Creek had forked off eastward toward the slopes of Anakeesta Knob. Shortly afterward, cross the branch again, and then for a third time before passing through Arch Rock. (An old route, shown on the topo map, had the trail continuing along Alum Cave Creek to a switchback, then leading to Arch Rock without crossing Styx Branch.) Arch Rock is one of the most interesting geological features in the park. The trail climbs through an opening, an "arch" in the Anakeesta Formation. It's not an arch like those in Arches National Park or those in the valley and ridge provinces of Tennessee and Kentucky. In simplistic terms, those arches were formed by erosion from running water. Here, in the Anakeesta Formation, holes in the rock form from the expansion and crumbling caused by millions of years of freezing and thawing.

Beyond Arch Rock, you cross Styx Branch for the final time on a foot log and then pass by the site of a recent (1993) flash flood and landslide. The trail climbs steeply now, and soon you get a profile view of Little Duck Hawk Ridge. Farther up, at an especially scenic vista called Inspiration Point, you get another good view of the ridge. See if you can find both arches in the ridge. In summer, one of them may be hard to spot.

Alum Cave Trail leading through Arch Rock, with Styx Branch in the foreground.

From Inspiration Point it's a short ascent to the bluffs. It's not a cave, as the name suggests, but rather an overhanging rock ledge. However, this isn't your average, ordinary rock overhang. Andy Griffith fans may recall a popular line of Barney's when they see the bluff for the first time: "It's big, really big." It's geologically unique, too. The bluffs create a very dry environment below the overhang, which is responsible for the thick, flourlike powder you walk through. Several very rare minerals have been found here, some not known to occur anywhere else in the world. What isn't here, though, is a lot of alum. In prepark days, several attempts were made to mine the bluffs for various minerals. The full extent of those mining operations isn't known, but none of them had any significant success.

Alum Cave Bluffs is home not only to rare minerals but rare birds as well. Ravens and peregrine falcons make a home on the bluffs. Ravens are relatively frequent at many high-elevation sites in the Southern Appalachians, particularly around rocky bluffs like Alum Cave. Peregrine falcons are another story. Having been under federal protection since 1970, peregrine falcons were just removed from the endangered species list in 1999. Between 1984 and 1986, the Park Service released thirteen young peregrines in the park. In 1997 a pair of peregrines raised three chicks in a nest on Alum Cave Bluffs, the first recorded nesting of peregrines in the park since 1942. Today the bluff continues to support the only verified peregrine nesting site in the Smokies.

The bluffs mark the end of this hike. Alum Cave Trail continues 2.7 miles to Mt. LeConte. See the options below if choosing to continue.

Options: Many persons hike the Alum Cave Trail all the way to Mt. LeConte and back as a day hike. I've seen overweight and out-of-shape people huffing and puffing up the trail. There seems to be a mystique about having "made it" to LeConte.

Here are some better options that allow you to see LeConte's summit without backtracking. Arrange for a shuttle and start at Newfound Gap, returning along Alum Cave Trail (see Hike 31: Mt. LeConte via The Boulevard), or have the shuttle take you to the Grotto Falls trailhead and hike up Trillium Gap Trail to the summit and return on Alum Cave Trail. Hike 35 outlines a third route to Mt. LeConte via Rainbow Falls Trail and a return by Bull Head Trail.

30

Charlies Bunion

Highlights: *Spectacular views*

(See map for Hike 29: Alum Cave Bluffs.)

Type of hike: Out-and-back; day hike or over-nighter
Total distance: 8.2 miles round-trip
Difficulty: Moderate

Best time of year: Winter, for fewer people and less smog
Maps: Trails Illustrated; USGS Clingmans Dome, Mt. LeConte, and Mt. Guyot

Special considerations: This is an extremely popular hike, so expect to rub shoulders along the entire trail. Snow and ice cover the trail in winter, and the rocky hiking is challenging any time of year. Charlies Bunion has dangerous drop-offs.

Finding the trailhead: The trailhead is located at the Newfound Gap Overlook on the Smokies crest. Drive 15.5 miles north on Newfound Gap Road from Oconaluftee Visitor Center or 12.7 miles south from Sugarlands Visitor Center. The trailhead is on the northeast end of the parking lot, between the rest rooms and the Rockefeller Memorial.

Parking and trailhead facilities: Newfound Gap has a very large parking lot that rarely fills completely. Rest rooms are available here, but you might find the woods a cleaner, less odorous option.

Key points:

1.7 Junction with Sweat Heifer Creek Trail.
2.7 Junction with The Boulevard Trail.
3.0 Icewater Spring Shelter.
4.0 Side path to Charlies Bunion.

The hike: Nearly everyone who visits the Smokies spends a little time at New-found Gap, and it seems as though they all have to go to the rest room at the same time. You'll want to park and hit the trail quickly, but don't expect to get away from

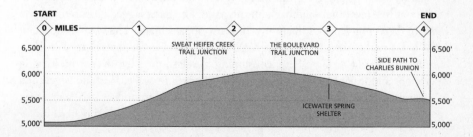

people here. Charlies Bunion is a classic Smokies hike and can be crowded any time of year except winter. Winter hiking along this trail is very rewarding, with great vistas and the opportunity for seeing interesting ice formations, but only experienced hikers should attempt it.

Begin hiking the Appalachian Trail (AT) from the northeast corner of the parking area. The trail starts out level and wide but soon begins a 1.5-mile steady ascent to a grassy knoll. You're walking through high-elevation spruce-fir forest. Occasional openings provide vistas of Mt. LeConte to the north. In late April and early May, the ground is covered in places with spring beauty.

From the knoll descend 0.2 mile to a gap and the junction with Sweat Heifer Creek Trail at a huge, gnarled birch tree. For a short and interesting side trip, take this trail a few hundred feet to a large skeleton forest of hundreds of dead trees. The lack of foliage provides great views into the Oconaluftee watershed.

Back on the AT, head east and begin a steep ascent. You soon pass an open view into North Carolina, taking in Clingmans Dome, Newfound Gap Road, and a glimpse of Bryson City. At 2.7 miles you reach the junction with The Boulevard Trail. The Boulevard Trail forks left (north) and leads to Mt. LeConte. For a side trip, go a short distance on this trail to an uprooted tree. Look here for a side path to the right and possibly a rock cairn in the trail. The rugged side path leads about 0.5 mile to an overlook called The Jumpoff, which provides a great view of Charlies Bunion. The view from The Jumpoff is a must-see.

Now back on the AT at the junction with The Boulevard Trail, go right on the AT (northeast). After 0.3 mile, a short side path on the right leads to the Icewater Spring Shelter, situated in an open, grassy area with good views. You'll probably see other day hikers here, posing for pictures in front of the shelter. One thing you won't see at this shelter is heavy-gauge wire fencing on the front like that at some other park shelters. The Park Service is attempting to provide a true wilderness experience, void of any zoolike atmosphere regarding bears. In times past, hikers would retreat behind the fencing and watch the bear show created by the ignorant tossing and storage of food. Now campers are on their own—and expected to exercise responsibility.

Just beyond the shelter, the trail passes literally over Icewater Spring. A rusty old pipe provides a drop so that you can fill a water bottle, but there's something unappealing about drinking water that comes out of a heavily trodden trail. *Caution:* Be sure to treat all drinking water in the Smokies, no matter the source.

Beyond the spring it's an easy hike to the side trail for Charlies Bunion. There's no marker for the side trail, but don't worry, you can't miss it. Charlies Bunion stands out like few other landmarks in the park. The bare, jagged cliffs remind you more of the young Rockies than the old, worn Appalachians. The obvious question is "Where are the trees?" The answer is a sad testament to Smokies history. In 1925 a raging fire swept through here, consuming the slash piles left over from logging operations and leaving not a twig or blade of grass in its wake. With no vegetation to secure the soil, the cliffs were vulnerable to erosion, and a 1929 rainstorm scoured the soil from the cliffs to create the site you see today. Noted writer Horace

Hikers enjoying the view from Charlies Bunion.

Kephart, who joked that the jagged cliffs reminded him of the foot ailment of his friend, Charlie Conner, supposedly coined the name Charlies Bunion soon after the storm.

The views are spectacular. To the west is The Jumpoff; to the northwest is the unmistakable Mt. LeConte; and northeast is Greenbrier Pinnacle. You'll want to spend some time here, but take extra precaution. Many people have fallen while climbing on the rocks.

The side path circles the knoll and comes back to the AT. Turn right (west) and backtrack to the trailhead.

Options: You can do this hike as an overnighter by staying at Icewater Spring Shelter. This provides you with the opportunity to view the sunset from Charlies Bunion, an experience few people have. Don't stay too late, though. You don't want to have to hike back to the shelter in the dark.

31
Mt. LeConte via The Boulevard

Highlights: *Exceptional views, high-elevation old-growth forest, geology*
(See map for Hike 29: Alum Cave Bluffs.)

Type of hike: Shuttle; day hike or overnighter
Total distance: 13.2 miles one-way
Difficulty: Difficult

Maps: Trails Illustrated; USGS Clingmans Dome and Mt. LeConte

Special considerations: While winter is a wonderful time to make this hike (less smog, better views), it's also a very dangerous time at these high elevations. You might start out at Newfound Gap in flurries, only to find yourself wading in 2 feet of snow on Mt. LeConte. Only experienced and well-prepared hikers should attempt this hike in winter.

Some of the very qualities that make this hike so appealing—precipitous drop-offs and paths carved out of solid rock—also make it very dangerous, especially with snow or ice on the trail. This is a hike for surefooted hikers wearing ankle-supporting hiking boots. Leave the sandals in the car. If hiking with children, keep a close rein; there are many hidden drop-offs.

Finding the trailhead: The trailhead is located at the Newfound Gap Overlook on the Smokies crest. Drive 15.5 miles north on Newfound Gap Road from Oconaluftee Visitor Center or 12.7 miles south from Sugarlands Visitor Center. The trailhead is on the northeast end of the parking lot, between the rest rooms and the Rockefeller Memorial.

You need to arrange a shuttle for this hike unless you have two vehicles. Park your car and have the shuttle pick you up at the Alum Cave trailhead on Newfound Gap Road, 4.2 miles north of Newfound Gap and 8.5 miles south of Sugarlands Visitor Center.

Parking and trailhead facilities: Newfound Gap has a very large parking lot that rarely fills completely. Rest rooms are available here, but in summer you might find the woods to be a cleaner, less odorous option. The Alum Cave trailhead (no facilities) has two large parking areas that fill quickly on summer weekends.

Key points:
1.7 Junction with Sweat Heifer Creek Trail.
2.7 Junction with The Boulevard Trail.
2.8 Side path to The Jumpoff.
7.6 Side path to Myrtle Point.
7.9 Mt. LeConte Backcountry Shelter.

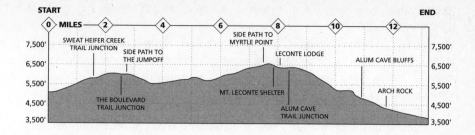

START   END

0   MILES   2   4   6   8   10   12

7,500'   SIDE PATH TO   7,500'
          SWEAT HEIFER CREEK   MYRTLE POINT
          TRAIL JUNCTION   SIDE PATH TO
6,500'   THE JUMPOFF   LECONTE LODGE   ALUM CAVE BLUFFS   6,500'

5,500'   MT. LECONTE SHELTER   5,500'

          THE BOULEVARD   ARCH ROCK
4,500'   TRAIL JUNCTION   ALUM CAVE   4,500'
                                                        TRAIL JUNCTION
3,500'   3,500'

8.1 Junction with Trillium Gap and Rainbow Falls Trails. LeConte Lodge is immediately beyond the junction.

8.2 Junction with Alum Cave Trail.

10.9 Alum Cave Bluffs.

11.8 Arch Rock.

The hike: If you have to choose only one hike in the Smokies, this might be the best choice. It gives you nearly everything the park is famous for, and by starting at an elevation of 5,046 feet and ending at close to 3,800 feet, it's not overly strenuous. You're going to get a good workout, but you won't think you're in boot camp. (Before reading any further, see Hiking to Mt. LeConte at the beginning of this chapter.)

The hike begins on the Appalachian Trail at the northeast corner of Newfound Gap. (See Hike 30: Charlies Bunion for the trail narrative covering the section from here to The Boulevard Trail.) A short distance after turning left (north) on The Boulevard Trail, you come to an uprooted tree across from a side path on the right. There might be a rock cairn marking this spot. The rugged path leads about 0.5 mile to a spectacular overlook of Charlies Bunion called The Jumpoff. If planning to overnight on Mt. LeConte, this side trip is highly recommended. If you're doing this trip as a day hike, you may not want to take the extra time.

From the side path, the trail ascends a bit and then begins a long, fairly steep descent along the northwest flank of Mt. Kephart, crossing over the upper reaches of Walker Camp Prong and finally reaching a narrow ridgeline. This is The Boulevard, and you follow it all the way to Mt. LeConte. Along the ridge are occasional open views to the right (north) into the Porters Creek watershed and leafy peeks left (south) into the Walker Camp Prong watershed. At about 2.5 miles from the Appalachian Trail, you swing sharply around to the right over Anakeesta Ridge. Look down at your feet. That gray, slatelike rock you're standing on is the Anakeesta Formation, and it and its orientation are responsible for the incredible geologic features encountered along this hike. You can see how easily this rock might fracture and break apart. Later on this hike, you'll see the effects of such fracturing.

Notice also the uprooted tree on the ridge. You've already passed several such trees, and you'll see many more before you finish. Thin soil (making for shallow root systems), heavy rainfall, and extreme winds constantly threaten the trees at these elevations.

Descend from the ridgeline to a small landslide and look back behind you to see the summit of Anakeesta Knob and Anakeesta Ridge extending from it. Now go on an undulating course and come to a sharp left swing around a ridge, with open views to the north. You're now ascending the flanks of Myrtle Point, and you pass massive cliffs with sand myrtle clinging in cracks.

At this point you must cross a massive landslide. What a horrific sight this must have been while the landslide was occurring. You see several more landslides on the remainder of the hike, but few places in the Smokies allow you to experience one of these scars so intimately. A steel cable helps with the footing on the treacherous path through the slide and is a necessity with ice or snow on the trail. Beyond the slide you make a sharp left turn and come to a very dangerous section of trail. Back at the slide, at least you could see the danger and act accordingly. Here a thin veil of vegetation hides the sheer vertical drops created by landslides.

Soon the excitement and exhilaration of the hike turns to depression as you near LeConte's highest peak, High Top, and pass through its graveyard of fir trees. Every mature tree is dead; many still stand like ghostly skeletons, while others lie in a jumbled tangle like chopsticks. (See Hike 51: Clingmans Dome for a discussion about what's going on here.) Shortly after entering the graveyard, the side path to Myrtle Point leads off to the left. Just beyond the side path, you cross the highest point on Mt. LeConte at 6,593 feet and the second highest point reached by maintained trail in the Smokies. Clingmans Dome, at 6,643 feet, is a mere 50 feet higher, but some people want Mt. LeConte to be the highest in the park. Look over to the left on High Top's summit. That pile of rocks looks very out of place, doesn't it? It's a lighthearted attempt by some persons to make LeConte higher than Clingmans Dome. They have a long way to go. At my last visit, the pile was only about 5 feet high.

After topping out on High Top, you pass the best view so far, toward Newfound Gap and Clingmans Dome. The parking area where you began this hike is clearly visible behind Anakeesta Ridge. Shortly beyond the vista is the Mt. LeConte Backcountry Shelter, one of only three such shelters not located near the Appalachian Trail. Just beyond the shelter you pass a side path to Cliff Top on the left and then reach the three-way trail junction at LeConte Lodge.

Trillium Gap Trail goes right (northeast), and Rainbows Falls Trail continues straight ahead. The Boulevard Trail officially ends here. The scattered collection of buildings making up LeConte Lodge lie just beyond the trail junction on the right. Our hike now follows the Rainbow Falls Trail past the lodge and a little farther to the junction with Alum Cave Trail, on the left (west).

Alum Cave Trail starts out level, but that quickly changes as the trail swings around to the east and skirts beneath the sheer cliffs of Cliff Top. Steel cables serve as helpful handholds with the wet rocks and are crucial when there's ice on the trail. The 2.5 miles of descent between here and Alum Cave Bluffs are steep and rocky, with several stretches of trail carved out of solid rock. Along the way are several landslide scars and several good views. Two features along this stretch stand out. At

Log steps on Alum Cave Trail.

one point you come to an ingenious solution to navigating a steep, rocky slope. The trail engineers angled a large, long tree trunk down the slope and sawed steps into it. Tar and gravel give traction to the steps.

The second feature is farther down. The trail actually ascends a bit, and where it swings to the left and begins descending again, a side path leads a few yards to a viewpoint known as Gracies Pulpit. Avid LeConte buffs know Gracie McNichol well. At the age of ninety-two she made her 244th trip to LeConte Lodge. Although a stroke forced her to make eighty-nine of those trips on horseback, the feat is still extraordinary. The unobstructed view of Mt. LeConte from this viewpoint serves as a fitting memorial to this remarkable woman.

From Gracies Pulpit the trail climbs very steeply down a rock slope and soon comes to Alum Cave Bluffs. Hike 29: Alum Cave Bluffs covers the remaining 2.3 miles of the hike in reverse order.

32 Noah "Bud" Ogle Nature Trail

Highlights: *Historic farmstead, wildflowers, mossy rocks*
(See map for Hike 28: Sugarlands Valley Nature Trail.)

Type of hike: Loop; day hike
Total distance: 0.75 mile round-trip
Difficulty: Easy

Best time of year: Spring
Maps: Trails Illustrated; USGS Mt. LeConte

Finding the trailhead: From U.S. 441 in Gatlinburg, turn at traffic light #8 onto Historic Nature Trail–Airport Road and drive 0.6 mile to a confusing intersection. Stay to the right and continue straight ahead. You soon enter the park on Cherokee Orchard Road. Reach Noah "Bud" Ogle Place on the right, 2.6 miles from traffic light #8. The parking area is on the right, just before the cabin. The nature trail starts behind the cabin.

Parking and trailhead facilities: Ample parking is available at the cabin, but there are no facilities.

Key points:
    0.3   Twin Creeks Trail goes to the right.

The hike: As a self-guiding nature trail, this hike doesn't get a lot of attention from the "hard-core" hiking crowd. Nature trails are for tourists, some might say. That's a shame, because Noah "Bud" Ogle Nature Trail, for its length, is one of the best hikes in the park. I don't know of many other 0.75-mile sections of trail that offer what this one does.

Noah "Bud" Ogle tub mill.

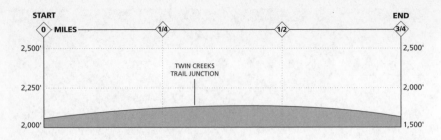

START

0 MILES — 1/4 — 1/2 — 3/4

END

2,500'

2,500'

TWIN CREEKS
TRAIL JUNCTION

2,250'

2,000'

2,000'

1,500'

In early spring, wildflowers are abundant. You might even spot a cluster of yellow lady's slipper orchids if you look closely. The trail passes by LeConte Creek, tumbling along in a picturesque setting. Situated by the creek is the Ogle Tub Mill, operating today just as it did in the late 1800s. Beyond the mill, the trail passes through a forest of large hemlock and yellow-poplar trees set amidst a jumble of huge, mossy boulders. At some places, rock and trail are the same. Finally, there's the "Bud" Ogle Place itself, a restored cabin and barn open for exploring.

Those hard-core hikers don't know what they're missing.

33

Twin Creeks

Highlights: *Easy family walk*

(See map for Hike 28: Sugarlands Valley Nature Trail.)

Type of hike: Shuttle; day hike; a great split-party hike
Total distance: 2.4 miles one-way
Difficulty: Easy

Best time of year: Spring, before the poison ivy appears
Maps: Trails Illustrated; USGS Mt. LeConte and Gatlinburg

Special considerations: Poison ivy grows abundantly along the entire route. Make sure the kids (and their parents) know how to identify it before making this hike.

Finding the trailhead: From U.S. 441 in Gatlinburg, turn at traffic light #8 onto Historic Nature Trail–Airport Road and drive 0.6 mile to a confusing intersection. Stay to the right and continue straight ahead. You soon enter the park on Cherokee Orchard Road. Reach Noah "Bud" Ogle Place on the right, 2.6 miles from traffic light #8. The parking area is on the right, just before the cabin. The hike begins on the Noah "Bud" Ogle Nature Trail, starting behind the cabin.

Parking and trailhead facilities: Ample parking is available at the cabin, but there are no facilities. Back in Gatlinburg, though, is everything you need—plus a whole lot of what you might not need.

Key points:

0.3 Junction with Twin Creeks Trail.
1.0 Junction with paved road that leads to Twin Creeks facility.

The hike: While there's no such thing as a bad hike in the Smokies, this one isn't one of the best. The forest here is scraggly and seems to be struggling to recover from years of prepark farming and clearing. Poison ivy covers the trail, and you're within earshot (sometimes eyesight) of the road the entire way. That said, one attribute of this hike makes it worth including in this guidebook: It makes a great split-party hike. Go with the family to visit Noah "Bud" Ogle Place, maybe hiking the nature trail, and then let them go back to the hotel in Gatlinburg while you laze your way back on foot. The trail ends at the common boundary between the park and Gatlinburg.

Twin Creeks Trail begins about 0.3 mile into the Noah "Bud" Ogle Nature Trail (Hike 32). Hike the nature trail even if you don't do this hike. Just past marker #6 on the nature trail, turn right onto Twin Creeks Trail (north) and descend gently. You go by rock walls, boxwoods, and other signs of settlement. About a mile into the hike, you pass through a rock wall and have to cross a paved road. The road leads to Twin Creeks Resource Center, a science facility for the park.

Soon cross a small creek branch at the junction with Grassy Branch Trail. That trail, and a few others, weaves through the mountains between here and the park entrance on Newfound Gap Road. These trails are open to the public, but their primary use is for equestrians.

From the creek crossing it's a short walk to the trail's end on Cherokee Orchard Road. A right turn takes you back to Noah "Bud" Ogle Place in 1.75 miles. A left turn takes you into the asphalt and concrete morass of Gatlinburg.

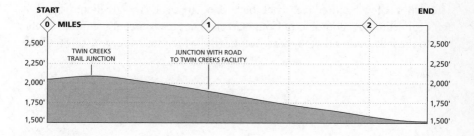

115

34

Rainbow Falls

Highlights: *Big trees, Rainbow Falls, cascades*

Type of hike: Out-and-back; day hike
Total distance: 5.4 miles round-trip
Difficulty: Difficult

Best time of year: April
Maps: Trails Illustrated; USGS Mt. LeConte

Special considerations: Climbing the rocks at the waterfall can be dangerous. Also pay careful attention if you visit the falls in cold weather and scramble up under the ledge. Icicles form on the overhanging rocks and constantly break off, hitting the ground like missiles. The trail is very rocky; leave the sandals in the car.

Finding the trailhead: From U.S. 441 in Gatlinburg, turn at traffic light #8 onto Historic Nature Trail–Airport Road and drive 0.6 mile to a confusing intersection. Stay to the right and continue straight ahead. You soon enter the park on Cherokee Orchard Road. Reach the parking area for Rainbow Falls and Bull Head Trails at 3.3 miles from traffic light #8. The Rainbow Falls Trail begins from the western end of the parking area.

Parking and trailhead facilities: Although there's room for several vehicles, the parking area can fill up quickly on summer weekends. Additional parking is available 0.1 mile farther on Cherokee Orchard Road. There are no facilities available on Cherokee Orchard Road, but Gatlinburg has more than everything you need. Of course you'll probably have to pay for parking. The rest rooms and parking are free at Sugarlands Visitor Center.

Key points:
   0.1   Junction with Trillium Gap Trail.

The hike: A few hundred feet from the parking area you cross Trillium Gap Trail and begin climbing alongside LeConte Creek. The steady ascent continues all the way to the falls, and so do the rocks. You might be tempted to rename this trail the

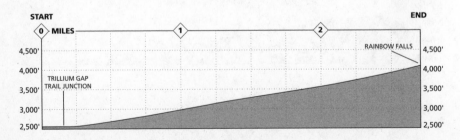

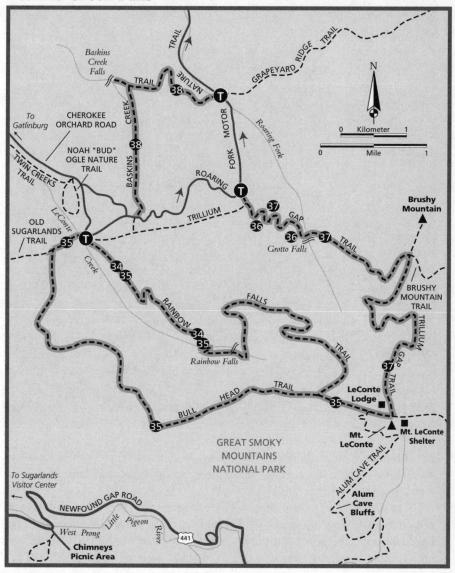

"Rocky Falls Trail" before you finish. LeConte Creek keeps close company most of the way. Only at a few places does the trail get out of earshot of the creek.

After a mile or so, the trail swings away and comes to a sharp right switchback. In winter there's a view back toward Gatlinburg. You can see the Space Needle and the Park Vista Hotel. Work your way back toward the creek and come to a high overlook at a left-hand turn in the trail. There's a perfect sitting rock here at a silverbell

Rainbow Falls.

tree. From here the trail makes a quick swing away from the creek then returns to parallel it on a high bench before making the first crossing on an asphalt-covered foot log.

Now the big trees start to appear. There are several large hemlocks and a huge cherry tree with the top blown out. Farther up there's a massive hemlock right beside the trail. This is one of the largest hemlocks I've seen in the park. After crossing a couple of side streams—one below a small waterfall—you cross LeConte Creek on another foot log. From this crossing, Rainbow Falls is visible high above. Continue up the trail to a final crossing below the falls.

LeConte Creek at this point is a rather small stream and not capable of creating a thundering, crashing waterfall. What you have here is a misty, lacy type of waterfall. The creek spills over an overhanging ledge some 80 feet to the rocks below. Much of the water changes to mist before it reaches bottom, and with the proper angle on a sunny day, you can see rainbows in the mist. In winter, after prolonged cold spells, the waterfall can freeze from bottom to top.

Although the view from the foot log is great, many persons scramble up the rocks to get closer and to find different vantage points for photographs. Exercise extreme caution if you do this.

Options: Rainbow Falls Trail continues on to the Mt. LeConte summit, but most hikers turn around at the falls. (To plan a Mt. LeConte excursion, see Hiking to Mt. LeConte at the beginning of this chapter.)

35 Mt. LeConte via Rainbow Falls and Bull Head

Highlights: *Falls, old-growth forest, exceptional views, wildflowers*

(See map for Hike 34: Rainbow Falls.)

Type of hike: Loop; long day hike or overnighter
Total distance: 13.6 miles round-trip
Difficulty: Difficult

Best time of year: April for spring wildflowers, August for summer wildflowers
Maps: Trails Illustrated; USGS Mt. LeConte

Finding the trailhead: From U.S. 441 in Gatlinburg, turn at traffic light #8 onto Historic Nature Trail–Airport Road and drive 0.6 mile to a confusing intersection. Stay to the right and continue straight ahead. You soon enter the park on Cherokee Orchard Road. Reach the parking area for Rainbow Falls and Bull Head Trails at 3.3 miles from traffic light #8. The Rainbow Falls Trail begins from the western end of the parking area.

Parking and trailhead facilities: Although there's room for several vehicles, the parking area can fill up quickly on summer weekends. Additional parking is available 0.1 mile farther on Cherokee Orchard Road. There are no facilities available on Cherokee Orchard Road, but Gatlinburg has more than everything you need—everything, that is, except free and convenient parking. The rest rooms and parking are free at Sugarlands Visitor Center.

Key points:
- **0.1** Junction with Trillium Gap Trail.
- **2.7** Rainbow Falls.
- **6.1** Junction with Bull Head Trail.
- **6.6** Junction with Alum Cave Trail.

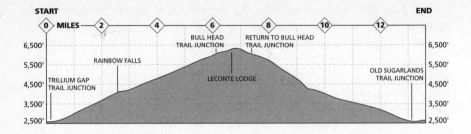

6.7 LeConte Lodge and junction with Trillium Gap and The Boulevard Trails.

7.3 Return to junction with Bull Head Trail.

13.2 Junction with Old Sugarlands Trail.

The hike: The only way to hike to Mt. LeConte and return to your car without backtracking or long road-walking is by utilizing Rainbow Falls and Bull Head Trails. For a detailed narrative of the first 2.7 miles to Rainbow Falls, see Hike 34. Most people turn around at the falls, so the rest of the hike will be less crowded.

From Rainbow Falls the trail swings away from LeConte Creek and crosses a side stream twice before working back to the creek. This is the final crossing of LeConte Creek. There's no foot log, but you don't need one. Often the creek runs underground, so this is a dry crossing.

Now you leave the creek and begin a long ascent on switchbacks that takes you to Rocky Spur, the prominent ridge separating the LeConte Creek and Roaring Fork watersheds. As you cross the ridgeline, look to the left and you might catch a glimpse of Gatlinburg. It's better, though, to pay attention to the trail and its many nuances. Notice the difference, for instance, in the vegetation now that you've rounded the ridge to the north-facing slope. Here are hemlocks and rhododendron, and the forest is darker, cooler, and wetter. Back on the south-facing slope, you passed through mountain laurel, with a ground cover of galax and trailing arbutus.

Continue on the north side of Rocky Spur for about a mile, make a switchback, and continue a short distance before rounding back to the south side. Look up ahead at that mountaintop. That's Cliff Top; you'll watch the sunset from there if staying overnight on LeConte's summit. Pressing on, a side path turns off to the left and rejoins the main trail a few yards ahead. By now your energy is sapped, and exploring side trails is probably not an appealing thought. Don't worry, you didn't miss a lot.

Soon the trail swings around to the right and begins skirting Mt. LeConte's summit. Cross the trickling headwaters of LeConte Creek (oops, that previous crossing wasn't the final one after all) and look north for great views of Rocky Spur, which you just ascended. To the west is an open view of Gatlinburg and its Space Needle.

Now you come to the junction with Bull Head Trail, coming in from the right. From here it's a little more than 0.5 mile on a very rocky course to LeConte Lodge.

At the lodge, pat yourself on the back. You've made a near continuous climb from the parking area on a long, difficult, rocky trail. Tomorrow, or in a little while if doing this hike in one day, you'll head back down Rainbow Falls Trail and turn west on Bull Head Trail. Fill up your water bottle before you start, though. Bull Head Trail is dry as a bone.

Now on Bull Head Trail heading west, two things immediately come to mind. First, this trail is not nearly as steep as Rainbow Falls Trail; second, it's not nearly as rocky. The steepness increases later on, but you can enjoy a long stretch of easy hiking. This section of trail is great for summer wildflowers. Farther down, it's better for spring wildflowers.

As the trail approaches Balsam Point, it switches to the south side of the ridge, begins descending much more steeply, and continues to do so until reaching a flat spot on the ridge leading to Bull Head. Just before here you passed through what must be the longest rhododendron and mountain laurel tunnel in the park. On the ridge is the "Pulpit"—a stack of rocks made by the crews who built this trail. There's a fair view off the north side, but it's not as good as the views you had farther back up the trail.

Now enjoy a surprisingly long and level stretch; as you turn toward the south, look back up the trail to see Balsam Point far above that rhododendron tunnel you just passed through. Now the trail descends through a stand of pines killed by the Southern pine beetle, a native insect. The vegetation is indicative of the dry southern exposure: galax, wintergreen, trailing arbutus, and mountain laurel.

The trail swings around to a northern exposure, and the vegetation changes instantly. Here it's cool and moist. Moss covers the rocks; rhododendron grows densely among hemlock trees. This is a typical cove forest and a terrific spot to see spring wildflowers. Farther down, you pass two huge rock overhangs, one right after the other. They project completely over the trail and would provide wonderful protection during a storm. Trouble is, there's never one of these things around when you need it.

The trail starts a serious descent now and continues that way to the junction with Old Sugarlands Trail. A left turn here takes you to Newfound Gap Road near Sugarlands Visitor Center. You want to go right and enjoy the easy 0.4-mile walk along the old road to the trailhead.

Options: To plan a Mt. LeConte excursion, see Hiking to Mt. LeConte at the beginning of this chapter.

36

Grotto Falls

Highlights: *Old-growth forest, Grotto Falls, llamas*

(See map for Hike 34: Rainbow Falls.)

Type of hike: Out-and-back; day hike
Total distance: 2.6 miles round-trip

Difficulty: Moderate
Maps: Trails Illustrated; USGS Mt. LeConte

Special considerations: Everyone wants to see Grotto Falls, so expect lots of company. The access road (Roaring Fork Motor Nature Trail) is closed from December 1 to March 31.

Finding the trailhead: From U.S. 441 in Gatlinburg, turn at traffic light #8 onto Historic Nature Trail–Airport Road and drive 0.6 mile to a confusing intersection. Stay to the right and continue straight ahead. You soon enter the park on Cherokee Orchard Road. At 3.6 miles from traffic light #8, you come to Roaring Fork Motor Nature Trail on the right. This one-way road passes old homesites and several trail-heads before looping back to Gatlinburg. At 1.7 miles from the start of the Motor Nature Trail, you come to the large parking area on the left for Grotto Falls. The trail begins across the road, at the far end of the parking area.

Parking and trailhead facilities: The parking area holds quite a few cars, but it fills up on summer weekends and people spread all along the road. Try to get here early; it isn't safe to park alongside this road, and it damages the environment. There are no facilities along Roaring Fork Motor Nature Trail or Cherokee Orchard Road.

Key points:

0.1 Junction with Trillium Gap Trail.

The hike: Start on the path from the parking area and hike a little more than 0.1 mile to join Trillium Gap Trail. You could have begun 2.4 miles back at the Trillium Gap trailhead on Cherokee Orchard Road, but why add 4.8 humdrum miles to the

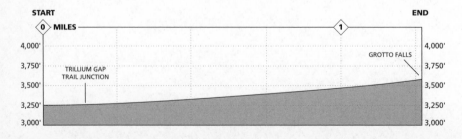

122

Llama train passing behind Grotto Falls on the way to Mt. LeConte Lodge.

hike when you don't have to? Trillium Gap Trail leads to the summit of Mt. LeConte, 6.6 miles and nearly 4,000 vertical feet from here. Don't worry, this hike barely makes a dent in either the elevation or total distance of the trail.

The trail climbs moderately on hard-packed dirt all the way to the falls. Along the way you pass through an impressive old-growth hemlock forest that takes on an ethereal look in fog. In and out you weave until finally rounding a ridge into the Roaring Fork drainage and making a short, level approach to the falls.

Grotto Falls is appropriately named. Roaring Fork spills from an overhanging ledge some 20 feet into a small pool, creating a dry space behind the falls for the trail to pass. The waterfall is lovely and makes a terrific photo subject, and the post-card racks in Gatlinburg hold many different scenes of the falls.

For a special treat, try to time your trip to coincide with the Mt. LeConte llama schedule. Every week, in season, a llama train passes behind Grotto Falls on its way to supply LeConte Lodge with fresh food, laundry, and other necessities. The schedule may vary; during 2002 they made the trip every Monday, Wednesday, and Friday. You can call the lodge (865–429–5704) to learn the current year's schedule.

This hike ends at the falls. If you decide to continue on the Trillium Gap Trail to Brushy Mountain or on up to Mt. LeConte, see the narrative in Hike 37: Mt. LeConte via Trillium Gap.

37 Mt. LeConte via Trillium Gap

Highlights: *Grotto Falls, old-growth forest, llamas, views, wildflowers*
(See map for Hike 34: Rainbow Falls.)

Type of hike: Out-and-back; day hike or over-nighter
Total distance: 13.4 miles round-trip

Difficulty: Difficult
Best time of year: April for wildflowers
Maps: Trails Illustrated; USGS Mt. LeConte

Special considerations: For a special treat, try to time your trip to coincide with the Mt. LeConte llama schedule. Every week, in season, a llama train heads up Trillium Gap Trail to supply LeConte Lodge with fresh food, laundry, and other necessities. The schedule may vary; during 2002 they made the trip every Monday, Wednesday, and Friday. You can call the lodge (865–429–5704) to learn the current year's schedule. If planning to spend the night on Mt. LeConte, you can schedule to return on the day the llamas head up the mountain. That way, you're sure not to miss them.

Finding the trailhead: From U.S. 441 in Gatlinburg, turn at traffic light #8 onto Historic Nature Trail–Airport Road and drive 0.6 mile to a confusing intersection. Stay to the right and continue straight ahead. You soon enter the park on Cherokee Orchard Road. At 3.6 miles from traffic light #8, you come to Roaring Fork Motor Nature Trail on the right. This one-way road passes old homesites and several trail-heads before looping back to Gatlinburg. At 1.7 miles from the start of the Motor Nature Trail, you come to the large parking area on the left for Grotto Falls. The trail begins across the road, at the far end of the parking area.

Parking and trailhead facilities: The parking area holds quite a few cars, but it fills up on summer weekends. If you don't find a parking spot, it isn't safe to park

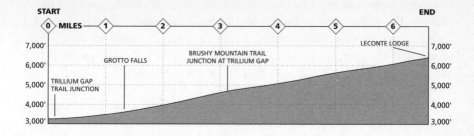

alongside this road. There are no facilities along Roaring Fork Motor Nature Trail or Cherokee Orchard Road.

Key points:

0.1 Junction with Trillium Gap Trail.

1.3 Grotto Falls.

3.1 Junction with Brushy Mountain Trail at Trillium Gap.

6.7 LeConte Lodge on Mt. LeConte summit.

The hike: Hike 36: Grotto Falls covers the first 1.3 miles of this hike in detail. Start on the path from the parking area and hike a little more than 0.1 mile to join Trillium Gap Trail. You could have begun 2.4 miles back at the Trillium Gap trailhead on Cherokee Orchard Road, but that adds an unnecessary 4.8 round-trip miles. Trillium Gap Trail climbs moderately on hard-packed dirt all the way to Grotto Falls. Along the way you pass through an impressive old-growth hemlock forest.

Grotto Falls is appropriately named. Roaring Fork spills from an overhanging ledge some 20 feet into a small pool, creating a dry space behind the falls for the trail to pass. The waterfall is lovely and makes a terrific photo subject.

Beyond the falls the trail is a little steeper and rockier, but it's pleasant hiking through a lush forest. You cross a couple of small streams, but you might want to hold off on filling your water bottle from them. The llamas have a habit of using the creeks as their rest room facilities. You should treat all water in the Smokies, but after you see an entire llama train doing their business in one of these creeks, filtering and boiling just won't cut it. There are several springs farther up, the last one on LeConte's summit.

When you start to see grassy patches along the trail, you know you're nearing Trillium Gap. This is a typical beech gap, covered in dense grass and dominated by American beech trees. In early spring, spring beauty carpets the ground with so many blossoms that it looks like freshly fallen snow. Brushy Mountain Trail intersects at the gap, having climbed up the opposite side, and it continues on the left to the summit of Brushy Mountain. If you have time, perhaps on the hike back down, the short side trip to Brushy is highly recommended (see Hike 40).

Water, rocks, and verdancy characterize the remaining 3.6 miles to LeConte's summit. The trail is steep and rocky, but the luxuriant vegetation takes your mind off the climb. Mosses, lichens, ferns, wildflowers, shrubs, and trees cover every square inch of ground except the rocky trail under your feet. You cross several creek branches, one below a postcard scene of a tiny waterfall flowing through mossy rocks.

When you enter a fir tunnel, you're getting close to trail's end. Soon you pass a horse hitching rack on the right and then a spring on the left. LeConte Lodge is on the right, and the junction with The Boulevard and Rainbow Falls Trails is just ahead.

38 Baskins Creek Falls

Highlights: *Baskins Creek Falls*
(See map for Hike 34: Rainbow Falls.)

Type of hike: Out-and-back; day hike
Total distance: 6.0 miles round-trip, including side trip to falls

Difficulty: Difficult
Maps: Trails Illustrated, USGS Mt. LeConte

Special considerations: Roaring Fork Motor Nature Trail is closed from December 1 to March 31.

Finding the trailhead: From U.S. 441 in Gatlinburg, turn at traffic light #8 onto Historic Nature Trail–Airport Road and drive 0.6 mile to a confusing intersection. Stay to the right and continue straight ahead. You soon enter the park on Cherokee Orchard Road. At 3.6 miles from traffic light #8, you come to Roaring Fork Motor Nature Trail on the right. This one-way road passes old homesites and several trailheads before looping back to Gatlinburg. At 2.8 miles from the start of the Motor Nature Trail, you come to a small parking area on the left, just before the Jim Bales Place. The obvious trail begins from the middle of the parking area.

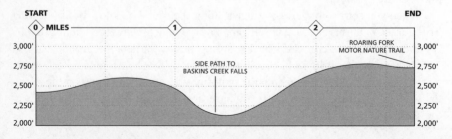

Parking and trailhead facilities: The parking area holds a half dozen cars, but it rarely fills up. There are no facilities along Roaring Fork Motor Nature Trail.

Key points:
1.3 Side path to Baskins Creek Falls.
2.7 End of hike at Roaring Fork Motor Nature Trail.

The hike: The Roaring Fork area is popular, but you won't feel too crowded on this hike. Most people never get out of their cars, and those who do are usually exploring the historical structures or hiking to Grotto Falls.

The trail passes a cemetery at the start of the hike before climbing to a ridge-line. After a short run on the ridge, you descend steeply to Baskins Creek. Don't take the side trail that forks right and heads downstream. Instead, cross the creek (tricky in high water) and make a short, steep climb over a small ridge. On the ridge crest, look out to the right to see the remains of an old chimney.

In summer, cardinal flowers grow in a tiny meadow below the ridge; just beyond the meadow on the right is an obvious side path leading to the falls. A trail sign was here at my visit, but it only said 1.3 miles back to the trailhead and 1.4 miles continuing. Someone had written FALLS on the post along with AND GROUND WASPS. BEWARE! I didn't see any wasps, but you might want to keep an eye out.

The side path leads about 0.3 mile to the base of the falls, passing an old home-site on the right, and finally descending very steeply down the cliff at the falls. The waterfall is picturesque and well worth the difficult scramble. It's about 30 feet high and, interestingly, is located on Falls Branch not Baskins Creek. Falls Branch joins Baskins Creek a short distance downstream.

Back on the main trail, you may wish to head back to the car or continue 1.4 miles to the trail's end near the beginning of the Motor Nature Trail. If choosing this option, begin a gradual ascent and soon pass another side path on the right, this one leading to Baskins Cemetery. Pressing on, the trail climbs steeply for a good distance, finally topping out on a ridge with winter views toward Gatlinburg. From here you have a rather easy walk through a nice hardwood forest to the road. The trail crosses the road here and continues a few yards to its official terminus on the Trillium Gap Trail.

Options: With two vehicles, this hike makes a good shuttle. Just remember that Roaring Fork Motor Nature Trail is one-way only. This might make a better split-party hike. Have your group drop you off at trail's end and hike it in reverse, meeting back up with your party at the other end.

39
Porters Creek

Highlights: *Spring wildflowers, Fern Branch Falls*

Type of hike: Out-and-back; day hike or overnighter
Total distance: 7.2 miles round-trip
Difficulty: Moderate

Best time of year: April
Maps: Trails Illustrated; USGS Mt. LeConte and Mt. Guyot

Finding the trailhead: From U.S. 441 in Gatlinburg, turn at traffic light #3 and drive east on U.S. 321. At 5.9 miles turn right (south) onto Greenbrier Road. This road follows scenic Middle Prong of Little Pigeon River, changing to gravel just past the ranger station. Drive slowly, and watch for pedestrians in summer. At 3.1 miles, the road to the Ramsay Cascades trailhead turns left. Stay straight and continue another 0.9 mile to a traffic loop. Park at the far end of the loop, at the road gate. The trail is a continuation of the gravel road.

Parking and trailhead facilities: There's room for several vehicles scattered along the traffic loop, but there are no facilities. Portable toilets are available at the two picnic areas on the gravel road leading to the trailhead.

Key points:
- **1.0** Junction with Brushy Mountain Trail and side trail to historic farmsite.
- **1.5** Cross Porters Creek.
- **1.8** Fern Branch Falls.
- **3.6** Campsite 31.

The hike: It would be hard to pick a better spring hike than this one. For wildflower lovers, this is the stuff. Start up the gravel road and soon come to a great view of Porters Creek at a washout. A little farther along, you begin noticing relics of life before the park was established: rock walls and homesites. Cross a small creek branch on a bridge and pass a nice patch of crested dwarf iris, just up the hill. An old cemetery lies to the right, and just beyond there's an old rusty vehicle sitting 100

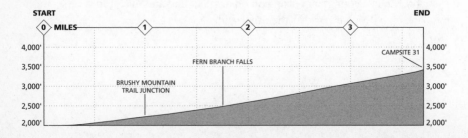

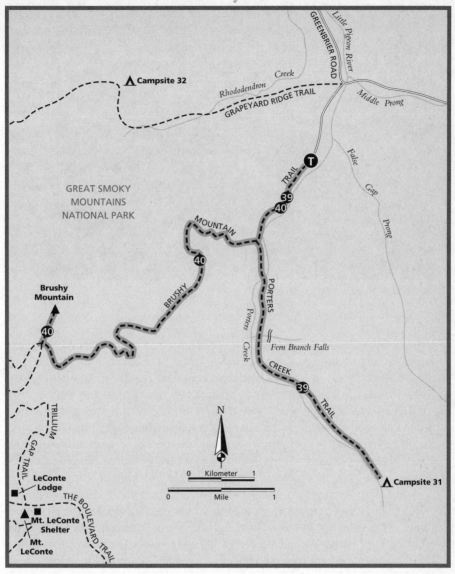

feet in the woods. The road soon crosses a larger stream, this one with the option of wading the ford or crossing on a foot log. Kids love this one.

At 1.0 mile, you reach the old traffic turnaround and the junction of three trails. On the far left, heading south along Porters Creek, is Porters Creek Trail. To the far right (west end) is a side trail leading a short distance to a historic farmsite. (For a description of the site see Hike 40: Brushy Mountain.) In the middle of the two is the trailhead for Brushy Mountain Trail.

Take Porters Creek Trail, and after 0.5 mile cross Porters Creek on two foot logs. Now you start to see what all the fuss is about. There's fringed phacelia,

Stone steps along Porters Creek Trail.

bishop's cap, several trillium and violet species, mayapple, blue cohosh, geranium, Fraser's sedge, toothwort, phlox—countless more. Less than 0.5 mile farther, as if the wildflowers were not enough, you cross Fern Branch at the base of Fern Branch Falls. This surprisingly high waterfall tumbles over mossy rocks and logs.

Beyond the falls the wildflower displays continue, with the species variety depending upon the angle to the sun and the surrounding vegetation. At 3.6 miles the official trail ends at Campsite 31, a lovely site situated on a bank above Porters Creek. If you're planning to spend a lot of time studying or photographing the wildflowers, a good option is to spend the night here and backtrack the following day.

Some trail narratives state that Porters Creek Trail continues as an unmaintained route from Campsite 31 all the way to the Appalachian Trail at Dry Sluice Gap, 2,000 feet higher. I don't recommend hiking on any unmaintained trails in the Smokies, but I particularly advise against hiking this one. The trail peters out in a short distance, and then it's a full mile of very steep rock scrambling. Even experienced hikers should reconsider such a trek.

Options: The short side trip to the historic farmsite is highly recommended.

40

Brushy Mountain

Highlights: *Historic structures, views*

(See map for Hike 39: Porters Creek.)

Type of hike: Out-and-back; day hike
Total distance: 11.8 miles round-trip
Difficulty: Moderate

Best time of year: June for the mountain laurel bloom, August for the blueberries
Maps: Trails Illustrated; USGS Mt. LeConte

Finding the trailhead: From U.S. 441 in Gatlinburg, turn at traffic light #3 and drive east on U.S. 321. At 5.9 miles turn right (south) onto Greenbrier Road. This road follows scenic Middle Prong of Little Pigeon River, changing to gravel just past the ranger station. Drive slowly, and watch for pedestrians in summer. At 3.1 miles the road to the Ramsay Cascades trailhead turns left. Stay straight and continue another 0.9 mile to a traffic loop. Park at the far end of the loop, at the road gate. The trail is a continuation of the gravel road.

Parking and trailhead facilities: There's room for several vehicles scattered along the traffic loop, but there are no facilities. Portable toilets are available at the two picnic areas on the gravel road leading to the trailhead.

Key points:

    1.0   Junction with Brushy Mountain Trail and side path to farmsite.
    5.5   Junction with Trillium Gap Trail at Trillium Gap.
    5.9   Summit of Brushy Mountain.

The hike: Start up the gravel road and soon come to a great view of Porters Creek at a washout. A little farther along, you begin noticing relics of life before the park was established: rock walls and homesites. Cross a small creek branch on a bridge and pass a nice patch of crested dwarf iris, just up the hill. An old cemetery lies to the right, and just beyond there's an old rusty vehicle sitting 100 feet in the woods. The road soon crosses a larger stream, this one with the option of wading the ford or crossing on a foot log.

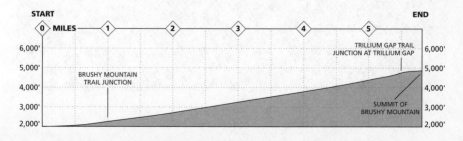

Rhododendron tunnel on Brushy Mountain.

At 1.0 mile you reach the old traffic turnaround and the junction of three trails. On the far left, heading south along Porters Creek, is Porters Creek Trail. To the far right (west end) is the side trail leading a short distance to a historic farmsite. In the middle of the two is the Brushy Mountain Trail. The side trip to the farmsite is recommended. The reconstructed buildings accurately represent structures that were common in prepark days. There's a cantilevered barn, springhouse, and cabin. The Smoky Mountains Hiking Club used the cabin as a hiking base camp for many years, but camping is now prohibited.

After exploring the farmsite, take the Brushy Mountain Trail and ascend through an area known as Porters Flat. Pass rock walls and other artifacts of early settlement, and cross a few small creek branches. The grade is easy at first but soon picks up and stays moderate the rest of the way.

Long Branch flows down the north side of a ridge, and you get within earshot of it before turning to remain on the south side. Just beyond here is Fittified Spring, about 100 feet off the left side of the trail on a faint and easily missed path. Supposedly, an earthquake in 1916 caused this spring to flow intermittently, or in "fits," thus the name. With summer vegetation, you might pass right by the spring and never see it.

If you're making this hike in late May and June, the blooming mountain laurel tunnels up ahead are a highlight of the trip. Farther up on a rocky ridge, the trail opens up to a nice view. Look for several table mountain pines growing here. They grow in dry, exposed, rocky ridge areas like this and occur only in the Southern Appalachians. Look for the upwardly curving spines on the cones to identify this tree.

Now you enter a lush, scenic forest with good-sized hemlocks and cross several small creek branches. One particularly scenic pool on Trillium Branch looks as though it could harbor a good-sized brook trout. A good distance farther up, you cross Trillium Branch again. This time the creek creates a postcard-worthy scene as it slides and tumbles over mossy rocks.

Trillium Gap is a short distance from this last creek crossing. At the gap, Trillium Gap Trail goes straight ahead down the other side, and to the left it goes to Mt. LeConte. Our hike goes right (north) on a deeply rutted trail and passes through a rhododendron tunnel, then a mountain laurel tunnel. The tunnels soon open up to great views of Mt. LeConte behind you and the Porters Creek watershed to the right. Continue along the trail to a fork. The right fork leads a few feet to a restricted view toward the east. The left fork leads a few yards to a near-180-degree view toward the north. From that view, straight ahead (north) and below is the imposing Mt. Winnesoka, to the right is Greenbrier Pinnacle, and to the left is Gatlinburg and the Space Needle. To the northeast, English Mountain looms in the distance. On a clear, smog-free day (a rare occurrence in the Smokies), you can see Pigeon Forge and Douglas Lake far to the northwest.

Brushy Mountain itself is worth the hike even if the views aren't clear. On its summit is a heath bald. Heath plants include mountain laurel, Catawba rhododendron, sand myrtle, wintergreen, blueberry, and huckleberry—all shrubs or groundcover plants. From a distance the low-growing assemblage of plants appears smooth, and old timers referred to them as "laurel slicks."

Options: With a second vehicle or shuttle, an excellent choice is to combine this hike with Hike 37: Mt. LeConte via Trillium Gap, omitting the section from Trillium Gap to Mt. LeConte.

Ramsay Cascades

Highlights: *Wildflowers, old-growth forest, Ramsay Cascades*

Type of hike: Out-and-back; day hike
Total distance: 8.0 miles round-trip
Difficulty: Moderate

Best time of year: Early spring for wildflowers and high stream flows
Maps: Trails Illustrated; USGS Mt. Guyot

Special considerations: It is tempting to climb the ledges that make up Ramsay Cascades; however, it is very dangerous to do so. A sign at the falls lists the number of people killed here.

Finding the trailhead: From U.S. 441 in Gatlinburg, turn at traffic light #3 and drive east on U.S. 321. At 5.9 miles turn right (south) onto Greenbrier Road. This road follows scenic Middle Prong of Little Pigeon River, changing to gravel just past the ranger station. Drive slowly, and watch for pedestrians in summer. At 3.1 miles the road to the Ramsay Cascades trailhead turns left and crosses Porters Creek. Drive 1.5 miles along this road to the trailhead parking area.

Parking and trailhead facilities: The trailhead has room for several cars, but there are no facilities. Portable toilets are available at the picnic areas on Greenbrier Road.

Key points:
   1.5 Old jeep road ends.

The hike: Ramsay Cascades Trail provides an exceptional Smokies experience and is a good choice if you have only one day to hike in the park. The trail, which is a

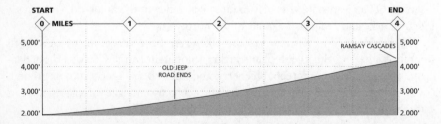

Ramsay Cascades; Old Settlers Trail

Ramsay Cascades.

continuation of the gravel road, begins east of the parking area. If you make this trek in April, the first thing you notice is a large patch of crested dwarf iris right beside the trail on the left. You then cross Little Laurel Branch on a culvert and immediately afterward cross Middle Prong of Little Pigeon River on a long footbridge. This crossing provides a great view of the cascading stream.

For the next 0.25 mile beyond the bridge, you pass through a terrific spring wildflower display. Showy orchis, creeping phlox, yellow trillium, and wild geranium grow here; a little farther up the trail, there are nice patches of dwarf iris. The hiking is easy as the trail follows an old jeep road with only moderate grades. At 1.5 miles, the jeep trail ends at a turnaround on the banks of Ramsay Prong, just before it enters Middle Prong. The old Greenbrier Pinnacle Trail cuts sharply to the left (north) just before the road ends. That trail leads to the sight of a former fire tower on the pinnacle, but the park no longer maintains the path. Ramsay Cascades Trail continues on the far side of the turnaround and follows Ramsay Prong upstream (east) through a dense understory of rhododendron.

You are now hiking on a bona fide Smokies trail, complete with slippery roots, rocks, and dense forest. At about 2.1 miles, a side stream crosses the trail and the forest opens up to a photogenic view of a rhododendron-framed cascade on Ramsay Prong. Just past this view, the trail crosses Ramsay Prong on an angled, slippery foot log. This is a tricky crossing in wet weather. Beyond the crossing the trail turns left and follows Ramsay Prong closely upstream. This section of trail is not very scenic because of the many downed trees and snags in the creek, and it can be a muddy mess during rainy weather. Soon, however, the forest makes you forget about mud and snags. Many large trees grow along the trail, and at 2.6 miles you pass between two huge yellow-poplars and enter a cove with more big trees and carpets of wildflowers. Another yellow-poplar, a massive one, is just ahead on the left. After a steep section and several rock steps, the trail crosses Ramsay Prong for the last time at 2.9 miles, this time on an asphalt-covered foot log that provides sure footing.

Leave the creek and rock-hop a side stream twice within a few hundred yards. (The route shown on the USGS map is not correct.) The next 0.5 mile passes through a very scenic, open, old-growth forest. As you near the falls, the trail approaches Ramsay Prong, and the sound of crashing water makes you think you've arrived at Ramsay Cascades. It's only a tease, though, as the most difficult part of the hike is still to come. The next 0.3 mile is a continuous scramble over rocks and roots. You come to a side stream that enters Ramsay Prong just below the falls. Rock-hop the stream and scramble a few feet up to the base of the waterfall.

Ramsay Cascades is one of the highest major falls in the park, and maybe the prettiest. Unfortunately, at my last visit a large tree had fallen over the falls just to the right of the main drop, and several large snags clogged the stream at the vantage point downstream from the base. If you're expecting to take wide-angle photographs, prepare yourself for disappointment.

Options: You could hike the first 0.5 mile and return, making for an easy family walk past numerous spring wildflowers and huge, mossy boulders.

42

Albright Grove

Highlights: *Exceptional old-growth forest*

Type of hike: A "lollipop" loop; day hike
Total distance: 6.8 miles round-trip
Difficulty: Moderate

Best time of year: Early April
Maps: Trails Illustrated; USGS Jones Cove and Mt. Guyot

Special considerations: The trailhead may not be a safe place to leave your car. In the past several vehicles have been stolen or vandalized, and while such activity has subsided recently, you are still taking a chance parking here. You might be able to park at a business back on U.S. 321, but be sure to ask permission beforehand and be prepared to pay a small fee.

Finding the trailhead: From U.S. 441 in Gatlinburg, turn at traffic light #3 and head east on U.S. 321. Drive 15.5 miles and turn right onto Baxter Road. Baxter road is about 0.1 mile beyond Yogi Bear's Jellystone Park Campground. Stay on the paved Baxter Road for 0.3 mile and turn sharply right onto a gravel road. Go a few hundred feet to a gated dirt road on the left. Park here, but don't block the gate.

Parking and trailhead facilities: There is room for only a few vehicles, but that's usually only a problem on summer weekends. Service stations and convenience stores are scattered along U.S. 321.

Key points:

1.2 Junction with Old Settlers and Gabes Mountain Trails.
2.9 Lower junction with Albright Grove Trail.
3.2 Upper junction with Albright Grove Trail.
3.9 Return to Maddron Bald Trail.

The hike: Do some things before you make this hike. Return your phone calls, do your grocery shopping, clean your camp, drop your postcards in the mail box—anything that might cause your mind to swirl with thoughts other than the path ahead of you. Albright Grove deserves your complete and undivided attention.

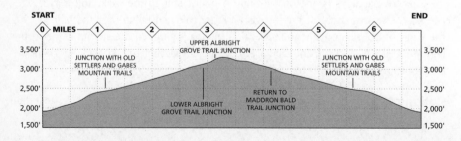

138

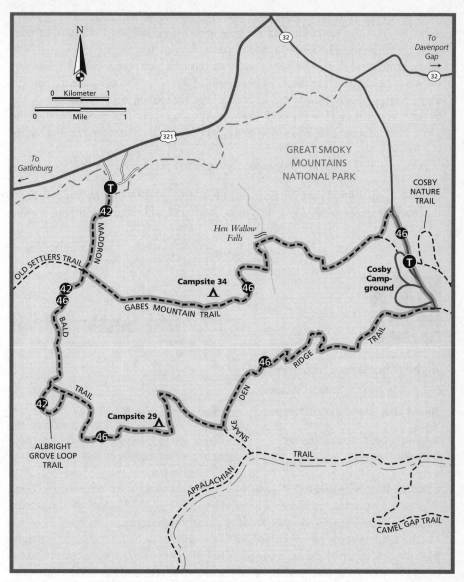

Begin on the Maddron Bald Trail, which starts as an old wagon road, and climb gently about 0.7 mile to the one-room Willis Baxter Cabin on the right. Beyond the cabin the grade increases noticeably. At 1.2 miles reach the junction with Old Settlers Trail on the right (see Hike 43) and Gabes Mountain Trail on the left (see Hike 46). Our hike continues straight ahead on the old roadbed. About a mile farther, the wagon road ends at an old traffic circle and the path becomes a real hiking trail. A little more than 0.5 mile farther, Maddron Bald Trail meets the lower end of Albright Grove Loop Trail.

You can go either way at the junction, since it's a loop hike. I recommend going left, staying on the Maddron Bald Trail and ascending another 0.3 mile to the upper junction with Albright Grove Loop Trail. This way, it's easier to laze your way through the good stuff. And what good stuff this is! Many people consider Albright Grove to be the finest example of old-growth forest in the park. (The old growth along Baxter Creek Trail is my favorite.) In early spring, wildflowers carpet the ground, seeming to compete with the trees for attention. The crown jewel of the grove is a yellow-poplar measuring more than 25 feet in circumference and standing 135 feet high.

Once back at the lower trail junction, retrace your steps to the trailhead.

Options: Hike 46: Maddron Bald and Hen Wallow Falls—a one- to two-night backpacking trip—passes Albright Grove Loop Trail and other old-growth stands.

43

Old Settlers Trail

Highlights: *Solitude, settlement history*

(See map for Hike 41: Ramsay Cascades.)

Type of hike: Shuttle; long day hike or over-nighter
Total distance: 17.0 miles one-way
Difficulty: Moderate

Best time of year: Winter
Maps: Trails Illustrated; USGS Jones Cove, Mt. Guyot, and Mt. LeConte (trail not shown on USGS maps and not accurate on Trails Illustrated map)

Special considerations: Poison ivy is abundant along most of this hike. Consider making this hike in winter, when the leaves are gone. Wintertime also reveals rock walls, cemeteries, and other artifacts of early settlement.

You need a shuttle to make this hike. If you use two vehicles, note that the trailhead off U.S. 321 may not be a safe place to leave your car. In the past several vehicles have been stolen or vandalized, and while such activity has subsided recently, you still take a chance parking here. You might be able to park at a business back on U.S. 321, but be sure to ask permission beforehand and be prepared to pay a small fee. The best option is to leave your vehicle at the Greenbrier trailhead and have a shuttle bring you to the trailhead off U.S. 321.

Finding the trailhead: The hike ends at the trailhead in the Greenbrier section of the park. You need to leave a vehicle here and drive to the starting trailhead or arrange for the shuttle to pick you up here. To get here from U.S. 441 in Gatlinburg, turn at traffic light #3 and drive east on U.S. 321. At 5.9 miles turn right (south) onto Greenbrier Road. This road follows scenic Middle Prong of Little

Stone chimney along Old Settlers Trail.

Pigeon River, changing to gravel just past the ranger station. Drive slowly, and watch for pedestrians in summer. At 3.1 miles the road to the Ramsay Cascades trailhead turns left and immediately crosses Porters Creek. Take this road and cross three bridges in the first 0.1 mile. Park just beyond the third bridge, on the left.

To get to the start of the hike, go back to U.S. 321 and turn right. Drive 9.6 miles from the Greenbrier entrance (15.5 miles from Gatlinburg) and turn right onto Baxter Road. Baxter Road is about 0.1 mile beyond Yogi Bear's Jellystone Park Campground. Stay on the paved Baxter Road for 0.3 mile and turn sharply right onto a gravel road. Go a few hundred feet to a gated dirt road on the left. Park here, but don't block the gate.

If you arrange for a commercial shuttle service, don't worry about finding the starting trailhead. The service will not only take you there without fear of getting lost, but you might also get a history lesson to complement your hike.

Parking and trailhead facilities: Both trailheads hold only a few vehicles, but that shouldn't be a problem. Neither trailhead has facilities, but U.S. 321 has many convenience stores and service stations.

Key points:
1.2 Junction with Old Settlers and Gabes Mountain Trails.
10.4 Campsite 33.
17.0 Trailhead on Ramsay Cascades Road.

The hike: This hike isn't for everyone. In summer it's hot, buggy, overgrown, and infested with poison ivy. The views aren't good, and the forest is mostly second growth. It's long and tiring, though only a few sections are steep. So, why would you want to make this hike? If you're a history buff, this trail was made especially for you. The Old Settlers Trail passes by (and through) more evidence of settlement history than does any other trail in the park. There are old rock walls, cemeteries, chimneys, wagon traces, rotting structures, and pieces of old stoves and dishes scattered about. Some of the stone walls are remarkable, as though the builders were trying to show off instead of just clearing a plot for planting.

The Old Settlers Trail is an assemblage of old paths and wagon roads, with many side paths leading off. A few of these side paths connect the trail with U.S. 321, creating the possibility of breaking this hike into smaller segments. However, it's frustrating trying to find the trailheads, and the current widening work on U.S.

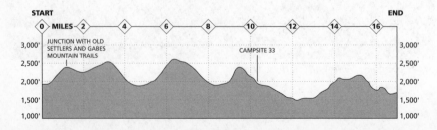

321 has all trailheads in a state of flux. The best bet is to stick with the hike as presented here and stay on the main trail. Signs mark all questionable trail junctions along the Old Settlers Trail.

Begin on the Maddron Bald Trail, which starts as an old wagon road, and climb gently about 0.7 mile to the one-room Willis Baxter Cabin on the right. Beyond the cabin the grade increases noticeably. At 1.2 miles you reach the junction with Gabes Mountain Trail on the left and Old Settlers Trail on the right. Maddron Bald Trail continues straight ahead, but you want to turn right (north) onto the Old Settlers Trail and stay on it for the rest of the hike.

Descend through a hemlock forest to pick up an old wagon road (a common theme on this hike). Look closely from now on. There are some old metal pieces (stove?) on the left and remnants from a chimney on the right. A side path leads from the chimney to a cemetery that has only slabs of rock as headstones. Now cross a small creek branch, and shortly afterward cross Indian Camp Creek on a sturdy foot log. Next comes a rock-hop of Dunn Creek, which could be tricky in high water. Notice the fine rock wall on the left just beyond the crossing. Now begin a long, gradual ascent up a small drainage and swing around sharply to the right on a switchback. Now it's a climb up and around Snag Mountain (look for mountain laurel blooms in June) and a descent to a small tributary of Webb Creek. An old homesite sits on the left, just beyond the creek. Pick up an old wagon road and follow it down a small ridge to another crossing of the tributary.

You soon meet up with Webb Creek and follow alongside it. There are rock walls everywhere—to the right, across the creek, even one across the trail that you have to walk through. Where the trail crosses the creek, a sign says that the T. McCarter Barn is 600 feet to the right. The side path leads to a left turn onto an old road that leads to the barn. Behind the barn another path leads several yards to the foundation remains of a homesite and a standing springhouse. Be careful; the path is overgrown with poison ivy. You're not far from U.S. 321 at this point, and you can hear the traffic.

Back on the main trail, cross Webb Creek and pass an impressive rock wall on the left that's nearly 6 feet high. The best rock wall of the entire hike (and probably in all the park) is just ahead. It's 5 feet high, 3 feet thick, and about 100 yards long. No stone seems out of place, as though they were placed according to a computer-generated master plan.

Now cross several small creek branches and come to Texas Creek, where the trail joins an old roadbed and heads upstream. (A side path at this point follows the creek downstream to U.S. 321.) About 0.25 mile upstream, you pass a homesite on the left with two chimney remains and some rotten timber lying in one corner. Now climb (steeply in places) high into the Texas Creek drainage, crossing several feeder streams and finally crossing Texas Creek before swinging out of the drainage. The trail then climbs to a ridge and descends through a scenic forest with some good-sized hemlocks and yellow-poplars. In this forest is the greatest concentration of fallen (some standing) American chestnut trees I've seen in the park.

After crossing Tumbling Creek, you quickly climb over a ridge and descend steeply to pick up an old roadbed along Noisy Creek. Soon you cross the creek twice in quick succession and a third time a little farther down. After the third crossing the trail continues to follow the roadbed along the creek to a fork. The path on the right follows the creek downstream to U.S. 321; our trail turns left and heads away from the creek.

Pass more rock walls and a chimney on the left, and then swing around into the Ramsey Creek drainage and follow that creek upstream, crossing it five times and passing two chimneys. After the fifth crossing the trail begins a brutal climb, the steepest of the hike, and passes a chimney on the left. After moderating the ascent and rounding a broad ridge, the trail descends through a dry forest of pines (killed by Southern pine beetles), oaks, sourwood, and mountain laurel to a crossing of Redwine Creek.

Just beyond the creek crossing lies Campsite 33, situated directly on top of an old homesite. You can pitch your tent in the former living room. Rocks from the crumbling chimney have been commandeered for the fire ring and as chairs. Park rules strictly forbid such activity, so don't contribute.

Shortly beyond the campsite the trail swings left around a ridge, while another path goes right and follows the ridge. Staying left on the main trail, you pass more rock walls and then a chimney right beside the trail. Just past the chimney the trail crosses an old roadbed. To the left about 25 yards sits an old log structure without a roof. Was this once a corncrib? Maybe a chicken coop? A right turn on the roadbed leads to U.S. 321. You want to go straight and descend to cross Timothy Creek. Shortly beyond the creek crossing, the trail descends steeply for a short distance before moderating and following a drainage downstream. As the grade begins to level out, an obvious path goes right, but you need to stay to the left as the sign indicates. Shortly beyond here, the terrain flattens and you experience the rare occurrence of a totally level hike in the Smokies. This was prime bottomland for early settlers.

Once through the bottomland, the trail ascends alongside Soak Ash Creek and follows it high into the drainage, crossing it a few times and passing another homesite. Finally, the trail leaves the drainage and goes on a long, gradual climb to cross Copeland Divide. In doing so, you climb some, level some, descend some, and cross Snakefeeder Branch. But mostly you climb.

Once over Copeland Divide you descend to pick up the Little Bird Branch drainage, eventually crossing the branch and following it downstream before swinging away, crossing an unnamed branch, and then arriving at Bird Branch. Cross Bird Branch and enjoy the level 0.3-mile final push to the trailhead.

Cosby Nature Trail

Type of hike: Loop; day hike
Total distance: 1.0 mile round-trip
Difficulty: Easy

Maps: Trails Illustrated; USGS Hartford (trail not shown)

Finding the trailhead: From the U.S. 321 and Tennessee Highway 32 junction in Cosby, drive 1.2 miles and turn right at the sign for Cosby Campground. Follow this road 2.2 miles to the parking lot on the left at the campground amphitheater. The trail begins from the parking lot.

Parking and trailhead facilities: The parking lot holds only a few vehicles, but you shouldn't have a problem. If it's full you can park at the hiker parking lot behind the campground registration building, which is where you want to park for any extended hiking in the area. Rest rooms are available in the campground.

The hike: The Cosby Self-guiding Nature Trail makes a great outing for families staying at the nearby campground. Start from the parking lot and in a few feet meet Low Gap Trail. Low Gap Trail starts at the hiker parking area behind the campground registration building and creates part of the loop for the nature trail on its way to the Appalachian Trail. Turn right, but do not take the immediate side path that leads down to Cosby Creek. Continue straight; in a short distance another path turns to the left. Take this path and wind through a scenic forest and over numerous foot logs. You come back to Low Gap Trail a short distance above where you broke off from it. Turn right and cross Cosby Creek on a foot log and then come to a side path cutting sharply left that leads to the road. Stay to the right and hike a short distance back to the trailhead.

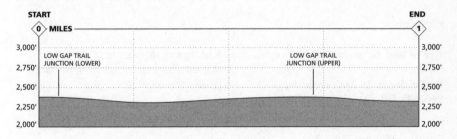

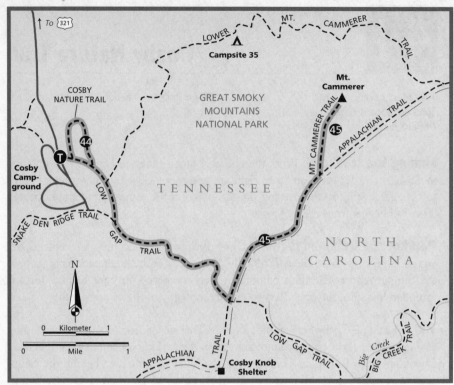

To 321

LOWER MT. CAMMERER TRAIL

Campsite 35

COSBY NATURE TRAIL

GREAT SMOKY MOUNTAINS NATIONAL PARK

Mt. Cammerer

MT. CAMMERER TRAIL

APPALACHIAN TRAIL

45

44

T

Cosby Camp-ground

LOW

TENNESSEE

SNAKE DEN RIDGE TRAIL

GAP

TRAIL

45

NORTH CAROLINA

N

0 Kilometer 1

0 Mile 1

APPALACHIAN

TRAIL

LOW GAP TRAIL

Cosby Knob Shelter

Big Creek

BIG CREEK TRAIL

45

Mt. Cammerer

Highlights: *Terrific views*

Type of hike: Out-and-back, with loop option; day hike
Total distance: 11.2 miles round-trip
Difficulty: Difficult

Best time of year: October
Maps: Trails Illustrated; USGS Hartford and Luftee Knob

Finding the trailhead: From the U.S. 321 and Tennessee Highway 32 junction in Cosby, drive 1.2 miles and turn right at the sign for Cosby Campground. Follow this road 2.1 miles to the campground registration building. Drive past the building and turn left to loop back to the hiker parking area. The Low Gap Trail starts on the south end of the parking area.

Parking and trailhead facilities: The hiker parking lot is plenty large enough most of the time; if it's full, the picnic area parking is right behind it. Rest rooms are available in the campground.

Key points:
- **0.1** Lower junction with Cosby Self-guiding Nature Trail.
- **0.3** Upper junction with Cosby Self-guiding Nature Trail.
- **0.4** Junction with Lower Mt. Cammerer Trail.
- **2.9** Junction with Appalachian Trail.
- **5.0** Junction with Mt. Cammerer Trail.
- **5.6** Mt. Cammerer Lookout.

The hike: This hike provides the shortest route to the Mt. Cammerer Lookout, a restored 1930s fire tower on the rocky summit of Mt. Cammerer. The panoramic view from the lookout is spectacular at any time, but if you can make this hike in mid-October when the autumn foliage peaks, you'll have a hard time pulling yourself away.

The Low Gap Trail begins from the hiker parking area and soon passes behind the campground amphitheater and the Cosby Self-guiding Nature Trail. Pay attention to the signs through here, because a number a paths lead off from the main trail. At 0.4 mile you come to what looks like an old traffic turnaround. A right turn here takes you over a ford of Cosby Creek to the campground. Don't turn right. Go left a few yards to the junction with Lower Mt. Cammerer Trail. Turn right (south) at this junction to stay on Low Gap Trail.

At 0.8 mile pass a side path on the right that leads back to the campground. The next 2.1 miles is a steady uphill grind through a scenic forest to Low Gap on the Appalachian Trail (AT), with most of this distance on a loose parallel of Cosby Creek. At Low Gap turn left (north) and make a steady climb for about a mile before leveling out for an easy section. Climb again before reaching the junction with Mt. Cammerer Trail at a fork. The AT goes to the right and descends, while our hike goes left (actually more straight) and continues to follow the ridgeline. A 0.6-mile hike on Mt. Cammerer Trail takes you to the lookout.

The term "lookout" typically refers to observation structures that are at or near ground level, while "tower," as in Mt. Sterling Tower, refers to structures built to

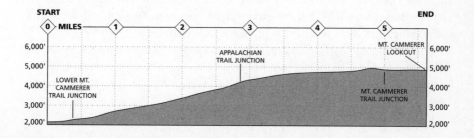

Mt. Cammerer Lookout.

rise above the trees. The Civilian Conservation Corps built the fire lookout in the 1930s, using the same design as the lookouts on the treeless and rocky mountains of the western states. After falling in disrepair, the lookout was restored in 1995 and is now open for hikers to enjoy. When you see the view from here, you won't care whether it's a lookout, a tower, or just an overlook. You can go inside, but the view is not good through the stained and scratched windows. The wraparound deck allows you to experience the views without distraction.

Options: This hike is the shortest route to the lookout. A longer route that does not require backtracking uses Lower Mt. Cammerer Trail. You take it at the junction with Low Gap Trail near Cosby Campground and hike about 7.5 miles to the AT. A right turn on the AT takes you to the Mt. Cammerer Trail in 2.3 miles. Complete the loop by taking the AT down to Low Gap Trail and then following it back to the trailhead. Total round-trip mileage for this option is about 18.7 miles. That's tough for a day hike. You could overnight at Campsite 35 on Lower Mt. Cammerer Trail to break up the hike, but the extra weight from camping gear makes the hike just as difficult to do in two days as in one day unencumbered.

Another route to Mt. Cammerer is from Davenport Gap. You hike 5.3 miles on the AT to the Mt. Cammerer Trail junction. This route is more strenuous, and it may not be safe to leave a vehicle at Davenport Gap. For a day hike, the route presented here is the best option.

Hike 80: Big Creek Perimeter Loop passes Mt. Cammerer on its route.

46

Maddron Bald and Hen Wallow Falls

Highlights: *Old-growth forest, Hen Wallow Falls, wildflowers*

(See map for Hike 42: Albright Cove.)

Type of hike: Loop; long day hike, overnighter, or two-night backpack
Total distance: 17.9 miles round-trip
Difficulty: Difficult

Best time of year: Spring
Maps: Trails Illustrated; USGS Hartford, Luftee Knob, Mt. Guyot, and Jones Cove

Finding the trailhead: From the U.S. 321 and Tennessee Highway 32 junction in Cosby, drive 1.2 miles and turn right at the sign for Cosby Campground. Follow this road 2.1 miles to the campground registration building. Drive past the building and turn left to loop back to the hiker parking area. To reach the trailhead for Snake Den Ridge Trail, you have to walk 0.1 mile up the road from the registration building and turn right into the campground. Go straight into the B section for about 0.2 mile. Just before reaching site B51, the gated road marking the trailhead turns to the right.

Parking and trailhead facilities: The hiker parking lot is plenty large enough most of the time; if it's full, the picnic area parking is right behind it. Rest rooms are available in the campground.

Key points:

0.3 Snake Den Ridge Trail begins from campground registration building.
4.9 Junction with Maddron Bald Trail.
6.5 Campsite 29.
9.0 Upper junction with Albright Grove Trail.
9.3 Lower junction with Albright Grove Trail.
11.0 Junction with Old Settlers and Gabes Mountain Trails.
12.8 Campsite 34.
15.5 Hen Wallow Falls.
17.6 Junction with Cosby Road.

The hike: For people who like trees, this may be the best backpacking trip in the park. Much of the hike passes through old-growth forest, including what many

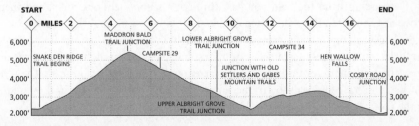

people believe to be the finest "virgin" woods in the park, at Albright Grove. Throw in a high, pretty waterfall and spring wildflowers, and you have a grand adventure ahead of you.

The adventure begins from Cosby Campground, directly opposite site B51. Snake Den Ridge Trail enters the forest here and climbs gradually along an old roadbed. Soon you pass the Cosby Horse Trail, which comes in from the left. The horse trail serves as a connector to Low Gap Trail. Stay to the right and continue climbing along the old roadbed. You soon pass an old graveyard on the right and shortly afterward reach an old turnaround. A side path on the right leads a few feet to a concrete slab and an overlook of Rock Creek. Look for clumps of showy orchis in April.

A few feet from the side path, Snake Den Ridge Trail continues past three boulders on the right and is now a bona fide trail. Hike through a scenic forest of hemlock and basswood with an understory of rhododendron, and soon cross Rock Creek on a foot log. The forest continues to be picturesque, with good-sized trees. There's yellow-poplar, silverbell, hemlock, and maple. Spring wildflowers carpet the ground.

About a mile above the Rock Creek crossing, you come to a crossing of Inadu Creek above a small waterfall. Inadu means snake in Cherokee, and it's one of the few Native American names retained in the park. As you leave the creek and begin ascending the ridge, the vegetation changes to plants more adapted to a drier environment—pine, galax, trailing arbutus, and mountain laurel. Climbing on, you pass through a moist cove with big hemlocks and numerous painted trilliums in spring. Beyond here, you climb a short knife ridge with nearly 360-degree views. Mt. Cammerer is prominent. Soon you enter a darker, cooler forest and begin to see red spruce; as you climb higher you pass through a ground cover of spring beauty with patches of trout lily, both blooming in April.

The junction with Maddron Bald Trail is not far ahead. From the junction, Snake Den Ridge Trail continues another 0.7 mile to the Appalachian Trail, but our hike turns right (west) and follows Maddron Bald Trail. Enjoy the first significant downhill section of the hike as you travel through a dark spruce forest to Maddron Bald.

Maddron is typical of many "balds" in the Smokies, but it might not be what you expected. In the Southern Appalachians, a bald can be one of two types. They can be open and grassy like Andrews and Gregory Balds or covered in shrubby heath vegetation like on Brushy Mountain and here at Maddron Bald. Although the vegetation on Maddron Bald restricts the vistas somewhat, the views are great to the south and west.

Descending from the bald you pass through a scenic hemlock forest and then arrive at Campsite 29 beside Otter Creek. This is your first night's stay on a two-night backpack or your only stay on an overnighter. The site sits in a mossy boulder field—not the best terrain for camping, but pleasant enough. It isn't private, since the trail encircles the site, but it's far enough from any trailhead that you're not likely to have any walk-by traffic unless you hang out at the site in the middle of the day.

Pressing on from the campsite, the trail weaves a bit and then swings around a ridge separating the Otter Creek and Copperhead Branch drainages. An obvious side path on the right leads a few yards to a wonderful view. Soon cross Copperhead Branch and then Indian Camp Creek at a photogenic cascade amongst huge, mossy boulders. Farther down you cross a side branch, then cross Indian Camp Creek again; 50 yards farther, cross Copperhead Branch again. Now you pass between two giant hemlocks, one on each side of the trail, and soon begin a high parallel course above Otter Creek.

Here you pass what must be the oddest-looking stump in the Smokies. It's huge—so huge that four people could pack themselves into the hollow center. It has several rhododendron trees growing all over it and a hemlock or two. Shortly beyond the stump, you cross Indian Camp Creek once more and arrive at the upper junction with Albright Grove Trail. It's 0.3 mile from here on the Maddron Bald Trail to the lower junction with Albright Grove Trail, but you don't want to hike that part of the trail. Instead, turn left and follow the Albright Grove Trail 0.7 mile through one of the most magnificent old-growth forests in the Smokies (see Hike 42: Albright Grove).

At the lower end of Albright Grove Trail, you rejoin Maddron Bald Trail and soon cross Indian Camp Creek for the final time on an asphalt-covered foot log. Farther down, the trail joins an old roadbed and follows it down to the junction with Old Settlers and Gabes Mountain Trails in a small clearing.

Our hike follows the Gabes Mountain Trail to the right (south) and begins climbing again, though not too steeply. For the next 1.8 miles you cross over small creek branches and hike through a beautiful forest with yellow-poplar, buckeye, beech, Fraser magnolia, and silverbell. At your feet are numerous species of spring wildflowers, and you pass huge American chestnut stumps.

Reach Campsite 34 right beside Greenbrier Creek. The forest here is pleasantly open, and the tent sites have a little more privacy than Campsite 29. This is your home on the second night of a two-night backpack.

For the most part you're finished climbing once you leave Campsite 34. There's some gradual ascending, but nothing significant. The forest remains outstanding, and there are scenic stream crossings. At the third crossing of Lower Falling Branch, you can't help but realize that you're looking out over the top of Hen Wallow Falls. Hiking in this direction, you might be tempted to attempt a scramble down the bank for a close view, but save your energy. A short distance farther, a side path to the left leads safely (but steeply) to the base of the falls. Lower Falling Branch at this point is a continuous set of cascades and drops. The side path comes out at the base of the uppermost drop, which is about 50 feet high. No path leads to views of the lower drops, and any attempt to get down there would risk life and limb.

Back on the main trail, you can take heart that the huffing and puffing is all behind you. Except for a few minor humps, it's downhill from here. As you near the end, the trail forks, with the left fork leading 0.3 mile to the picnic area and the right fork going 0.3 mile to the campground at site A44. Take the left fork and come out on Cosby Road. Turn right and follow the road 0.2 mile to the parking area.

Southwest
SECTION

Grinding corn in Mingus Mill.

47

Mingus Mill and Newton Bald

Highlights: *Solitude, wildflowers*

Type of hike: Shuttle; day hike or overnighter
Total distance: 11.4 miles one-way
Difficulty: Moderate
Best time of year: April for wildflowers

Maps: Trails Illustrated (the first 2.9 miles are not shown on the 1999 version); USGS Smokemont

Special considerations: You might be tempted to turn this hike into a loop by walking 2.8 miles on Newfound Gap Road. You can do this, but I don't recommend it. In many places, there isn't much of a shoulder, and the traffic is looking out for scenery, not you.

Finding the trailhead: From Oconaluftee Visitor Center drive 0.4 mile south on Newfound Gap Road and turn left at the sign for Mingus Mill. Reach the parking area immediately. The road ends beyond the parking area at a turnaround, and the trail begins as a continuation of the road.

If leaving a second vehicle at hike's end, go to the trailhead for Newton Bald Trail, located 2.8 miles farther south on Newfound Gap Road, just beyond the entrance to Smokemont Campground. There is no official parking area at the trailhead. Instead, turn onto the campground road and park on the right just after crossing the river.

Parking and trailhead facilities: The Mingus Mill parking area fills up on weekends, but if you get there by midmorning, you should be okay. Rest rooms are available at the trailhead.

Key points:
1.25 Fork leads to cemetery.
2.9 Junction with Deeplow Gap Trail.
5.8 Junction with Newton Bald Trail on Newton Bald.

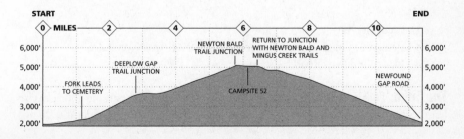

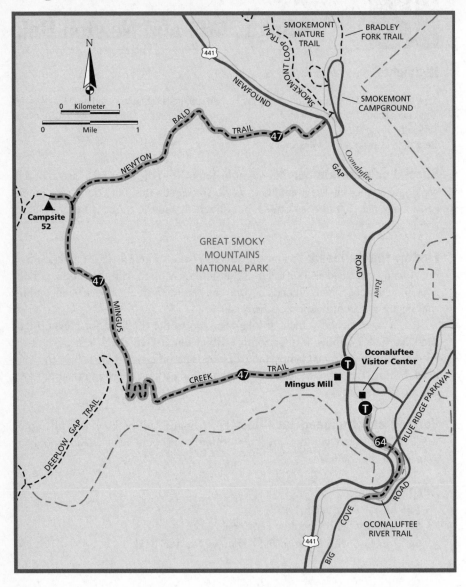

6.1 Campsite 52.

6.4 Return to junction with Newton Bald and Mingus Creek Trails.

11.4 Newfound Gap Road.

The hike: Don't worry about all the people you see in the parking lot. They're here to see Mingus Mill, a restored late-nineteenth-century gristmill. You'll have the hike to yourself. You can explore the mill before you hike or, since it is so near the parking area, save it for another day when you have more time. The mill still operates using the originally installed water-powered mechanism. Hours may vary, but generally the mill opens daily in summer and on weekends in spring and fall.

From the mill's grounds you can walk along the raceway to Mingus Creek and cross to get on Mingus Creek Trail, but this could be a wet crossing in high water. The parking area marks the official start of Mingus Creek Trail. Take the gravel road that begins from the turnaround and follow it along Mingus Creek behind the mill. Cross the creek two times on auto bridges and pass a firing range. (If the range is in use, the trail may be closed temporarily.) Continue on the service road, ascending gradually, and cross the creek once more just before passing an old water plant with an ugly metal building.

The service road ends here, and the trail becomes rocky. Soon cross Madcap Branch on a foot log and come to a fork. A right turn takes you to an old cemetery. Our hike goes left and follows Madcap Branch upstream. (Pay attention at the fork; the most trodden path goes to the right, and at my last visit Mingus Creek Trail to the left was not signed.) After rock-hopping the branch and then a feeder, you start to climb. Look for large patches of sharp-lobed hepatica along the trail. The wildflower is unusual in that its distinctive three-lobed leaves remain throughout the winter. The trail continues on a long, sometimes steep ascent, crossing Madcap Branch or its branchlets many times before swinging away and climbing the ridge on switchbacks.

At a small gap in the ridgetop, Deeplow Gap Trail goes straight ahead and down the other side. Our hike goes right and follows up the ridgeline. It starts out surprisingly level and then begins climbing—moderately at first, but with a few steep stretches later on. Occasional views are off both sides of the trail. After following on or near the ridgeline for nearly 3 miles, you arrive at Newton Bald and the junction with Newton Bald Trail. Newton Bald is no longer a bald. Trees have completely covered the summit, and it's hard to tell that it was once open.

Turn left (north) onto Newton Bald Trail and hike an easy 0.3 mile to Campsite 52, straddling a small saddle. The trail passes right through the tiny site. Water is available from a very small spring 75 yards down the northeast side. If you're doing this hike as an overnighter, this is home for tonight.

Backtrack to the junction with Mingus Creek Trail, but stay on Newton Bald Trail. You now have a 5.0-mile near-continuous descent (sometimes steep) to Newfound Gap Road. Look out for wildflowers in spring; this trail is a good one for them. About 0.25 mile before reaching the road, you pass a bridle path on the right; a short distance farther there's another horse trail on the right. Stay to the left at both junctions. Once back at the road, you are 0.1 mile north of the Smokemont Campground entrance.

Options: This hike is a good day hike for campers staying at Smokemont Campground. Arrange for a shuttle to the trailhead, make the hike, and walk back to the campground in time for dinner.

48

Deep Creek

Highlights: *Wildflowers, Deep Creek*

Type of hike: Shuttle; day hike, overnighter, or extended backpacking trip
Total distance: 14.2 miles one-way
Difficulty: Moderate

Best time of year: April for wildflowers
Maps: Trails Illustrated; USGS Clingmans Dome and Bryson City

Special considerations: In high water, some of the creek crossings could be a little tricky and might require wading. Try not to hike this trail in the rain. The upper section is heavily overgrown with dog hobble, and the wet foliage constantly brushing against you is irritating.

Finding the trailhead: From Oconaluftee Visitor Center drive 13.9 miles north on Newfound Gap Road to a gravel pullout on the left. This is 1.7 miles south of the Newfound Gap. The Deep Creek Trail begins from the pullout.

Parking and trailhead facilities: The pullout has room for only a couple of vehicles. A larger, paved parking area is located 0.1 mile south of the pullout. It's probably safer to park here even if the pullout is empty. Newfound Gap has rest room facilities. In peak season, stick a clothespin over your nose, and don't touch anything.

Leave a second vehicle (or have the shuttle pick you up) at the lower trailhead for Deep Creek Trail. Follow the signs from downtown Bryson City to Deep Creek Campground. As you enter the park, continue on the paved road past the campground entrance and the picnic area to where the road ends at a turnaround. A paved parking area is on the left.

Key points:
3.9 Campsite 53 and junction with Fork Ridge Trail.
6.5 Campsite 54.
7.4 Campsite 55 and junction with Pole Road Creek Trail.

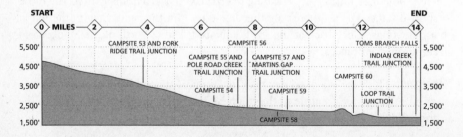

158

Deep Creek; Noland Divide

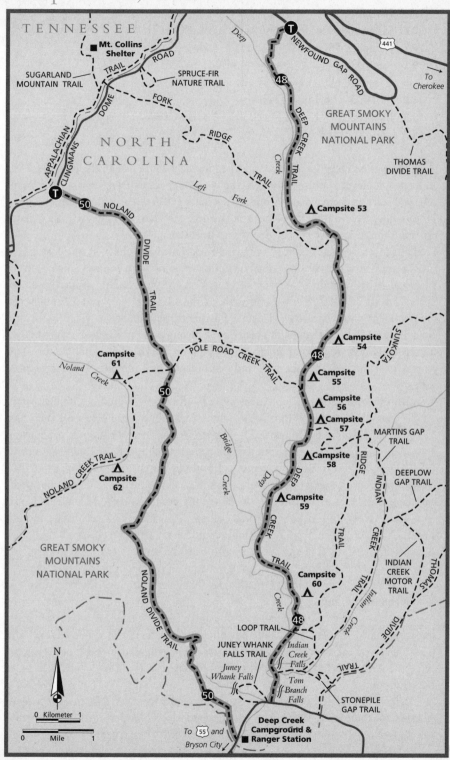

TENNESSEE

Mt. Collins Shelter

SUGARLAND MOUNTAIN TRAIL

SPRUCE-FIR NATURE TRAIL

DOME ROAD

FORK

TRAIL

APPALACHIAN

CLINGMANS

NORTH CAROLINA

RIDGE

TRAIL

Left Fork

Deep

Creek

DEEP CREEK TRAIL

NEWFOUND GAP ROAD

441

To Cherokee

GREAT SMOKY MOUNTAINS NATIONAL PARK

THOMAS DIVIDE TRAIL

Campsite 53

NOLAND

50

DIVIDE

TRAIL

Campsite 61

Noland Creek

POLE ROAD CREEK TRAIL

50

NOLAND CREEK TRAIL

Campsite 62

Bridge

Creek

Deep

CREEK

TRAIL

SUNKOTA

Campsite 54

48

Campsite 55

Campsite 56

Campsite 57

Campsite 58

RIDGE

INDIAN

CREEK

MARTINS GAP TRAIL

DEEPLOW GAP TRAIL

INDIAN CREEK MOTOR TRAIL

Campsite 59

TRAIL

Indian Creek

TRAIL

THOMAS

DIVIDE

TRAIL

GREAT SMOKY MOUNTAINS NATIONAL PARK

NOLAND DIVIDE TRAIL

Campsite 60

Creek

48

LOOP TRAIL

JUNEY WHANK FALLS TRAIL

Juney Whank Falls

Indian Creek Falls

Tom Branch Falls

STONEPILE GAP TRAIL

50

N

0 Kilometer 1

0 Mile 1

To 55 and Bryson City

Deep Creek Campground & Ranger Station

7.6 Campsite 56.

8.1 Campsite 57 and junction with Martins Gap Trail.

8.7 Campsite 58.

9.1 Campsite 59.

11.6 Campsite 60.

12.5 Junction with Loop Trail.

13.5 Junction with Indian Creek Trail (Indian Creek Falls is nearby).

14.0 Tom Branch Falls.

The hike: The Deep Creek that most people see is more like a little river, but then most people never venture as far into the headwaters as you will on this hike. Actually, you start on the headwaters and follow the creek downstream, watching it grow by the mile. By the time it reaches the Deep Creek Campground area, it's a major stream, though not any deeper than other park streams.

Descend from the trailhead on switchbacks through a lush, scenic forest, and cross several small stream branches. Wildflowers abound in the wet spots. Lettuce saxifrage grows here; look for its blooms in May and June and its distinctive lance-shaped, coarsely toothed leaves throughout the summer. At about 1.5 miles you enter a boggy and surprisingly flat cove. Passing through the cove, you cross several branches and then meet up with Deep Creek. Swing away from the creek and go on a long stretch where you parallel the creek high on the bank. Dog hobble threatens to take over the trail through here and continues to be a nuisance for several more miles.

Continue downstream, sometimes close by the creek, sometimes high above it. At 3.9 miles you come to the first of eight backcountry campsites on the Deep Creek Trail; this one is Campsite 53. The site is not very pleasant—a cleared-out spot in a brier patch with the trail passing right through it. Fork Ridge Trail turns off to the right here, crossing Deep Creek without benefit of a foot log.

Continuing on Deep Creek Trail, you follow along the creek closely but without many good views of it through the dense dog hobble and rhododendron. Come to Cherry Creek and make a tricky rock-hop in normal flows or a wade in high water. Once across Cherry Creek, climb up and away from Deep Creek then back down to it. Here the trail and creek are the same for several yards, and in very high water this stretch could be dicey. Look for a fallen hemlock by the creek that has several small trees growing from its trunk. There are birches, rhododendron—at least a half dozen species.

Now leave the creek a bit and pass through a forest with some impressive hemlock and yellow-poplar trees. On returning to the creek, the ground is wet and boggy and you cross over two out-of-character corrugated metal pipes. Past the pipes the trail turns left and goes through a rerouted section that avoids even more boggy ground.

At about 6.5 miles you cross two creeks in quick succession (the first crossing of Nettle Creek might be tricky) and arrive at Campsite 54, just after the crossings. It's

Garter snake along Deep Creek.

another small site but much more attractive than Campsite 53. Less than a mile farther you come to Campsite 55, a horse camp, on the left. Just beyond the campsite Pole Road Creek Trail turns off to the right and crosses Deep Creep on two foot logs on its way to Upper Sassafras Gap on Noland Divide. Stay straight on Deep Creek Trail.

After a short up-and-down segment, pass right through Campsite 56, a very small site in a hemlock grove. Soon the trail swings away from the creek and climbs a little to Campsite 57 at the junction with Martins Gap Trail. Campsite 57 is named Bryson Place and is the site of Horace Kephart's last permanent camp in the Smokies. A few hundred feet off the right side of the trail lies a millstone and plaque honoring Kephart, placed in 1931 by the Horace Kephart Boy Scout Troop. (See Hike 68: Kephart Prong for more on Horace Kephart.) This isn't the best site. It's open and on a slope—and it's a horse camp. If here in May, look around the horse hitching area for pink lady's slipper orchids; they're everywhere. Martins Gap Trail goes to the left, between the campsite and hitching area. Again, stay on Deep Creek Trail.

Reach Campsite 58 in another 0.6 mile. It offers no privacy, but its setting right beside Deep Creek makes it appealing. Beyond the site the trail does its typical up-and-down routine; on the down side, you come to Campsite 59, also beside Deep Creek. It has no privacy either, although a screen of dog hobble offers a little isolation. From here you go on a roller-coaster ride of ups and downs and then make a long, somewhat steep climb (the longest climb of the hike). After the climb an even longer descent takes you to Campsite 60, the prettiest one of all. It sits off the trail enough for a little privacy and has a ground cover of soft pine needles.

Cross Bumgardner Branch on a foot log just past the campsite, make a final climb, then descend to the old road turnaround. From here it's an easy 2.1-mile walk along the old roadbed to the trailhead. See Hike 56: Deep Creek Loop for more detail about this segment.

Options: With eight campsites and five intersecting trails (each offering other hike possibilities), it's hard to decide how to plan a hike. If doing an overnighter, you might want to stay at Campsite 56, which is about halfway into the hike. On a lazy two-night backpack, I'd camp at 54 the first night and 60 on the second. Truthfully, unless you plan to fish, this hike is better done as a day hike. There are better backpacking hikes in the park.

49

Spruce-Fir Nature Trail

Highlights: *Clinton's lily*

(See map for Hike 4: Chimney Tops.)

Type of hike: Loop; day hike
Total distance: 0.5 mile round-trip
Difficulty: Easy

Best time of year: May
Maps: Trails Illustrated; USGS Clingmans Dome

Special considerations: Clingmans Dome Road is closed from December 1 to March 31.

Finding the trailhead: At Newfound Gap, turn west onto Clingmans Dome Road and drive 2.6 miles to one of the two small pullouts on the left. The trail begins from the first pullout at the interpretive sign. Interpretive brochures (50 cents to keep) are available from the trailhead.

Parking and trailhead facilities: The pullouts are small, but finding space is rarely a problem. Often-malodorous rest rooms are available at Newfound Gap and at the end of Clingmans Dome Road.

The hike: I don't recommend this hike. It's included in this guidebook only because I wanted to include all the park's self-guiding nature trails, which provide great opportunities to learn about the park ecosystem without investing a lot of effort. However, the Spruce-Fir Nature Trail provides little more than a case of depression.

Not too many years ago, I hiked a few dozen yards away from the road along this trail and felt as though I was in the middle of a wilderness. It was dark, cool, dense, and mysterious. Today it's open, hot, weedy, and depressing. The fir trees are dead and the spruces uprooted. Briers invade the open areas—a common scene in spruce-fir forests today. For an explanation of what's to blame for this destruction, see Hike 51: Clingmans Dome.

In an effort to find something nice to say, the Spruce-Fir Nature Trail is one of the best places in the park to find Clinton's lily, a high-elevation plant with greenish-

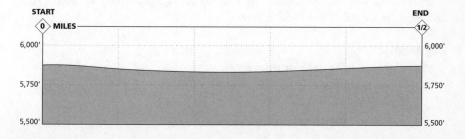

yellow bell-like flowers and distinctive elliptical basal leaves. Dense patches of the wildflower, which blooms in May, occur along this trail.

If you decide to make this hike despite my glowing comments, ignore the sign that says there are steep (12 percent) grades on this trail. This is an easy walk in the park.

Options: The best option is to skip this hike and do Hike 51: Clingmans Dome instead. That hike introduces you to the same heartbreak seen along this hike but provides distant views as a redeeming quality.

Noland Divide

Highlights: *Views, wildflowers, forest diversity*
(See map for Hike 48: Deep Creek.)

Type of hike: Shuttle; day hike
Total distance: 11.6 miles one-way
Difficulty: Moderate

Maps: Trails Illustrated; USGS Clingmans Dome and Bryson City

Special considerations: Clingmans Dome Road is closed from December 1 to March 31.

Finding the trailhead: Drive 5.5 miles west of Newfound Gap on Clingmans Dome Road to the small pullout on the left. The Noland Divide Trail begins beyond the gate.

Parking and trailhead facilities: There's limited parking at the pullout, but you usually don't have a problem. Rest rooms are located 1.5 miles farther on Clingmans Dome Road.

Leave a vehicle or have your shuttle meet you at the lower trailhead. Follow the signs from downtown Bryson City to Deep Creek Campground. As you enter the park, continue to the campground entrance on the right. Directly across the road on the left is a large gravel parking area.

Key points:
0.5 Roadbed ends and footpath begins.
3.7 Upper Sassafras Gap and junction with Pole Road Creek and Noland Creek Trails.
8.1 Lonesome Pine Overlook.

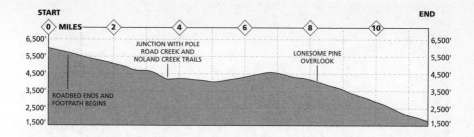

6,500'
5,500'
4,500'
3,500'
2,500'
1,500'

6,500'
5,500'
4,500'
3,500'
2,500'
1,500'

JUNCTION WITH POLE
ROAD CREEK AND
NOLAND CREEK TRAILS

LONESOME PINE
OVERLOOK

ROADBED ENDS AND
FOOTPATH BEGINS

The hike: Few other hikes in the Smokies provide the diversity that this one does. Starting at 5,929 feet and ending at just under 1,800 feet, the hike is roughly equivalent (ecologically) to driving from Canada to North Carolina. In spring or fall it can be 55 degrees at the lower trailhead and snowing at the upper.

The first 0.5 mile descends on a service road and passes an acid rain monitoring tower. Just beyond the tower, the footpath leads off to the left (southeast) and the grade lessens considerably. For many persons (myself included) this segment is the best part of the hike. It passes through one of the most scenic spruce-fir (mostly spruce) forests in the park. Since it's not a pure stand of fir, you don't feel as though you're in a tree graveyard like you do up on Clingmans Dome. In April and early May the ground is alive with spring beauty and trout lily. Patches of Clinton's lily bloom in May, and bluets bloom throughout the warm season. Look for a huge yellow birch on the left, a few feet off the trail.

When you leave the ridgetop and begin skirting the west side of Roundtop Knob, you leave the spruce-fir behind and enter a forest of oak, beech, hemlock, and maple. Continue descending, pass through rhododendron and mountain laurel tunnels, and reach Upper Sassafras Gap at mile 3.7. At the gap, Pole Road Creek Trail heads down the left side to Deep Creek. On the right, Noland Creek Trail descends very steeply to Campsite 61. You want to go straight and stay on the ridge.

Now begin an ascent through a burned area. A huge fire in November 2001 scorched this forest, and you pass through several more blackened areas on the remainder of the hike. In this section, many of the mountain laurels and most of the rhododendrons are dead. In May look for pink lady's slippers making a comeback. (The fire probably helped them.) At one point you pass through a 50-foot swath of forest that somehow escaped the flames. Notice the difference in ground cover and leaf litter here. After topping out on the ascent, you begin a long stretch that mostly follows the contour line. Next is a long, gradual, continuous descent to Lower Sassafras Gap. Look for rhododendron growing here with impressively thick trunks.

Now you begin climbing again, not too steeply, but long and continuously. You go around several knobs before leveling out on a ridge. After a mostly level walk, begin climbing again around the southeast side of Coburn Knob. After passing over a broad ridge, you come to a left-hand switchback at mile 6.7. A small spring gurgles right on the trail—the only water source encountered so far. At my last visit, it was flowing pretty well, but it doesn't look to be too dependable.

Noland Divide Trail after forest fire.

From here on, it's all downhill except for a few quick ups and some level stretches. At mile 8.1 the trail veers left to skirt a small, rocky ridge, while a side path goes straight a short distance to an opening on the top of the ridge. This is the Lonesome Pine Overlook, but don't look for a solitary pine up here. Pines and mountain laurel cover the ridge, though many are dead from the fire. The view south toward Bryson City is spectacular. You're probably happy to finally get a good view—for such a long ridge walk, the views to here are disappointing. Look down to the left. That narrow ridge (Beaugard Ridge) is the one you descend to the trail-head.

Now on Beaugard Ridge, enjoy more views. Here you can see farther to the west and off the left side of the trail back toward the Smokies crest. The fire damage is more evident here than anywhere else. Descend a steep section on switchbacks and soon leave the burned area and begin a long, continuous descent. In places you pass through great spring wildflower habitat, and complementing the flowers is a small waterfall that you cross in its middle. Just past the falls on the right bank is a large patch of speckled wood lily. Look for its white flowers in May and its distinctive dark blue fruit in August. Other wildflowers along this segment include Vasey's trillium, bloodroot, wild geranium, Solomon's seal, and spiderwort.

Farther down you pass through a drier area that has yellow-eyed grass, trailing arbutus, mountain laurel, and a few flame azaleas. Finally, after the long downhill stretch, meet up with Deep Creek Horse Trail and a foot log crossing Durham Branch. A short walk takes you to the parking area.

51

Clingmans Dome

Highlights: *The best (or worst) views in the park, high-elevation ecosystem*

Type of hike: Loop; day hike
Total distance: 1.5 miles round-trip
Difficulty: Difficult

Best time of year: November
Maps: Trails Illustrated; USGS Clingmans Dome
and Silers Bald

Special considerations: You have to make this hike early in the morning to avoid the crowds on the 0.5-mile portion leading to the tower. The Clingmans Dome Road is closed from December 1 to March 31. Read the narrative below for other considerations.

Finding the trailhead: At Newfound Gap turn west onto Clingmans Dome Road and drive 7.0 miles to the Forney Ridge parking area at the end. The paved trail begins on the far western end of the parking area at the water fountain.

Parking and trailhead facilities: The parking lot is huge, but it's often not big enough to accommodate weekend traffic. Try to get here early in the morning or on a weekday. There is a large rest room facility at the beginning of the hike.

Key points:
0.5 Clingmans Dome Observation Tower and junction with Appalachian Trail.
0.8 Junction with Clingmans Dome Bypass Trail.
1.3 Junction with Forney Ridge Trail.
1.5 Forney Ridge parking area.

The hike: Hiking to the top of the highest mountain in the park (6,642 feet), and the third highest in the East (Mt. Mitchell is first at 6,684 feet, Mt. Craig second at 6,647 feet), is bittersweet. On one hand you experience the extremes of life at this elevation—wind, rain, snow, fog, cold. It's not uncommon to leave Gatlinburg in sunshine and 55-degree temperatures and find it snowing on Clingmans Dome. On

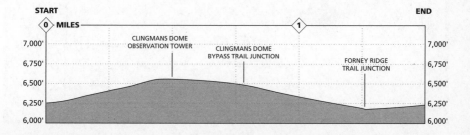

Clingmans Dome; Andrews Bald; Forney Ridge and Noland Divide; Silers Bald and Forney Creek

the other hand you experience the extremes of man's negative influence on the environment—smog, introduced pests, crowds, and bulldozed mountainsides. Clingmans Dome is an outdoor classroom, and everyone ought to study here at least once.

You can't help but notice that something's not right up here. All the trees are dead. Some stand like skeletons in a graveyard, and many are uprooted and lying on the ground like pickup sticks. These are—or were—Fraser firs, the dominant tree species at this elevation. Farther down, the firs mix with red spruce. The culprit usually cited is the nonnative insect balsam woolly adelgid, *Adelges piceae*. Introduced from Europe in the early 1900s, the adelgid, which feeds on Fraser firs, reached the Smokies in the 1950s. For decades there was no critical cause for alarm, but that changed dramatically in the 1980s when trees began dying at an alarming rate all over the Southern Appalachians.

So what's the problem? As with most things related to ecosystem health, a combination of factors is to blame. However, the overriding problem is pollution in the form of acid rain and ozone. The acidity level of the rain and fog on Clingmans Dome and other high-elevation mountains is extreme, somewhere between 2.5 and 3.5 pH. Acid rain and ozone weaken the tree's root system to the point that the tree cannot fight off normal stresses such as drought, extreme winds, and native pests. And with something as abominable as the nonnative balsam woolly adelgid in the mix, the trees don't stand a chance.

The natural environment isn't the only thing in danger up here. People breathe the same air that the trees do. The park constantly monitors ozone and issues warnings when the concentrations reach unsafe levels. Sadly, those warnings are a regular occurrence during summer. During summer 1999, the park recorded fifty-two days when the air exceeded health standards. Young persons and those with asthma or other breathing problems are especially at risk.

Begin the hike on the paved path at the water fountain. After you pass the rest room building, the grade becomes very steep. Numerous benches provide rest stops. Just before the path levels off, a short connector to the Appalachian Trail (AT) turns off to the left. Continue on the paved path a short distance to the tower.

A long circular ramp leads to an observation deck 54 feet above the ground. Not too many years ago, the view from the deck was limited, with Fraser firs blocking much of the panorama. But today, with the trees dead and falling over, the view is open all around. Today, it's air pollution that limits the views. Studies from records kept since 1948 show that visibility in the park has decreased 40 percent in winter, and a horrifying 80 percent in summer. The annual average visibility in the park is 22 miles, compared with 93 miles in natural conditions. The winter months provide the clearest views, but since Clingmans Dome Road is closed from December to March, November is the best month. When the view is good, it's *really* good.

As you head back down, turn right onto the connector path you passed on the way up and follow it a few yards to the Appalachian Trail. Turn left (west) and find yourself alone. Few persons leave the paved path, so you might have the rest of the hike to yourself. Follow the AT 0.3 mile to the junction with Clingmans Dome

Clingmans Dome Observation Tower.

Bypass Trail. There are views along the way, but you already had the best possible views back up on the tower.

Turn left (southeast) on the Bypass Trail, and on a clear day you can see the Forney Ridge parking area up ahead. The next 0.5 mile is extremely rocky and extremely depressing, even more so than what you've already seen. Dead trees are everywhere. You have to pass under them where they lean over the trail and clamber over them if park crews haven't cut them out of the way. The steep mountainside on the left is a jumble of bleached fir trunks.

The junction with Forney Ridge Trail is a fork. The right fork leads down and eventually to Andrews Bald. You want to go left and make the 0.2-mile climb back to the parking area.

52

Andrews Bald

Highlights: *Spruce-fir forest, views*
(See map for Hike 51: Clingmans Dome.)

Type of hike: Out-and-back; day hike
Total distance: 3.6 miles round-trip
Difficulty: Difficult

Best time of year: Mid- to late June
Maps: Trails Illustrated; USGS Clingmans Dome

Special considerations: Clingmans Dome Road, which leads to the parking area, is closed from December 1 to March 31.

Finding the trailhead: At Newfound Gap, turn west onto Clingmans Dome Road and drive 7.0 miles to the Forney Ridge parking area at the end. The trail begins on the far western end of the parking area and leads between the water fountain and the paved path to the Clingmans Dome Tower.

Parking and trailhead facilities: The parking lot is huge, but it's often not big enough to accommodate weekend traffic. Try to get here early in the morning or on a weekday. There is a large rest room facility near the beginning of the hike.

Key points:
- **0.2** Junction with Clingmans Dome Bypass Trail.
- **1.1** Junction with Forney Creek Trail.
- **1.8** Andrews Bald.

The hike: On the open and grassy Andrews Bald grow flame azaleas and Catawba rhododendron, both peaking their blooms sometime around the middle to end of June. That's when you want to make this hike, but hordes of other people do the same. The best plan is to arrive at the Forney Ridge parking area early and watch the sunrise. After sunrise you can hike to Andrews Bald before most people are stirring.

At the beginning of the paved path leading to Clingmans Dome Tower, there is a water fountain. Just past it, an unpaved trail drops down to the left. This is For-

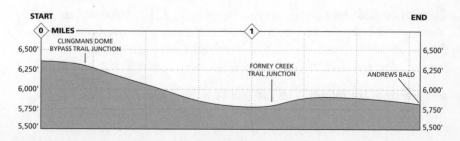

ney Ridge Trail, which you will take to Andrews Bald. The first 0.2 mile is a steep and rocky descent to the junction with Clingmans Dome Bypass Trail. You need to cut sharply back to the left (south) to remain on Forney Ridge Trail. The trail is absurdly rocky and not well drained. Heavy rains (common here) turn the trail into a creekbed. Unfortunately, it's pretty much like this for the entire hike. Only in a few brief spots is the trail not rocky—and then it's muddy.

Descend for a little more than a mile, and in a small clearing reach the junction with Forney Creek Trail on the right. Stay straight (south) on Forney Ridge Trail. The forest here is darker and denser than you see in many other spruce-fir forests today. Mature Fraser firs are dead, but there are more young trees here than in some places. The forest here provides a hint at what once was on these mountaintops.

After a moderate ascent you exit the woods on the descent to the bald. If you've been to Gregory Bald (Hikes 24 and 63), you might be disappointed in Andrews. Andrews is like a smaller cousin to Gregory—fewer azaleas, restricted views, and encroaching vegetation. Don't let that stop you from coming, though. Andrews makes one of the finest relatively short day hikes in the park. On a clear day the views east into the Noland Creek watershed and southwest toward Fontana Lake are superb. The azalea show is the finest in the park except for Gregory Bald.

Options: The hike to Andrews Bald is the first 1.8 miles of Forney Ridge and Noland Divide (Hike 53), so you can do both of these hikes on the same (long) trip.

53 Forney Ridge and Noland Divide

Highlights: *Views, Andrews Bald, wildflowers, Noland Creek, spruce-fir forest*
(See map for Hike 51: Clingmans Dome.)

Type of hike: Loop; overnighter or killer day hike
Total distance: 18.4 miles round-trip
Difficulty: Difficult

Maps: Trails Illustrated; USGS Clingmans Dome, Silers Bald, Noland Creek, and Bryson City

Special considerations: Clingmans Dome Road is closed from December 1 to March 31. To complete the loop, you must walk the final 1.5 miles along the road. At least one crossing of Noland Creek is without a foot log or bridge. Count on its being a wade, and after heavy rains it is dangerous or impassable.

Finding the trailhead: At Newfound Gap, turn west onto Clingmans Dome Road and drive 7.0 miles to the Forney Ridge parking area at the end. The Forney

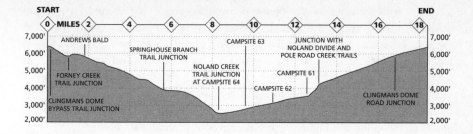

Ridge Trail begins on the far western end of the parking area and leads between the water fountain and the paved path to the Clingmans Dome Tower.

Parking and trailhead facilities: The parking lot is huge, but it's often not big enough to accommodate weekend traffic. Try to get here early in the morning or on a weekday. There is a large rest room facility at the beginning of the hike.

Key points:

0.2 Junction with Clingmans Dome Bypass Trail.

1.1 Junction with Forney Creek Trail.

1.8 Andrews Bald.

5.6 Junction with Springhouse Branch Trail.

8.4 Junction with Noland Creek Trail at Campsite 64.

9.8 Campsite 63.

11.0 Campsite 62.

12.6 Campsite 61.

13.2 Junction with Noland Divide and Pole Road Creek Trails.

16.4 Junction with service road.

16.9 Clingmans Dome Road.

The hike: This trip has most of what people look for in a Smokies adventure: high-elevation views, old-growth forests, cascading streams, wildflowers, and a challenging hike. On the latter point, if you're attempting this hike in one day, plan to start early and drag in late. Plan also to be one tired puppy by the end of the day.

Read the Andrews Bald (Hike 52) narrative for the first 1.8 miles of this hike to Andrews Bald. The many paths spreading out over the bald are confusing. Just keep heading down to the lower end until you see the sign marking the trail's exit from the bald. Pass a hog enclosure on the right after leaving the bald. The trail is steep and rocky and, if it's raining, full of puddles. Pass through a delightful rocky area with lush moss, ferns, lichens, and many wildflower species.

Here the footing changes from rocks to dirt and is fairly level (even some uphills). In places, briers overgrow the trail. After rounding over a ridge, you start a long descent, steep in places, to Board Camp Gap at mile 5.6. Forney Ridge Trail ends here and Springhouse Branch Trail takes over. You want to go sharply left (northeast) on the Springhouse Branch Trail.

For a while you follow the contour line, then you swing around a ridge and descend to the Springhouse Branch drainage, where you cross several branches in quick succession. The forest through here is old growth, and this is great wildflower habitat. In spring this area is a highlight of the hike. The last and largest stream in the immediate vicinity is Springhouse Branch. After crossing it you descend some- what steeply for about 0.75 mile to Mill Creek and cross it on a mossy foot log. Just before the crossing there's an old rock wall on the left and, just after, the remains of an old stone chimney. Obviously this place was once someone's home.

The next 0.75 mile or so is a loose parallel of Mill Creek all the way to Solola Valley and Campsite 64. The valley saw heavy settlement before the park was estab- lished, and even had its own post office. Today all that remain are scattered foun- dations, clearings, broken artifacts, and such. Campsite 64 is a horse camp, and although its setting at the confluence of Mill Creek with Noland Creek is pleasant enough, the site is not the best for backpackers. It's badly worn and receives heavy horse use. If you're doing this hike as an overnighter, you might want to continue to the next site.

At Campsite 64 is the junction with Noland Creek Trail, which follows Noland Creek 4.1 miles downstream to Lakeshore Drive. Our hike goes east on Noland Creek Trail and follows the creek upstream. A short ways upstream you cross the creek on a narrow foot log and, after ascending beside the creek, cross again. Come to Campsite 63 at mile 9.8 (1.4 miles from Campsite 64). The site is small and right beside the trail, but it's more appealing than site 64. This is a good place for an overnighter.

Soon cross the creek a third time on another foot log, and the trail becomes steeper and rockier. The next creek crossing is on what I hope is a temporary foot log—a small yellow-poplar tree lying very low to the water. It looks as though it could wash away at any time, and probably will before you get here. Prepare for a wade if the tree is gone and hasn't been replaced. Next come to Campsite 62, situ- ated beside Noland Creek.

Pressing on, rock-hop a side stream and right afterward come to another cross- ing of Noland Creek. There's no foot log here, and it's a tough rock-hop. In high water it might not be safe even to wade across. After hiking a segment away from the creek and making a couple of tributary crossings, arrive at Campsite 61, a small rationed site situated beside Noland Creek. Shortly beyond the campsite, the trail makes a sharp right switchback and begins a brutal ascent to Upper Sassafras Gap on Noland Divide. Noland Divide Trail intersects here. Turn left (northwest) on it and follow the ridgeline 3.7 miles to Clingmans Dome Road. (See Hike 50: Noland Divide for more detail about this segment.)

Once on the road, turn left and walk the remaining 1.5 miles to the trailhead.

Options: Several trails provide access to the Forney Creek and Noland Creek watersheds and the adjacent ridges. Experienced backpackers can plan extended trips using Clingmans Dome as a starting point. Silers Bald and Forney Creek (Hike 54) outlines one such route. This is tough country; don't plan to hike many miles each day, particularly on the way back up to Clingmans Dome.

Noland Creek.

54

Silers Bald and Forney Creek

Highlights: *Views, wildflowers, Forney Creek waterfalls and cascades*

(See map for Hike 51: Clingmans Dome.)

Type of hike: Loop; two- or three-night backpack or killer overnighter

Total distance: 20.4 miles round-trip

Difficulty: Difficult

Best time of year: Summer so that you can enjoy the creek crossings

Maps: Trails Illustrated; USGS Clingmans Dome and Silers Bald

Special considerations: Clingmans Dome Road is closed from December 1 to March 31.

Several unbridged creek crossings might be a little tricky even in low water; in high water they are dangerous or impassable. Do not make this hike after prolonged rains; at other times bring sandals or old sneakers to wear while crossing.

Read the introduction to the Appalachian Trail (AT) before making this hike. It contains important information about when to plan your trip. Silers Bald Shelter, your first night's stay on a two-night backpack, is one of the most popular shelters in the park. Make reservations early, no matter the season.

Finding the trailhead: At Newfound Gap, turn west onto Clingmans Dome Road and follow it 7.0 miles to its end at the Forney Ridge parking area. The trail begins on the extreme western end of the parking lot, near the water fountain.

Parking and trailhead facilities: The parking area is huge, but it still manages to fill up on summer and October weekends. Rest rooms are located near the start of the paved trail to the Clingmans Dome Tower. However, the facilities here, like those at Newfound Gap, aren't always in the most pleasant condition.

Key points:

0.2 Junction with Clingmans Dome Bypass Trail.

0.7 Junction with Appalachian Trail.

2.6 Junction with Goshen Prong Trail.

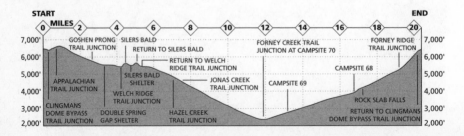

176

The hike: It would be hard to pick a better two-night backpack than this one. You get to sleep in a backcountry shelter (everyone needs to experience it at least once) and at a backcountry campsite. You have good high-elevation views, and you pass through scenic forests. And, finally, you experience a Smokies trademark: powerful cascading creeks that you have to figure out how to cross.

That said, this hike isn't for everyone. It's very strenuous, the high-elevation forest destruction is depressing, and the views are severely restricted by smog in summer. I discovered the hard way that these three negatives can make for an unpleasant experience after I chose this hike for an anniversary trip with my wife. Fortunately we're still married, but it's safe to say that we won't make this trip together again. Even that bottle of wine I lugged in my pack didn't smooth things over.

You can take the paved path to the Clingmans Dome Tower and pick up the Appalachian Trail from there or bypass the tower (and the crowds) by taking the Clingmans Dome Bypass Trail. (For the tower route, and to learn what's happening to the trees up here, see Hike 51: Clingmans Dome.) This hike description takes you on the bypass route, beginning on the Forney Ridge Trail, which starts between the water fountain and paved Clingmans Dome Trail. Follow it 0.2 mile and turn right (actually straight) onto Clingmans Dome Bypass Trail. This trail climbs moderately 0.5 mile to the AT, just west of the Clingmans Dome summit.

At the AT turn left (west), but take time to admire the view (if the smog allows) off the north side of the trail toward Mt. LeConte. The next 2.5 miles on the AT to the Double Spring Gap Shelter are relatively easy and provide numerous open vistas. About 0.6 mile before reaching the shelter you pass the junction with Goshen Prong Trail (described in Hike 11: Goshen Prong).

Not surprisingly, Double Spring Gap has two springs, one on each side of the gap and only a few yards from the shelter. If you're getting water, the spring on the south side is much better; the northern spring seeps through a boggy area. If you can't get reservations at Silers Bald Shelter, you could spend the night here instead.

Pressing on from the gap, the AT goes on its typical roller-coaster grade through a forest of beech, buckeye, and mountain ash. At one point the trail opens in a grassy spot, with fair views toward High Rocks. At this point you come to The Narrows—a knife-edge ridge with good views off both sides. The trail soon forks at the junction with Welch Ridge Trail, going left. You'll come back here and take Welch Ridge Trail tomorrow, but today you need to go right and stay on the AT. A 0.2-mile steep climb brings you to the 5,607-foot summit of Silers Bald at a small clearing. There's only one fair view from the clearing, back toward Clingmans Dome. On a sunny day you can see the light reflecting from the cars at the Forney Ridge parking area. An obvious path leads north from the summit a few hundred feet to a rock outcrop with wonderful open views to the north, as well as leafy views to the east and west.

From the summit descend on the AT to the Silers Bald Shelter, your home for tonight. The Smoky Mountains Hiking Club has upgraded the shelter recently. It now has an overhanging front roof, benches, and skylights. If the weather is clear, you can take in a show after dinner. Hike back up on the Silers summit and watch the sunset from the rock outcrop.

Next morning, backtrack to the Welch Ridge Trail and enjoy the next 2.5 miles—the easiest of the hike, although parts of the trail are heavily overgrown. Stay straight (south) at the Hazel Creek Trail junction, and in another 0.8 mile reach the junction with Jonas Creek Trail, cutting sharply left (east).

On Jonas Creek Trail you descend more than 2,000 feet in 4.1 miles—not an extreme descent, but keep in mind that every step down has to be made up, and that includes all the down steps you've already made from Clingmans Dome. During the descent you pass through a very scenic forest, though none of it is old growth. You also have to cross Jonas Creek five times without benefit of foot logs (the one rotten log hardly qualifies). In normal flows this isn't much of a problem. Just watch out for slick and wobbly rocks. In high water it could get a little dicey, especially with a heavy pack. I lost it on the final crossing and finished the day in wet boots. So did my wife, who tried to help me out of the water.

Reach Campsite 70 at the junction of Jonas and Forney Creeks. It's a large, unattractive site that gets a lot of horse use. Pass through the campsite and cross Forney Creek on a foot log. The old railroad grade on the far side is the Forney Creek Trail. Turn left (north) onto it, and begin your climb back up the mountain.

Campsite 69, your second night's camp (or only night's camp on an overnighter), is 1.4 miles ahead. To get there you must cross several small side streams on old rotten bridge supports and Forney Creek three times. In normal flows you might be able to rock-hop the crossings and keep your feet dry, but be careful. Some of the rocks are very slick. If the water is very high, you might not be able to cross at all. The thought of backtracking from here is not amusing, so plan this trip carefully. In the normal flows of summer, slip on the sandals and enjoy the cold water.

Arrive at Campsite 69 a few hundred feet beyond the third crossing. There are tent sites on the right between the trail and Forney Creek, or maybe you'll get lucky

Silers Bald Backcountry Shelter.

and the secluded spot on the left will be open. It sits beside Huggins Creek. Many old logging artifacts are scattered about the site. In fact, all along Forney Creek Trail you can see traces of logging history. Before the park was established, most of the Forney Creek watershed was logged to within a short distance of Clingmans Dome.

Shortly beyond the campsite, you have to cross Forney Creek once more, this crossing a little easier than the previous ones. The next 3.6 miles to Campsite 68 follow Forney Creek upstream, sometimes close, sometimes a little away. You cross numerous side streams and small ravines by way of rotten bridge supports, many of them studded with nails. You have to cross Forney Creek once more during this stretch, but it's the easiest crossing of all.

Currently, Campsite 68 has an upper and a lower site. The lower section, which you reach first, is a very small, open site, situated by Forney Creek. It may not have a signpost designating it, but don't worry about being confused about just where this site is. It's not a place to spend a week contemplating nature. As Kenneth Wise states in *Hiking Trails of the Great Smoky Mountains*, it has "all the charm of a disused construction site."

The trail climbs extremely steeply beyond the lower section of Campsite 68 and comes to an old railroad rail across the trail. Look in the creek below to see the wheels and axle of an old railroad car. Just beyond here you come to Rock Slab Falls—a long, high, sliding cascade on Forney Creek. Notice the crisscrossing quartz veins across the falls. The waterfall marks the upper section of Campsite 68.

There are food cables here, and this location is very scenic. However, it's small, and you may not find a tent spot. If no spots are available, you have to go back down to the lower site—and be sure to store your food properly.

Campsite 68 is unusual in that the two campsites are separated by 0.4 mile, and the lower one has no food suspension cables. The Park Service is reviewing the situation and may have made changes by the time you get here.

From Rock Slab Falls the trail makes a few switchbacks and creek crossings and becomes a real trail—a real steep trail. Then you come to the upper reaches of Forney Creek and actually walk in the streambed a few feet before you switchback to the left and away from the creek. The trail continues climbing steeply and becomes rocky, and you enter a dark forest of spruce, rhododendron, and birch. As you climb higher you begin to see young Fraser firs. With a heavy pack, this stretch is a killer.

Finally, reach the ridgeline and the junction with Forney Ridge Trail, but don't celebrate yet. You still have more than a mile of rocky climbing to go. Turn left (north) on Forney Ridge Trail and continue busting your lungs for 0.9 mile to the junction with Clingmans Dome Bypass Trail. Turn sharply right here, staying on Forney Ridge Trail, and climb 0.2 mile to the parking area.

Now you can celebrate, like my wife did. She even forgave me—somewhat.

Options: Fit and experienced hikers can make this trip as a day hike, but I don't recommend it. Even as a two-night backpack, that last day out is tough. You can extend the hike to three nights by staying the first night at Silers Bald Shelter, the second night at Campsite 70, and the third night at Campsite 68. However, this means staying the last two nights at less-than-desirable campsites. As an overnighter, you can save weight by staying at either Double Spring Gap Shelter or Silers Bald Shelter and not carrying a tent. But you'd still have a brutal second day. The best option is to go for the two-night backpack.

55

Juney Whank Falls

Highlights: *Juney Whank Falls*

Type of hike: Loop; day hike
Total distance: 0.7 mile round-trip

Difficulty: Moderate
Maps: Trails Illustrated; USGS Bryson City

Finding the trailhead: Downtown Bryson City has many signs that direct you to Deep Creek Campground. As you enter the park, continue on the paved road past the campground entrance and the picnic areas to where the road ends at a turnaround. A paved parking area is on the left. The trail begins from the upper end of the parking area at the sign for Juney Whank Falls.

Parking and trailhead facilities: If you get here in the middle of a sunny, summer weekday, you might not find a parking space in the paved lot, and on a weekend, you can forget it. Few other places in the park are as crowded. Rest rooms are available at the picnic areas.

Key points:
0.3 Juney Whank Falls.
0.6 Junction with Deep Creek Trail.

The hike: Don't worry about the crowds you see at the parking area. They're all headed up Deep Creek Trail, and except for a short segment at the end, you might have this hike to yourself.

The trail follows Juney Whank Branch upstream a short distance, then swings to the left away from the creek and climbs to a junction with a bridle path coming in from the left. Stay to the right and continue climbing up the old roadbed. You soon pass another side trail bearing off to the right; stay to the left, heading uphill. The waterfall is just ahead and clearly visible from the trail. A path leads down to a foot log crossing below the upper drop.

As waterfalls go, Juney Whank Falls isn't anything to get excited about. The trail is short, so it makes a good, quick hike, but the waterfall is not something you see

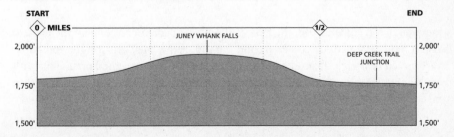

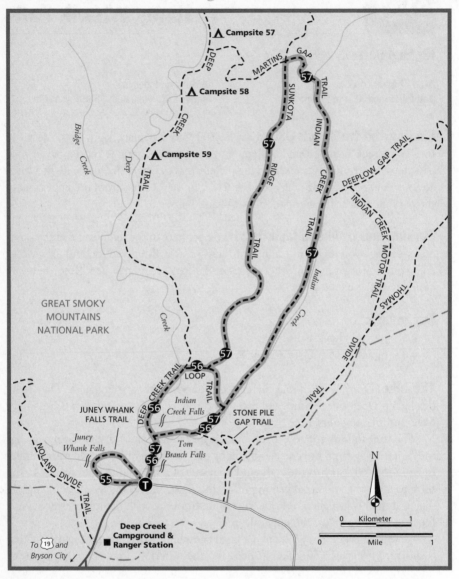

pictured in a calendar. From the falls you can backtrack or continue up the bank to rejoin the bridle path (it circles around the top of the falls). Turn right and go 25 yards, then bear right from the horse trail on an obvious, unsigned path. This path leads about 0.2 mile through a deep gully to Deep Creek Trail, where a right turn takes you back to the parking area.

Juney Whank Falls.

56   Deep Creek Loop

Highlights: *Tom Branch and Indian Creek waterfalls, Deep Creek*

(See map for Hike 55: Juney Whank Falls.)

Type of hike: A "lollipop" loop; day hike	**Best time of year:** Winter
Total distance: 4.4 miles round-trip	**Maps:** Trails Illustrated; USGS Bryson City
Difficulty: Easy	

Special considerations: In summer the first 0.7 mile of this hike is probably the most popular in the entire park. You'll see countless people, young and old, hiking along the easy roadbed to Indian Creek Falls. Many of them are toting inner tubes to float Deep Creek back to the parking area. You can't miss the roadside rental businesses vying for your attention as you approach the park's entrance. Pretty girls in swimsuits stand beside the road waving at every car that comes by, enticing you to stop and rent a tube from them. That's one reason for hiking this trail in winter: You might not see anybody else. The other reason is that both Tom Branch Falls and Indian Creek Falls look their best in winter, with higher water levels and less encroaching vegetation. Of course, those pretty girls in swimsuits might be incentive for some persons to choose this trail in summer.

Finding the trailhead: Downtown Bryson City has many signs that direct you to Deep Creek Campground. As you enter the park, continue on the paved road past the campground entrance and the picnic areas to where the road ends at a turnaround. A paved parking area is on the left. The trail is a continuation of the road, which turns to gravel beyond the turnaround.

Parking and trailhead facilities: If you get here in the middle of a sunny, summer weekday, you might not find a parking space in the paved lot, and on a weekend, you can forget it. Few other places in the park are as crowded. Rest rooms are available at the picnic areas.

Key points:

   0.2   Tom Branch Falls.

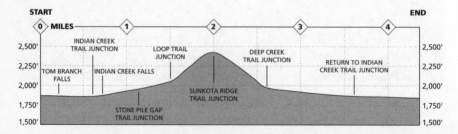

184

Indian Creek Falls.

0.7 Junction with Indian Creek Trail.
0.8 Indian Creek Falls.
1.2 Junction with Stone Pile Gap Trail.
1.5 Junction with Loop Trail.
2.0 Junction with Sunkota Ridge Trail.
2.7 Junction with Deep Creek Trail.
3.7 Return to junction with Indian Creek Trail.

The hike: The first couple of miles on Deep Creek Trail are along one of only four trail sections in the entire park open to bicyclists. So in summer you'll encounter backpackers, day hikers, fishers, tubers, baby strollers, scooters, and bicyclists.

Start up the gravel road that continues from the road turnaround. In 0.2 mile you pass Tom Branch Falls on the right, dropping directly into Deep Creek in the foreground. Only in fall and winter can you see much of this high waterfall. Foliage hides it in summer. Soon cross Deep Creek on an auto bridge and reach the junction with Indian Creek Trail on the right, just before Deep Creek Trail crosses Indian Creek. Turn onto Indian Creek Trail and follow it upstream. In a few hundred feet, you pass Indian Creek Falls—a long, steep, sliding cascade. You can see it from the trail or take a side path to the base for a closer view.

Continue on Indian Creek Trail, which is an old roadbed, and pass Stone Pile Gap Trail on the right, 0.5 mile from Deep Creek. Less than 0.25 mile farther, you come to Loop Trail on the left (west). At my last visit, the sign was missing, but the trail is obvious. Follow Loop Trail up a small drainage, pass the lower end of Sunkota Ridge Trail, then descend to Deep Creek Trail. Turn left, cross Deep

185

Creek on a bridge, and follow the trail downstream. Cross Deep Creek once more before reaching the Indian Creek junction. Retrace your steps from here.

Options: Indian Creek and Sunkota Ridge (Hike 57) is a longer loop hike that includes the lower section of this hike. Several other loop options exist in the Deep Creek area. Check a trail map for possibilities.

57 Indian Creek and Sunkota Ridge

Highlights: *Indian Creek Falls, wildflowers, winter views*
(See map for Hike 55: Juney Whank Falls.)

Type of hike: A "lollipop" loop; day hike
Total distance: 11.6 miles round-trip
Difficulty: Moderate

Best time of year: Winter, for solitude and best views
Maps: Trails Illustrated; USGS Bryson City and Clingmans Dome

Special considerations: See Hike 56: Deep Creek Loop.

Finding the trailhead: Downtown Bryson City has many signs that direct you to Deep Creek Campground. As you enter the park, continue on the paved road past the campground entrance and the picnic areas to where the road ends at a turn-around. A paved parking area is on the left. The trail is a continuation of the road, which turns to gravel beyond the turnaround.

Parking and trailhead facilities: If you get here in the middle of a sunny, summer weekday, you might not find a parking space in the paved lot, and on a weekend, you can forget it. Few other places in the park are as crowded. Rest rooms are available at the picnic areas.

Key points:
 0.2 Tom Branch Falls.
 0.7 Junction with Indian Creek Trail.

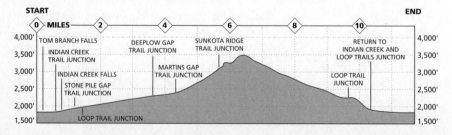

186

Foot log over Indian Creek.

0.8	Indian Creek Falls.
1.2	Junction with Stone Pile Gap Trail.
1.5	Junction with Loop Trail.
3.6	Junction with Deeplow Gap Trail.
4.3	Junction with Martins Gap Trail.
5.8	Junction with Sunkota Ridge Trail.
9.6	Junction with Loop Trail.
10.1	Return to junction of Indian Creek and Loop Trails

The hike: Hike 56: Deep Creek Loop covers the first 1.5 miles of this hike to the junction with Loop Trail. From that junction continue on the old roadbed of Indian Creek Trail past old homesites and cross the creek a few times on bridges. You reach the junction with Deeplow Gap Trail at mile 3.6. Stay on the roadbed and cross Indian Creek two more times, at which point the road becomes overgrown and seems more like a trail. Cross the creek once more and make a short, moderate climb to the old road turnaround and the junction with Martins Gap Trail. There's nowhere to go at the junction except straight ahead.

Now you're on a real trail, and you soon cross Indian Creek on foot logs twice more in quick succession. Farther ahead you cross the creek for the final time and begin a continuous, moderate climb to Sunkota Ridge at Martins Gap. Martins Gap Trail crosses over the ridge and descends to Deep Creek. Our route, though, goes left and follows the ridgeline on Sunkota Ridge Trail. (The topo map does not show the Sunkota Ridge Trail south of Martins Gap.) You have a short climb over a small knoll at first, then a longer ascent. After topping out on the ascent, it's mostly downhill all the way to the junction with Loop Trail. In winter there are decent views from the ridgeline.

At Loop Trail turn left (east) and descend along a small, narrow ravine back to the junction of Indian Creek and Loop Trails. At the junction retrace your steps to the trailhead.

58

Goldmine Loop

Highlights: *Lakeshore Tunnel, mountain laurel, Fontana Lake*

Type of hike: Loop; day hike or overnighter
Total distance: 3.1 miles round-trip
Difficulty: Moderate

Best time of year: June
Maps: Trails Illustrated; USGS Noland Creek (trail not shown)

Finding the trailhead: From U.S. 19 in downtown Bryson City, turn north onto Everett Street (the main drag) and follow it out of town. Outside Bryson City, the road is called Fontana Road, and when you enter the park, it's called Lakeview Drive. If you just stay on the same road and don't take any turns, you'll get it right. From U.S. 19 it is 8.7 miles to the end of the road at a parking area on the right.

Parking and trailhead facilities: There's plenty of room to park, but there are no facilities. The closest facilities are at Bryson City.

Key points:

0.3 Lakeview Drive Tunnel.
0.6 Junction with Tunnel Bypass Trail.
0.7 Junction with Goldmine Loop Trail.
1.6 Path to Campsite 67.
1.8 Fontana Lake.
2.7 Junction with Tunnel Bypass Trail.

The hike: The hike begins on Lakeshore Trail, which is a continuation of the road, and passes through the tunnel. You're probably wondering why in the world someone would build a thousand-foot-long tunnel wide enough for two lanes of traffic—and then use it for a hiking trail. Good question. The answer is that the government reneged on a 1943 agreement to build a road from near Bryson City to near Fontana Dam as part of mitigation for damming Little Tennessee River to create Fontana Lake. The state of North Carolina upheld its end of the bargain by building a road to the park boundary. The Park Service began its section of the road in

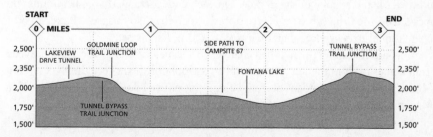

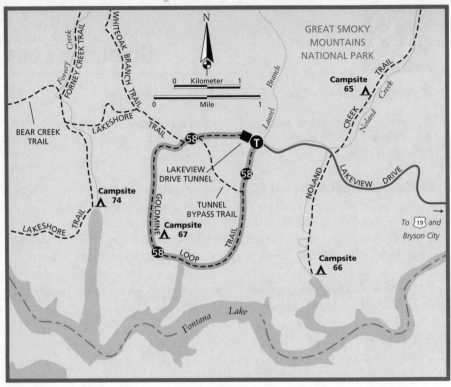

the 1960s but stopped after the construction uncovered rocks of the Anakeesta Formation. When exposed to air and water, these rocks can create sulphuric acid runoff, which is detrimental to aquatic life.

From the Park Service's point of view, it's a dead issue, contending that road construction is detrimental to the environment and the overall wilderness aspect of the Smokies. Furthermore, the road is no longer as important as it was in the 1940s because of North Carolina Highway 28 on the south shore of Fontana Lake. Efforts by some to compensate Swain County for the broken promise continue to fail, and the road has been dubbed THE ROAD TO NOWHERE. You might have noticed the sign at the park boundary, probably placed by a disgruntled Swain County resident.

The tunnel makes for a unique hiking experience. It's long enough that it gets pretty dark and spooky in the middle. On each end, particularly the beginning, the locals have used the tunnel walls to express themselves, so to speak. Better to do it on a "tunnel to nowhere" than on a rock outcrop, I suppose.

Beyond the tunnel the roadbed changes to a trail, and shortly the Tunnel Bypass Trail comes in from the left. Horses and claustrophobic hikers use the Bypass Trail. Mountain laurel is abundant here and along this entire hike. If you're hiking in late May and June, its blooms are a special treat.

Shortly beyond the Bypass Trail, you come to Goldmine Loop Trail on the left

Tunnel on Lakeview Drive (the ROAD TO NOWHERE).

(southwest). You won't find gold on this trail, and there is no mine—but the scenery sure is rich. Taking the trail, you descend steeply down the ridge spine to a small saddle, where the trail swings off the right of the ridge and heads down a drainage. You soon cross a tiny stream branch; look to the right in an open field to see an old chimney. There are walnut trees here, too. For the next little while you roughly parallel Goldmine Branch, and along the way you see other signs of settlement—clearings, wire fencing, and broken containers.

At a fork, Goldmine Loop Trail continues following the creek downstream, while a side path leads left a few hundred yards to Campsite 67—a very small site beside Hyatt Branch. Back on the main trail, it's a short distance to a small finger of Fontana Lake. After circling the embayment, you leave the lake and begin climbing along Tunnel Branch. Soon leave the creek and begin a steep climb up a ridge to meet up with the other end of Tunnel Bypass Trail. This is the official end of Goldmine Loop Trail. A left turn onto Tunnel Bypass Trail takes you to Lakeshore Trail in 1.2 miles (at the point you passed earlier in the hike). A right turn leads in 0.4 mile to Lakeview Drive, just below the parking area. Along the way you pass over a saddle and through good spring wildflower habitat.

59 Hazel Creek and Bone Valley

Highlights: *Fontana Lake, logging history, Hazel Creek, beaver dam*

Type of hike: Out-and-back; day hike or over-nighter
Total distance: 15.4 miles round-trip
Difficulty: Easy, except for stream crossings

Best time of year: Summer
Maps: Trails Illustrated; USGS Fontana Dam (lake portion only), Tuskeegee, and Thunderhead Mountain

Special considerations: All of this hike is on old roads, and the first 5 miles or so aren't much different from walking any of the drivable dirt roads in the park. If you're looking to hike a true trail, this hike will disappoint you.

Before you can make this trip, you must get to the trailhead on the other side of Fontana Lake. You could hike about 10 miles from Fontana Dam, but there's a better way. Take a boat shuttle from Fontana Marina, and the journey across the lake becomes a highlight of the trip. Call the marina at (828) 498–2211, ext. 277, to make reservations. The marina also rents handcarts for people who want to take more gear than they can carry. Hazel Creek Trail is one of only three in the park where you can use such carts. (The lower portions of Noland Creek and Forney Creek Trails are the others.)

If you plan to do this as a day hike, you'll want to head out on the boat as early as they'll take you—and don't dawdle on the hike in. You can pace yourself on the way back as time allows. There's nothing worse than having to run at the end to keep from missing the boat. (They won't leave you overnight, but they may have to leave for another pickup and come back to get you later. And they may charge you extra for that extra trip.)

If you plan to camp, I recommend getting a copy of *Hazel Creek from Then till Now* by Duane Oliver, or *Fontana, A Pocket History of Appalachia* by Lance Holland, both available from park sales outlets. When you're camping in the Fontana region, they make the best reading material you can have.

Four crossings of Bone Valley Creek require wading, which can be dangerous in high water.

Finding the trailhead: From the junction of U.S. 19/74 and North Carolina Highway 28 in the southwestern portion of the park, turn west onto NC 28 and go 21.1 miles to the stop sign at the entrance road for Fontana Dam. Turn right, go a short distance, and turn onto the first road to the right. This road leads 0.2 mile to the marina entrance.

Parking and trailhead facilities: Short-term parking is available along the slope leading to the marina, and there's plenty of parking in the gravel lot back atop the hill. Ancient rest rooms are available at the marina entrance. Backcountry camping permits are available at a kiosk near the rest room building.

Key points:
- **0.4** Campsite 86.
- **0.5** Bridge over Hazel Creek and junction with Lakeshore Trail.
- **3.4** Campsite 85.
- **5.1** Campsite 84 and junction with Jenkins Ridge Trail (formerly the Sugar Fork segment of Lakeshore Trail).
- **5.9** Campsite 83 and junction with Bone Valley Trail.
- **7.7** Hall Cabin.

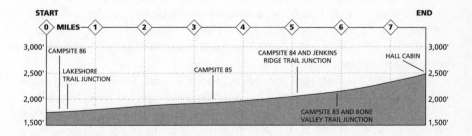

The hike: This is wonderful way to spend a summer day in the Smokies. It's great any time of year, but in summer you can enjoy the stream crossings and take advantage of Fontana Lake. If you get back to your pickup point a little early, you can take a dip in the lake while you're waiting for the boat.

Your hike begins when you step off the marina dock onto the boat. The boat captain knows the lake and the Smokies well, so ask lots of questions. The drop-off point varies according to water level, but the captain will make sure you know in what direction to hike.

The entire hike is along an old road; you could drive a Winnebago on the first 5 miles. Pass Campsite 86 on the left after about 0.4 mile. The site is popular with boaters, since it's so close to the lake. In a kayak or canoe, you can paddle right to it in summer. A short distance farther you come to a bridge over Hazel Creek and an interpretive post. If you don't already know a little about Hazel Creek's history, you're in for a surprise. The place you're standing is the old logging boomtown of Proctor. Today about all that's left is a frame house (you can see it across the creek), the concrete-and-brick carcass of the large dry kilns, a few small concrete structures, and a zillion artifacts and foundations scattered about and hidden in the leaf litter. It's hard to imagine that the photograph of Proctor you see on the post was taken here.

If you've been here before, you might be a little confused by the new trail signs. Continuing straight ahead, still on the right (east) side of Hazel Creek, is the Lakeshore Trail, as always. But after you cross the creek, no longer does the Lakeshore Trail go to the right. Now it goes left and follows a new course over Pinnacle Ridge to Eagle Creek. The old Lakeshore Trail segment that followed Pinnacle Creek is now closed. The trail on the right, heading upstream, is now the Hazel Creek Trail. (Locals have always called the trail by this name, but the official park name was Lakeshore Trail.) Before taking Hazel Creek Trail, go to the left and explore the Granville Calhoun House. It's open for you to walk through.

Now heading upstream, you soon pass a large concrete structure on the left. That was the dry kiln for the lumber operation. A few yards farther you pass a few smaller concrete ruins, and farther on there's a concrete water gauge station. Cross the creek two more times (on auto bridges) and come to Campsite 85, right beside the trail in an open area. If camping, sites 84 and 83, farther along, offer much better options.

Continuing on the road, you come to the fourth bridge over Hazel Creek at a particularly scenic spot with cascades and potholes. Take time to admire the scene, but pay attention to where you lean on the bridge railings in summer. The underside of the thick railings make choice sites for wasps, yellow jackets, and hornets. I speak from experience.

Just beyond the fifth (and last) bridge, the trail forks. On the left is Jenkins Ridge Trail (formerly Lakeshore Trail). You want to go right on Hazel Creek Trail and immediately cross Haw Gap Branch on a bridge. Campsite 84 sits on the right, between Hazel Creek and Haw Gap Branch. It's an attractive site set among white pines, with a pine needle ground cover. This is a good choice for a campsite.

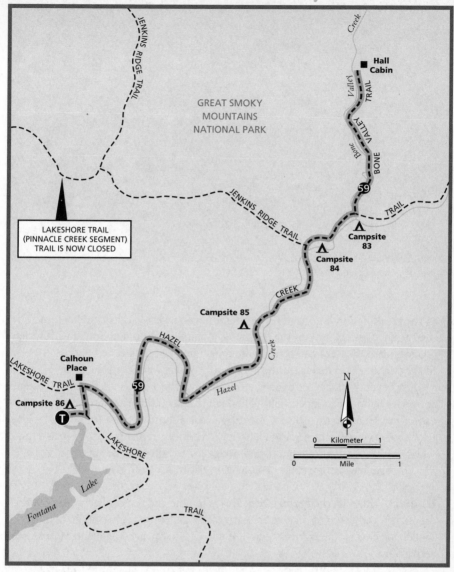

Continue about 0.8 mile from Campsite 84 and reach the junction with Bone Valley Trail just past the bridge over Bone Valley Creek. On the right, just before the creek crossing, sits Campsite 83. This site is also a great choice for camping. It's large, with the tent sites spread out. It's also a very attractive site; however, you might have to share it with a party of horse campers. As a rationed site, you have to make reservations if you decide to camp here.

After crossing Bone Valley Creek, turn left and follow the creek upstream, still using an old road. There are four creek crossings, all of which require wading. In normal flows you just need to be careful about walking on the extremely slick rocks

Hall Cabin in Bone Valley.

in the creek, but in high water, you might have to turn back. Just before and after the fourth crossing, look to the left to see a unique sight in the Smokies. Yes, that's a beaver dam. Beavers had historically inhabited the Smokies but had been absent in the twentieth century until the 1960s. It's good to have them back.

Just beyond the beaver dam, the trail follows Big Flats Branch a short distance and swings away to an open field. The Hall (Kress) Cabin sits here and is open for exploring. An obvious path near the cabin leads a short distance to the Hall Cemetery. In the vicinity are the foundation and chimney remains of the Kress House, which served as a hunting and fishing lodge for wealthy sportsmen.

The hike ends at the cabin. You have to backtrack from here.

Options: Although the Hazel Creek area is remote and not easily accessed, options for hiking and camping in the area are many and varied. One other hike in this guidebook covers some of this region: Eagle Creek, Spence Field, and Hazel Creek (Hike 60).

A terrific two-night backpack would be to take the boat shuttle to Hazel Creek and camp the first night at Campsite 86. The next day you would take the Lakeshore Trail to Eagle Creek and stay at Campsite 90. The boat would pick you up from there on the third morning.

To add more hiking to the trip, have the boat drop you off at Hazel Creek in the morning, then hike to Campsite 90 and overnight there. The next day you would hike 5.5 miles back to Fontana Dam on the Lakeshore Trail.

With a canoe or kayak you have wonderful flexibility. You can paddle into Campsite 86 or 90 and hike as much as you want during the day. Boaters can also use the unique Campsite 87, which lies on an island at the mouth of Eagle Creek.

Eagle Creek, Spence Field, and Hazel Creek

Highlights: *Fontana Lake, Eagle Creek, Spence Field, Hazel Creek, wildflowers*

Type of hike: Loop; extended backpacking trip
Total distance: 27.9 miles round-trip
Difficulty: Difficult
Best time of year: Summer

Maps: Trails Illustrated; USGS Fontana Dam, Cades Cove, Thunderhead Mountain, and Tuskeegee

Special considerations: You have a lot to consider before making this hike—possibly the most strenuous in this guidebook. First, you have to get to the trailhead at Campsite 90 on the Eagle Creek embayment. That requires hiking 5.5 miles from Fontana Dam or taking a boat shuttle across the lake. I definitely recommend the boat ride, which adds an interesting highlight to the trip. Call Fontana Marina at (828) 498–2211, ext. 277, to make reservations.

A key consideration is the many creek crossings. In all but the lowest water, most of them must be waded. In high water they can be dangerous or impassable. Generally, winter is not a good time to make this trip, but summer is ideal. The water is low, and getting your feet wet is not a problem. Plus, in summer you can take a dip in Fontana Lake at the Hazel Creek and Eagle Creek embayments.

You need to consider your physical abilities honestly before making this hike. The last part of Eagle Creek Trail is a tough climb, and most of the Jenkins Ridge Trail is a brutal descent that's hard on the knees.

No matter how you plan your campsites, it's likely that you'll stay one night at Spence Field Shelter. You need to reserve it, as with all park shelters. It receives a lot of use throughout the year, but in spring you probably want to avoid it altogether. (For more information see the special considerations in the introduction in the Appalachian Trail chapter.)

For camp reading, I recommend getting a copy of *Hazel Creek from Then till Now* by Duane Oliver or *Fontana, A Pocket History of Appalachia* by Lance Holland, both available from park sales outlets.

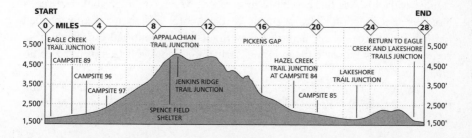

Finding the trailhead: From the junction of U.S. 19/74 and North Carolina Highway 28 in the southwestern portion of the park, turn west onto NC 28 and go 21.1 miles to the stop sign at the entrance road for Fontana Dam. Turn right, go a short distance, and turn onto the first road to the right. This road leads to the marina entrance in 0.2 mile.

Parking and trailhead facilities: Short-term parking is available along the slope leading to the marina, and there's plenty of parking in the gravel lot atop the hill. Ancient rest rooms are available at the marina entrance. Backcountry camping permits are available at a kiosk near the rest room building. Fontana Village is nearby with full services.

A special treat for backpackers is the hot showers located at the Fontana Dam Visitor Center. The showers are open all day, every day of the year.

Key points:
- **0.5** Junction with Eagle Creek Trail.
- **1.1** Junction with former Lakeshore (Pinnacle Creek) Trail.
- **2.0** Campsite 89.
- **3.1** Campsite 96.
- **4.6** Campsite 97.
- **9.1** Spence Field Shelter.
- **9.3** Junction with Appalachian Trail at Spence Field. Bote Mountain Trail is a few hundred feet away.
- **9.5** Junction with Jenkins Ridge Trail.
- **16.0** Junction with former Lakeshore Trail at Pickens Gap.
- **18.4** Junction with Hazel Creek Trail at Campsite 84.
- **20.1** Campsite 85.
- **23.0** Junction with Lakeshore Trail. Campsite 86 is nearby.
- **27.4** Return to junction of Eagle Creek and Lakeshore Trails.

The hike: Pick up the Lakeshore Trail, which runs through Campsite 90 and heads upstream along Eagle Creek. After about 0.4 mile you cross the creek on an elaborate metal footbridge. Just beyond the bridge is the junction of Lakeshore and Eagle Creek Trails. Lakeshore Trail turns off right and crosses Pinnacle Ridge to the Hazel Creek embayment. (You'll travel this trail at the end of the hike.) If you are familiar with this area but haven't been here in a while, you might be a little confused by this junction. This segment of Lakeshore Trail is a recently opened reroute. It replaces the segment of Lakeshore Trail that followed Pinnacle Creek, known locally as Pinnacle Creek Trail. That trail, along with Campsite 88, is no longer maintained.

Take Eagle Creek Trail at the junction. On it you soon cross the creek a second time on a footbridge. Enjoy this bridge; it is the last bridged crossing you have. There are twelve full crossings, and three crossings where the creek splits. In all but

Eagle Creek, Spence Field, and Hazel Creek

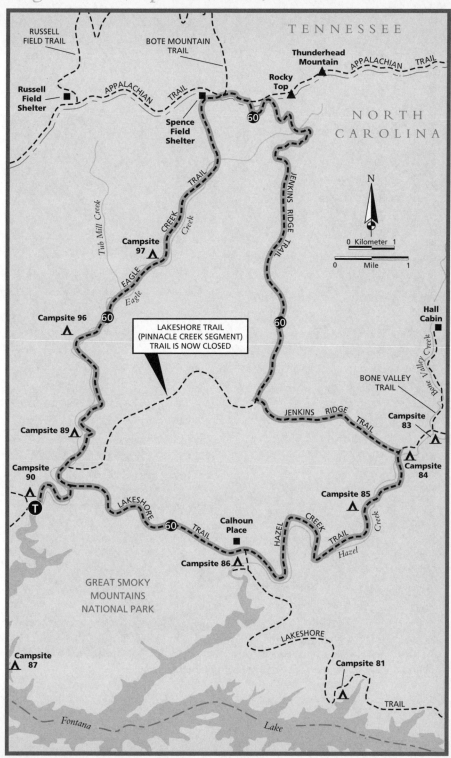

TENNESSEE

RUSSELL
FIELD TRAIL

BOTE MOUNTAIN
TRAIL

Thunderhead
Mountain

APPALACHIAN TRAIL

Russell
Field
Shelter

APPALACHIAN TRAIL

Rocky
Top

60

NORTH
CAROLINA

Spence
Field
Shelter

N

JENKINS RIDGE TRAIL

0 Kilometer 1

0 Mile 1

Tub Mill Creek

EAGLE CREEK TRAIL

Eagle Creek

Campsite
97

Campsite 96

60

60

Eagle

Hall
Cabin

Bone Valley Creek

LAKESHORE TRAIL
(PINNACLE CREEK SEGMENT)
TRAIL IS NOW CLOSED

BONE VALLEY
TRAIL

JENKINS RIDGE TRAIL

Campsite
83

Campsite 89

Campsite
90

T

LAKESHORE

Campsite
84

Campsite 85

HAZEL CREEK TRAIL

Hazel Creek

60 TRAIL

Calhoun
Place

Campsite 86

GREAT SMOKY
MOUNTAINS
NATIONAL PARK

Hazel

LAKESHORE

Campsite
87

Campsite 81

TRAIL

Fontana

Lake

Fontana Lake marina and departure point for boat shuttles.

the lowest water, all could be a wade. In high water the crossings are dangerous, if possible at all. If you aren't comfortable with the first one, turn around.

At 1.1 miles you pass the old Lakeshore Trail on the right. Not too far ahead is the first Eagle Creek crossing and, shortly afterward, crossing number two. A short ways ahead, just before you cross Ekaneetlee Creek, you pass Campsite 89 on the left. Situated in a grove of hemlock and white pine, this site has a soft pine needle ground cover. It's a nice site, but it has no privacy. A couple of old railroad rails remind you that this trail, like many others in the park, follows an old logging railroad grade.

At the sixth ford of Eagle Creek, you cross a split of the stream onto a narrow island. Campsite 96, a very small site, is located here. Conscientious people won't like camping here. Park regulations require that you answer Mother Nature's call at least 100 feet from any streams or trails. That means you have to wade across Eagle Creek every time you have to go. The Park Service puts a lot of trust in people with this one.

Just beyond Campsite 96 are two more fords that take you back to the left side of the creek. After five additional fords, you come to Campsite 97 on the left, right beside the creek. A 3-foot-diameter saw blade leans on a tree here. Just beyond the campsite is the final creek crossing. An illegal campsite sits on the left after this crossing. An old bed frame and several other artifacts lie scattered about. The grade to this point has been a piece of cake—uphill, but almost imperceptibly so. That changes now—gently at first, moderately later on.

Pressing on you pass a huge blowdown of trees off to the right and eventually make two crossings of Gunna Creek. Gunna Creek is the major headwater stream that creates Eagle Creek, and you've been following it for a while. The trail swings away from the creek a couple of times to a switchback, then comes to a fork. Go left (the right fork ends in a few yards) and climb much more steeply by an interesting rock on the right. It projects out of the ground as a monolith, and rock tripe lichens cover its surface.

Farther up, the trail swings away from Gunna Creek and begins tracing Spence Cabin Branch. The next 0.25 mile or so is insanely steep, very rocky, and overgrown in stinging nettle. This is the toughest part of the hike. Once beyond the steep part, the trail dips to cross the creek and continues following upstream before swinging away to the right and climbing steeply to Spence Field Shelter. Several hundred feet before the shelter, the trail crosses a spring—the shelter's water source.

Continue beyond the shelter about 0.2 mile to the junction with the Appalachian Trail at Spence Field. Turn right (east), and in 100 yards pass Bote Mountain Trail, which comes in from the left. When you top out on the grassy hump, strike out through the grass a few yards on the right to a rock cairn. There's a great view looking down the Eagle Creek drainage to Fontana Lake. Try as I might, this is the only good view I can find on Spence Field. And I've surely tried after reading several narratives about the "spectacular panoramic views," even in some recent publications. The views may exist, but I haven't seen them. That's not to say Spence Field isn't scenic. On the contrary, the open, grassy fields are fabulous, a highlight of this hike.

Descend from the hump a few yards and turn right (southeast) onto Jenkins Ridge Trail. The trail starts out heavily overgrown and at first skirts the flanks of Rocky Top, then crosses the headwaters of Gunna Creek and skirts the flanks of Blockhouse Mountain. After 2.8 easy miles and a final steep ascent, reach Haw Gap, marked by a small clearing overgrown in grass and weeds. Work your way to the other side of the field and reenter the forest.

For the next 3.7 miles the trail follows on or close to the spine of Jenkins Trail Ridge—a ridge interestingly named after a trail, rather than the other way around. There are a few short ascents, with a couple of them steep—one brutal—but this is mostly downhill now. This isn't your average, ordinary descent, however. In places the slope is wicked, and there's little grading—just a clear spot on the ground. With a heavy pack this stretch is murder on the knees. When it's raining, or after the autumn leaf fall, it could be dangerous. In snow, it's suicidal.

Reach Pickens Gap and celebrate the end of the difficult parts of this hike. The remainder is a comparative "piece of cake." The old Lakeshore Trail goes to the right here and meets Eagle Creek Trail in about 4 miles. You might be tempted to shorten the hike by taking this route, but remember, the park no longer maintains this trail, and there are more than a dozen unbridged creek crossings. I don't recommend hiking unmaintained trails. Go left instead, and follow Jenkins Ridge Trail (formerly the Sugar Fork segment of Lakeshore Trail) 2.4 easy miles to Hazel Creek Trail. Turn right (south) and follow Hazel Creek downstream. (See Hike 59: Hazel Creek and Bone Valley for more detail about the Hazel Creek segment.)

Once you reach the final Hazel Creek bridge at the horse pasture, continue on the right side of the creek (don't cross the bridge), pass the Granville Calhoun House and yard, and pick up the obvious roadbed. The next 4.4 miles follow along the new Lakeshore Trail segment. About half the route is on an old roadbed, but all of it is wide, well graded, and nowhere overly steep. It climbs alongside Sheehan Branch a good distance, swings away and crosses around a ridge, descends to cross a small branch, then makes a long ascent to cross Pinnacle Ridge before descending rather steeply to Eagle Creek. The last section passes through a forest with many dead pines—listen for the jungle call of the pileated woodpecker through here.

Options: A good plan is to take a boat shuttle to Campsite 90 in the afternoon and spend the night there. The next day, hike up to Spence Field and stay at the shelter. The third day, hike down to Campsite 86. Take a dip in the lake and camp there. The fourth day, you can laze your way back to Campsite 90 and lounge around the lake the rest of the day. The boat will pick you up on the fifth day. You could trim a day off this plan by having the boat pick you up at Hazel Creek on the fourth morning.

61

Shuckstack

Highlights: *Panoramic views, wildflowers, used car lot*

Type of hike: Loop; long day hike or overnighter
Total distance: 11.9 miles round-trip
Difficulty: Difficult

Best time of year: April for wildflowers and less smoggy views
Maps: Trails Illustrated; USGS Fontana Dam (the final 5.2 miles not shown)

Special considerations: Several creek crossings of Lost Cove Creek require wading in heavy flows and could be dangerous in very high water.

Finding the trailhead: From the junction of U.S. 19/74 and North Carolina Highway 28 in the southwestern portion of the park, turn west onto NC 28 and go 21.1 miles to the stop sign at the entrance road for Fontana Dam. Turn right and follow the road 1.1 miles to the dam. Drive over the dam and turn right at the fork. Continue 0.7 mile to the road's end at a trail information board. The Appalachian Trail leads behind the trail board.

Parking and trailhead facilities: Parking is limited here, but it's usually not a problem. Back at the Fontana Dam Visitor Center are rest rooms and a special treat for backpackers: hot showers. Fontana Village is nearby with full services.

Key points:

3.4 Junction with spur trail to Shuckstack Tower.
3.5 Shuckstack Tower.
3.6 Return to junction with Appalachian Trail and spur to tower.
4.0 Junction with Twentymile and Lost Cove Trails.
4.7 Campsite 91.
6.7 Junction with Lakeshore Trail.

The hike: For such a difficult and remote hike, a surprising number of people make the trek to Shuckstack Tower. Most people backtrack from the tower for a

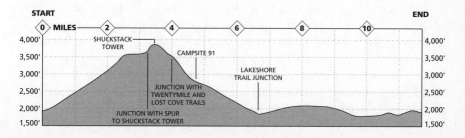

Shuckstack

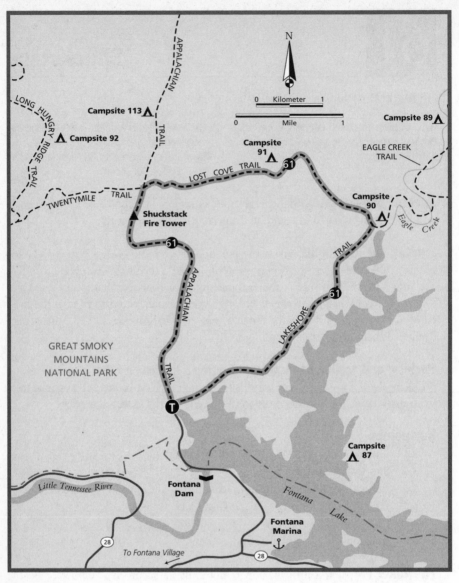

7.0-mile walk. This hike details a longer loop that experienced hikers can still do in a day. Two campsites provide the opportunity to turn this trip into an overnighter.

Begin at the trail information board and start climbing immediately. You'd better get used to it, because the first 3.5 miles are tough. There is one good view of Fontana Dam on the right and one great view on the left toward the Unicoi Mountains. Beyond this viewpoint, the trail climbs very steeply to pick up a ridge and continues steeply along the ridge spine. Spring wildflowers are abundant in this section.

A couple hundred yards below the tower, the Appalachian Trail veers off left, while a path continues climbing up the ridge to the tower.

Shuckstack Tower is an old fire tower, one of the few remaining in the park. At its base are the old tower-keeper's cistern and the foundation and chimney of the cabin. Six flights of stairs above you is one of the finest views in the park. The steps are in questionable shape; if you decide it's not safe to climb to the top, at least go high enough to look out over the trees. To the south are Fontana Lake and Dam, with the Snowbirds in the background; to the west are the Unicoi Mountains; and to the north is the crest of the Smokies. The views make you forget all about the strenuous climb required to get here.

After soaking in the views, backtrack to the Appalachian Trail and turn right, heading in the opposite direction from which you approached. A 0.4-mile easy descent takes you to Sassafras Gap. If you make this trip in mid-April, this is a highlight of the hike. Wildflowers are everywhere. There's mayapple, several trillium species, purple phacelia, false Solomon's seal—too many to count.

At the gap, turn right (northeast) onto Lost Cove Trail and descend through the Lost Cove Creek drainage. The trail is not well graded and in places is ridiculously steep. You pick up Lost Cove Creek when it's just a small branch, but a couple of miles downstream it becomes a respectable stream. The three or so crossings above Campsite 91 are easily negotiated. The campsite is small, right beside the trail, and looks rarely used. Below the campsite there are at least seven more creek crossings, some of them easy to rock-hop, some a little dicey. In high water all of them will demand your full attention.

Reach Lakeshore Trail at a nondescript junction. Straight ahead, continuing along Lost Cove Creek, Lakeshore Trail leads 0.3 mile to Fontana Lake at Campsite 90. To the right, and climbing up the bank, the trail leads 5.2 miles to the trailhead. It's a typical undulating course and rather boring much of the way. A section near the lake obviously follows part of old North Carolina Highway 288, which now lies mostly under Fontana Lake. If there's any doubt in your mind about that, it will be erased when you start seeing the abandoned cars along the trail. Unfortunately, the trail never gets close enough to provide good views of the lake—just the autos.

Options: If you're doing this hike as an overnighter, your two choices are Campsites 91 and 90. I'd choose 90. It adds only 0.6 mile to the total distance, and it's a much better site, being right on Fontana Lake. Plus, staying there puts all the creek crossings behind you.

Abandoned vehicle along Lakeshore Trail.

62

Twentymile Loop

Highlights: *Cascades*

Type of hike: A "lollipop" loop; day hike or over-nighter
Total distance: 7.6 miles round-trip
Difficulty: Easy (except for stream crossings)

Best time of year: Summer
Maps: Trails Illustrated; USGS Tapoco and Fontana Dam

Special considerations: Unless you hike during a drought, you're going to have to make several creek wades. Try doing this hike in summer and making the wades a highlight of the trip. In winter, or after heavy rains, the creek crossings can be unsafe, even impossible.

Finding the trailhead: The trailhead is at Twentymile Ranger Station, in the remote southwestern end of the park. Drive about 6 miles west from Fontana Dam on North Carolina Highway 28 and turn right at the sign for Twentymile. Pass the ranger station and park at the small gravel lot on the right, just before the gate. The trail is a continuation of the gravel road.

Parking and trailhead facilities: On summer weekends you might have to park back at the ranger station. There are no rest rooms or stores of any kind anywhere around here. The closest ones are at Fontana Village, near Fontana Dam.

Key points:

0.5 Junction with Wolf Ridge Trail.
1.6 Junction with Twentymile Loop Trail.
4.5 Junction with Twentymile Trail.
5.8 Campsite 93.
7.0 Twentymile Creek Cascades.
7.1 Return to junction with Wolf Ridge Trail.

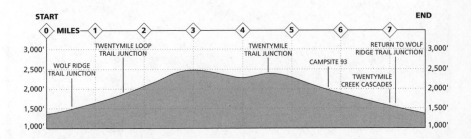

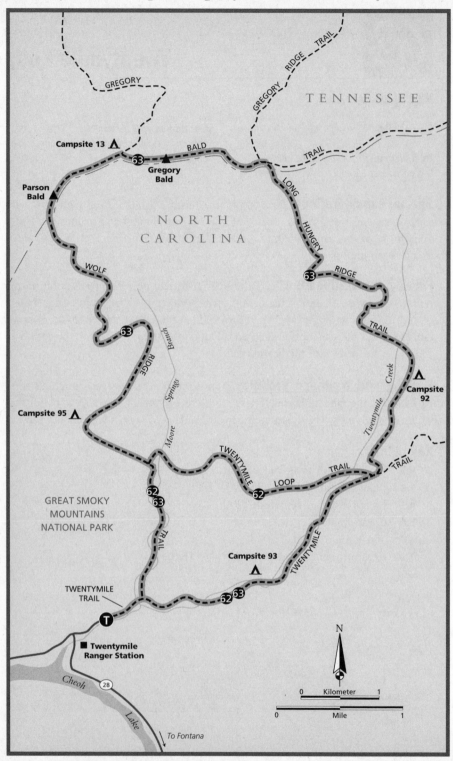

GREGORY

TENNESSEE

GREGORY RIDGE TRAIL

Campsite 13 △

BALD

63

Gregory
Bald

TRAIL

Parson
Bald ▲

LONG

HUNGRY

NORTH
CAROLINA

WOLF

RIDGE

63

63

RIDGE

Springs Branch

TRAIL

Twentymile Creek

△
Campsite
92

Campsite 95 △

Moore

TWENTYMILE

TRAIL

LOOP

TRAIL

62

62
63

TRAIL

GREAT SMOKY
MOUNTAINS
NATIONAL PARK

TRAIL

TWENTYMILE

Campsite 93

△

TWENTYMILE
TRAIL

62 63

T

■ Twentymile
Ranger Station

N

Cheoh

28

0   Kilometer   1

0   Mile   1

Lake

To Fontana

The hike: Although the Twentymile area is one of the more remote sections of the park, it receives a surprising amount of use. Expect some company on a summer weekend hike. Begin hiking up the gravel road on an old railroad grade. At 0.5 mile cross Moore Springs Branch on an auto bridge, and turn left onto Wolf Ridge Trail when you get to the other side.

The hike now follows Moore Springs Branch upstream, crossing it six times. Only the first crossing has a foot log, and in anything but drought conditions, Moore Springs Branch carries a healthy amount of water. Bring crossing shoes, go barefooted (carefully), or just plow on through in your boots. After the fifth crossing you soon come to the junction with Twentymile Loop Trail (not shown on the USGS map), forking right and continuing to follow the creek upstream. Wolf Ridge Trail turns left and swings away from the creek.

Take Twentymile Loop Trail and cross the creek for the sixth time just below a small cascade. If the water is high you'll want to scout a spot upstream or down, since the crossing here is a little dicey. Climb away from the creek on a long, moderate grade before leveling out on a contour run to a small saddle. Descend from the saddle and quickly cross a small branch, then cross a larger stream farther down and follow it downstream to an unbridged crossing of Twentymile Creek. This is the last wet crossing you have. Once across, begin a slight ascent and come to a rock-hop of Proctor Branch. Beyond this crossing it's a short, steep climb to the junction with Twentymile Trail.

Paths lead in four directions from the junction. Behind you is Twentymile Loop Trail. Immediately to the left is Long Hungry Ridge Trail, descended in Hike 63: Gregory Bald via Twentymile. On the well-graded roadbed in front of you, Twentymile Trail goes both ways. You want to go right on this trail and follow Twentymile Creek downstream.

It's 2.6 miles back to the junction with Wolf Ridge Trail, with Twentymile Creek as a constant companion. You cross the creek five times, but thankfully these crossings are on sturdy bridges. Just past the third crossing is Campsite 93, right beside the trail. It's a small site with zero privacy. You can camp here on an overnighter, but, truthfully, there are better backpacking trips in the Smokies. A few hundred feet before getting back to Wolf Ridge Trail, a signed side path to the left leads a few yards to the scenic Twentymile Creek Cascade.

Once back at the lower trail junction, backtrack the remaining 0.5 mile to your car.

Gregory Bald via Twentymile

Highlights: *Superb views, brilliant azalea displays*

(See map for Hike 62: Twentymile Loop.)

Type of hike: A "lollipop" loop; overnighter or tough day hike
Total distance: 15.5 miles round-trip
Difficulty: Difficult

Best time of year: Middle to late June
Maps: Trails Illustrated; USGS Tapoco, Fontana Dam, Calderwood, and Cades Cove

Special considerations: Unless you hike during a drought, you're going to have to make several creek wades of Moore Springs Branch. In winter, or after heavy rains, the creek crossings can be unsafe, even impossible.

Finding the trailhead: The trailhead is at Twentymile Ranger Station, in the remote southwestern end of the park. Drive about 6 miles west from Fontana Dam on North Carolina Highway 28 and turn right at the sign for Twentymile. Pass the ranger station and park at the small gravel lot on the right, just before the gate. The trail is a continuation of the gravel road.

Parking and trailhead facilities: On summer weekends you might have to park back at the ranger station. There are no rest rooms or stores of any kind anywhere around here. The closest ones are at Fontana Village, near Fontana Dam.

Key points:
- **0.5** Junction with Wolf Ridge Trail.
- **1.6** Junction with Twentymile Loop Trail.
- **2.5** Spur leads to Campsite 95.
- **6.1** Parson Bald.
- **6.8** Junction with Gregory Bald Trail at Campsite 13.
- **7.2** Gregory Bald.
- **7.9** Junction with Gregory Ridge and Long Hungry Ridge Trails at Rich Gap.

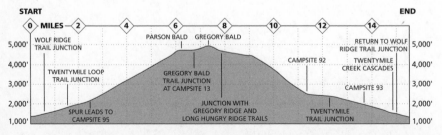

11.3 Campsite 92.

12.4 Junction with Twentymile Trail.

13.7 Campsite 93.

14.9 Twentymile Creek Cascades.

15.0 Return to junction with Wolf Ridge Trail.

The hike: Gregory Bald is one of the finest destinations in the Smokies backcountry; in the latter part of June, it's *the* finest. Most persons access the bald from the Tennessee side by taking either the Gregory Ridge or Gregory Bald Trail. This hike provides a less-traveled North Carolina access. (For the scoop on Gregory Bald and camping at Campsite 13, see Hike 24: Gregory Bald via Cades Cove in addition to this narrative.)

Begin hiking up the gravel road on an old railroad grade. At 0.5 mile cross Moore Springs Branch on an auto bridge, and turn left onto Wolf Ridge Trail on the far side.

The hike now follows Moore Springs Branch upstream, crossing it five times. Only the first crossing has a foot log, and in anything but drought conditions, Moore Springs Branch carries a significant amount of water. After the fifth crossing you soon come to the junction with Twentymile Loop Trail (not shown on the USGS map), continuing upstream. Wolf Ridge Trail turns left and swings away from the creek.

Take Wolf Ridge Trail; in a little less than a mile from the creek, come to a sharp right switchback. A side path leads a few hundred yards from the switchback to Campsite 95, a pleasant site in a second-growth mixed-hardwood forest. The site doesn't receive enough use for it to look trodden.

Wolf Ridge Trail begins climbing in earnest now, and it doesn't let up for the next 3.6 miles. (There's one tiny dip where the trail swings around a saddle, but that's it.) At several points you think you've reached Parson Bald, only to discover that you have to keep climbing. Once on the bald, you know it. It's mostly overgrown, but there are scattered open patches. Blueberries and black cherry trees are everywhere. If you want to see bears, come here in August when the fruit ripens. Parson Bald is an all-you-can-eat buffet to bears.

From the bald it's an easy and delightful walk through patches of tassel rue to Sheep Pen Gap and Campsite 13. Wolf Ridge Trail ends here at the junction with Gregory Bald Trail. Turn right (southeast) and climb 0.4 mile to Gregory Bald. It's 0.7 mile from the bald to Rich Gap and the junction with Gregory Ridge Trail on the left. A few hundred feet farther is the junction with Long Hungry Ridge Trail at a fork. Our hike follows the Long Hungry Ridge Trail to the right (south).

For nearly a mile the trail loses little elevation and is a joy to hike. Just before the trail drops off the east side of the ridge, you pass through Rye Patch, marked by an old sign at a tiny clearing. Rye Patch was much more open at one time and, as you would expect, planted in rye. Upon leaving Rye Patch, the descent increases noticeably, and the trail continues uneventfully. After a few creek crossings (some potentially tough in high water), you come to Campsite 92, 3.4 miles from Rich Gap. The site sits in a grove of hemlock and yellow-poplar and appears little used.

Just beyond the site you cross a small stream branch, spanned by the rotten remains of an old bridge. The steep grade is behind you now. Now you follow an easy course along an obvious logging grade and cross a few minor branches. A final crossing of Proctor Branch heralds the approach to Twentymile Trail at Proctor Field Gap. From the gap it's an easy 3.1 miles back to the trailhead. (See Hike 62: Twentymile Loop for details about this final segment.)

Options: Although this hike is certainly doable as a day hike, you'd be short-changing yourself. It's much better to overnight at Campsite 13. That way you can experience Gregory Bald at sunset and sunrise. You just don't know what you're missing until you do that.

Southeast
SECTION

Oconaluftee River

Highlights: *Easy walk along river*

(See map for Hike 47: Mingus Mill and Newton Bald.)

Type of hike: Out-and-back; day hike; a good split-party hike
Total distance: 1.6 miles one-way

Difficulty: Easy
Maps: Trails Illustrated; USGS Smokemont and Whittier (trail not shown)

Special considerations: Poison ivy is abundant along this trail.

Finding the trailhead: The trail starts at Oconaluftee Visitor Center.

Parking and trailhead facilities: The visitor center has ample parking, rest rooms, and a telephone.

The hike: This short, easy walk makes a good family hike. Just be sure to teach the kids how to identify poison ivy. From the visitor center walk to the Pioneer Farmstead and either skirt it by walking along the fence or pass through it, picking up the trail on the other side. You follow closely along the Oconaluftee River most of the way. Pass under the Blue Ridge Parkway then through a dense forest with a closed canopy, and cross a paved road before finally ending in Cherokee at a parking lot and footbridge leading to Chief Saunooke's Trading Post.

The trail is popular among locals as a fitness and dog-walking path. It's one of only two trails in the park that allow pets. (Gatlinburg Trail is the other.)

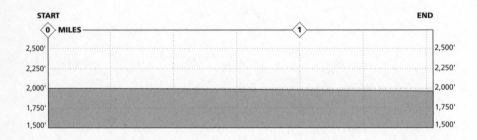

65

Smokemont Nature Trail

Type of hike: Loop; day hike
Total distance: 0.75 mile round-trip

Difficulty: Moderate
Maps: Trails Illustrated; USGS Smokemont

Finding the trailhead: Drive 3.1 miles north from Oconaluftee Visitor Center on Newfound Gap Road, and turn right at the sign for Smokemont Campground. Cross Oconaluftee River, turn left, and drive into the campground. The trail begins directly opposite Campsite B31.

Parking and trailhead facilities: Parking is available near both sides of the trailhead. Rest rooms are available in the campground.

The hike: Since it starts from the Smokemont Campground, this nature trail is a good choice for families who are camping. For those not staying at Smokemont, a better choice might be one of the many Quiet Walkways in the park.

The Smokemont Nature Trail crosses an overflow of Bradley Fork on a foot log, then crosses Bradley Fork and a split from the main stream. The trail loops after the crossings. If you're going right, it climbs rather steeply before descending back to Bradley Fork. The self-guiding trail leaflet (available at the trailhead; 50 cents to keep) discusses man's influence on the land and nature's resilience.

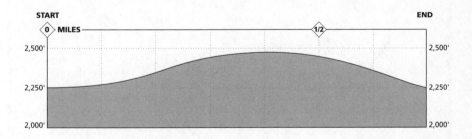

Smokemont Nature Trail; Smokemont Loop; Bradley Fork and Chasteen Creek

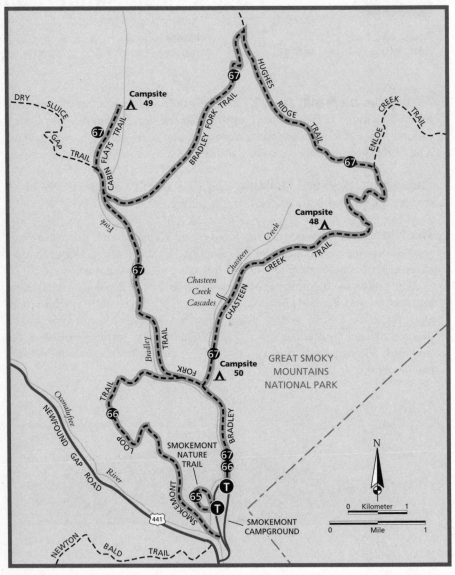

Campsite 49

Campsite 48

Campsite 50

DRY SLUICE GAP TRAIL

CABIN FLATS TRAIL

BRADLEY FORK TRAIL

HUGHES RIDGE TRAIL

ENLOE CREEK TRAIL

Chasteen Creek

CHASTEEN CREEK TRAIL

Chasteen Creek Cascades

GREAT SMOKY MOUNTAINS NATIONAL PARK

Bradley

Fork

BRADLEY FORK TRAIL

Oconaluftee River

NEWFOUND GAP ROAD

LOOP TRAIL

SMOKEMONT NATURE TRAIL

SMOKEMONT

SMOKEMONT CAMPGROUND

NEWTON BALD TRAIL

441

N

0   Kilometer   1

0   Mile   1

66 Smokemont Loop

Highlights: *Wildflowers*

(See map for Hike 65: Smokemont Nature Trail.)

Type of hike: Loop; day hike
Total distance: 6.1 miles round-trip
Difficulty: Moderate

Best time of year: Spring
Maps: Trails Illustrated; USGS Smokemont (most of trail not shown)

Finding the trailhead: Drive 3.1 miles north from Oconaluftee Visitor Center on Newfound Gap Road, and turn right at the sign for Smokemont Campground. Cross Oconaluftee River, turn left, and drive into the campground. Follow the road through the campground all the way to its farthest point at the end of "D" section, and park in one of the spaces around the loop. During winter "D" section is closed and you have to park at the end of "C" section and walk an additional 0.2 mile. You can also continue the loop around the campground and park at the old concrete bridge, just before leaving the campground.

Parking and trailhead facilities: Parking is at one of the three general-purpose parking areas described above. Since this is a loop, it really doesn't matter which you choose. Do not park in a designated camping space. The campground has a telephone and rest room facilities.

Key points:

- **1.2** Junction with Chasteen Creek Trail.
- **1.7** Junction with Smokemont Loop Trail.
- **5.4** Bradley Cemetery.
- **5.6** Return to Smokemont Campground.

The hike: For people staying at Smokemont Campground, this loop hike is a good way to spend part of the day. Begin by walking north through the campground, or the gate at the end of the campground, and follow the gravel road along Bradley Fork. It's an easy and popular walk along this stretch. At 1.2 miles

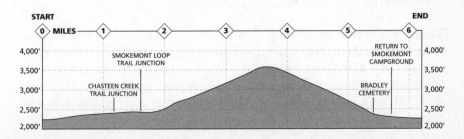

Chasteen Creek Trail forks right; stay to the left and continue following Bradley Fork upstream. At 1.6 miles you reach the junction with Smokemont Loop Trail, leading left (southwest). Take this trail and immediately cross Bradley Fork on a very long, bouncy foot log. On the other side the trail turns south and follows Bradley Fork downstream a few hundred yards to a fork, crossing a side branch along the way. Turn right (southwest) at the fork and begin a climb up Richland Mountain that continues steadily for nearly 2 miles. The varied forest allows many different species of wildflowers to grow. Open areas from downed trees contribute to brier patches and showy summer wildflowers.

After passing through a saddle, you begin climbing the west side of the ridge. You can hear Oconaluftee River now, but the peacefulness is probably short-lived, as you can also hear the cars along Newfound Gap Road. Newton Bald is visible through the trees off to the west.

At 3.4 miles a sharp bend to the left signals the end of the climbing and the beginning of a 2-mile downhill stretch. There are fewer wildflowers in this section, but the forest is more scenic. At about 5.1 miles you glimpse Bradley Cemetery down the slope to the right. If you want to visit the cemetery, don't take one of the eroded side trails. Instead, continue on to where the trail ends at a service road, about 0.2 mile farther. Turn right, then immediately right again onto another old road. Follow this road a few hundred feet to an obvious path on the right that leads to the cemetery.

To continue the loop hike, turn left (east) on the gravel road and follow it 0.2 mile back to the campground.

 Bradley Fork and Chasteen Creek

Highlights: *Cascading streams, wildflowers, big trees*
(See map for Hike 65: Smokemont Nature Trail.)

Type of hike: A "lollipop" loop; two-night backpack or difficult overnighter
Total distance: 17.2 miles round-trip

Difficulty: Moderate
Maps: Trails Illustrated; USGS Smokemont and Mount Guyot

Finding the trailhead: Drive 3.1 miles north from Oconaluftee Visitor Center on Newfound Gap Road, and turn right at the sign for Smokemont Campground. Cross Oconaluftee River, turn left, and drive into the campground. Follow the road through the campground all the way to its farthest point at the end of "D" section. During winter "D" section is closed and you have to park at the end of "C" section and walk an additional 0.2 mile.

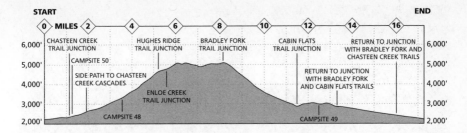

Parking and trailhead facilities: Parking is at the end of either "D" or "C" section in the campground. Do not park in a designated camping space. The campground has a telephone and rest room facilities.

Key points:

   1.2 Junction with Chasteen Creek Trail.
   1.3 Campsite 50.
   1.9 Side path to Chasteen Creek Cascades.
   3.6 Campsite 48.
   5.2 Junction with Hughes Ridge Trail.
   5.6 Junction with Enloe Creek Trail.
   8.1 Junction with Bradley Fork Trail.
 11.4 Junction with Cabin Flats Trail.
 11.7 Junction with Dry Sluice Gap Trail.
 12.3 Campsite 49.
 13.2 Return to junction with Bradley Fork and Cabin Flats Trails.
 16.0 Return to junction with Bradley Fork and Chasteen Creek Trails.

The hike: Some sections of this hike are very popular, so expect to meet lots of others hikers. The first 1.2 miles follow the gravel road beside Bradley Fork, along the same route as Hike 66: Smokemont Loop. At 1.1 miles the road crosses Chasteen Creek on a wide bridge and reaches a fork at 1.2 miles. Turn right (east) onto Chasteen Creek Trail. In less than 0.1 mile you pass Campsite 50, one of the nearest sites to a road in the park. It's a good choice for bringing young children on their first backcountry adventure.

Chasteen Creek Trail climbs gradually, loosely following Chasteen Creek, and at 1.9 miles comes to a horse-hitching rack on the left (creek side) of the trail. For a quick side trip, break off at this point and follow the narrow footpath by the hitching post. It leads a few hundred feet to scenic Chasteen Creek Cascades. Backtrack from the cascade; the footpath looks as though it might loop back to the main trail, but it peters out on the hillside.

Beyond the hitching rack the gravel road steepens on its approach to Campsite 48, reached in 3.6 miles. The campsite is scenic, nestled beside the headwaters of Chasteen Creek under a canopy of tall yellow-poplars and small hemlocks. This is the first night's stay on a two-nighter.

Rhododendron tunnel along Bradley Fork Trail.

Beyond the campsite the trail narrows and steepens as it passes through a headwater cove. Even though logging occurred here, the forest has grown back beautifully, and the spring flora display is impressive. In April look for larkspur, an uncommon wildflower with deep purple flowers.

Once you leave the headwater tributary streams, the trail goes through a series of tough switchbacks and reaches Hughes Ridge and Hughes Ridge Trail at 5.2 miles. At my last visit, the trail sign here indicated that a right turn on Hughes Ridge Trail (following the spine of Hughes Ridge) leads 7.3 miles back to Smokemont Campground, but that section of trail is now closed.

Turn left (north) and begin following the crestline of Hughes Ridge. At 5.6 miles you reach the junction with Enloe Creek Trail on the right. Continue along Hughes Ridge Trail for another 2.5 miles of typical ridge hiking (ups, downs, levels) to reach the junction with the upper terminus of Bradley Fork Trail—the same trail on which you started this hike. If hiking in winter, you'll probably notice the views of distant ridges from Hughes Ridge and possibly catch an occasional glimpse of Clingmans Dome.

Turn sharply left (south) on Bradley Fork Trail and descend steeply, passing through several laurel tunnels, and meet up with a finger of Taywa Creek on the left. The forest through here is similar to the cove forest along Chasteen Creek Trail. The trail remains steep and rocky until it crosses, on a wide bridge, another tributary coming in from the right. Now you're walking on an obvious roadbed, and the grade has become a gentle descent. A short distance later you cross the creek again on a culvert and then again on a wide bridge. After the third crossing you soon bear away from the creek and pass through drier ridges. As soon as you leave earshot of Taywa Creek, you begin to hear Bradley Fork. At 11.4 miles you see Bradley Fork at the junction with Cabin Flats Trail. The wide spot in the trail is the old turnaround for what used to be a motor nature trail.

Turn right (north) onto Cabin Flats Trail, and after 200 feet cross Bradley Fork on an out-of-character steel-truss bridge. Just beyond the bridge, an ascent takes you through an old-growth forest, with many large trees right beside the trail. You soon cross Tennessee Branch on an old foot log above a mossy cascade, and in a few feet you reach the junction with Dry Sluice Gap Trail on the left. Continue straight (north) for 0.6 mile to reach Campsite 49, your second night's destination.

The site is one of the largest backcountry campsites in the park, situated right beside Bradley Fork in a wide, flat bottomland. There are several tent sites scattered along the flat and a horse-hitching rack at the lower end. There's also a real oddity for the Smokies: a good-sized shingle beach that makes a great picnic and wading spot. Just downstream from the campsite is a huge logjam, the result of heavy flooding in 1994.

Now retrace your steps to the junction of Cabin Flats and Bradley Fork Trails. Continue straight (south) on Bradley Fork Trail, following Bradley Fork back to the trailhead.

Options: Experienced backpackers can do this trip as an overnighter, staying at Campsite 48. If you choose this option, you may want to skip the Cabin Flats Trail extension; but if you have the energy, it's worth it to see the trees.

Kephart Prong

Highlights: *Historical artifacts, wildflowers, Kephart Prong*

Type of hike: Out-and-back; day hike or overnighter
Total distance: 4.0 miles round-trip

Difficulty: Easy
Maps: Trails Illustrated; USGS Smokemont

Finding the trailhead: From Oconaluftee Visitor Center, drive 6.9 miles north on Newfound Gap Road and park in one of the pullouts on either side of the road. The trail begins on the right side of the road at the bridge over the Oconaluftee River.

Parking and trailhead facilities: Parking is usually sufficient at the two pullouts. Rest rooms are available at Oconaluftee Visitor Center.

Key points:

    2.0 Junction with Grassy Branch and Sweat Heifer Creek Trails at Kephart Shelter.

The hike: Kephart Prong is a popular hike that offers a little something for everyone. So you might want to avoid it on weekends or during the summer tourist season. Or you could begin the trek first thing in the morning and be back at your car before most people even begin their hike.

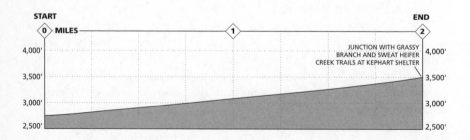

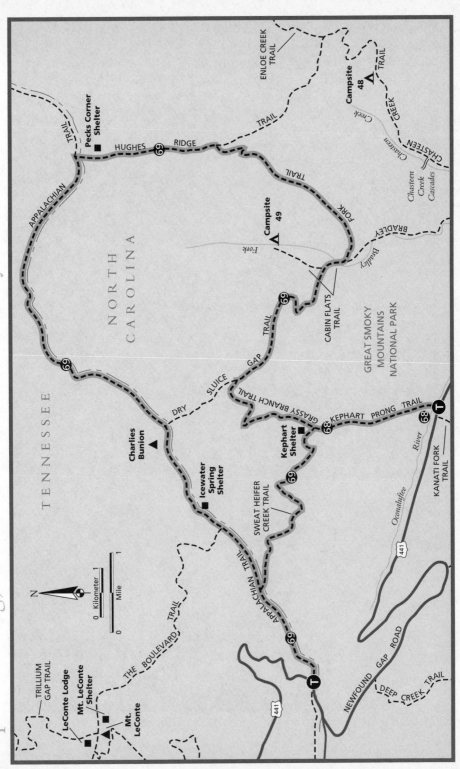

ENLOE CREEK TRAIL

CHASTEEN CREEK TRAIL

Campsite 48

Chasteen Creek

Chasteen Creek Cascades

CHASTEEN CREEK

Pecks Corner Shelter

APPALACHIAN TRAIL

HUGHES 69 RIDGE

TRAIL

FORK

BRADLEY

Bradley Fork

Campsite 49

NORTH CAROLINA

Fork

CABIN FLATS TRAIL

GREAT SMOKY MOUNTAINS NATIONAL PARK

69

TENNESSEE

69

DRY SLUICE GAP TRAIL

Charlies Bunion

GRASSY BRANCH TRAIL

KEPHART PRONG TRAIL

68 T

Icewater Spring Shelter

Kephart Shelter

69

SWEAT HEIFER CREEK TRAIL

Oconaluftee River

KANATI FORK TRAIL

N

0 Kilometer 1
0 Mile 1

TRILLIUM GAP TRAIL

LeConte Lodge

Mt. LeConte Shelter

Mt. LeConte

THE BOULEVARD TRAIL

APPALACHIAN TRAIL

69

441

T

441

NEWFOUND GAP ROAD

DEEP CREEK TRAIL

Oconaluftee River viewed from the Kephart Prong Trail bridge.

The trail begins on the east side of Newfound Gap Road and immediately crosses the Oconaluftee River on a wide bridge. Chances are good you'll see a trout fisher on the Oconaluftee and maybe on Kephart Prong as well. The trail is wide and with only a slight grade, owing to its once being a jeep road. You see bits of old asphalt here and there as further testament. At 0.2 mile you pass through the old Civilian Conservation Corps Camp, in operation in the 1930s and early 1940s. There are old chimneys, foundations, rock walls, and other artifacts from the camp. One of the largest chimneys I've seen in the park stands in a hemlock grove, making for a photogenic setting.

Beyond the CCC Camp the trail forks, with the right fork leading upstream and petering out. Turn left (west) and cross Kephart Prong on a sturdy foot-bridge. At 0.5 mile look for the remains of an old fish hatchery on the left bank. During the next mile you cross Kephart Prong three more times. Each time you can either wade at the ford or walk a few paces and cross on foot logs. You might also see other evidence that humans heavily used this area: old narrow-gauge railroad rails from the logging operations of the 1920s. The final push to the shelter is a little steeper and the trail rockier.

Kephart Shelter sits in a scenic cove beside Kephart Prong. The shelter has a rustic charm, but at my last visit, someone had strung ugly blue tarps over the front to block out the cold wind. The shelter, the prong, the trail, and Mt. Kephart, a few thousand feet higher up, all carry the name of one of the Smokies' most treasured friends, Horace Kephart. Kephart came to the Smokies in 1904 "to enjoy the thrills of single-handed adventure in a wild country." By 1913 he had written two books, *Camping and Woodcraft* and *Our Southern Highlanders*, both of which are still in print. He was particularly distressed by the massive logging operations and became a staunch advocate for the formation of the national park.

The shelter marks the junction with Grassy Branch Trail, which leads northeast behind the shelter, and Sweat Heifer Creek Trail, leading north and passing in front of the shelter. Hike 69: Charlies Bunion and Bradley Fork uses these two trails.

Options: You can spend the night at the shelter, but, like with all shelters in the park, you need a reservation.

69 Charlies Bunion and Bradley Fork

Highlights: *Spectacular high-elevation views, cascading streams, wildflowers, old-growth forest*

(See map for Hike 68: Kephart Prong.)

Type of hike: A "lollipop" loop; two-night back-pack, with option for overnighter or long day hike

Difficulty: Difficult

Total distance: 27.1 miles

Maps: Trails Illustrated; USGS Clingmans Dome, Mt. Le Conte, Mt. Guyot, and Smokemont

Special considerations: The 4.0 miles to Charlies Bunion are extremely popular, so expect to rub shoulders with other hikers. In winter, snow and ice cover the trail, and the rocky hiking is challenging any time of year. Charlies Bunion has dangerous drop-offs.

Finding the trailhead: The trailhead is located at the Newfound Gap Overlook on the Smokies crest. Drive 15.5 miles north on Newfound Gap Road from Oconaluftee Visitor Center or 12.7 miles south from Sugarlands Visitor Center. The trailhead is on the northeast end of the parking lot, between the rest rooms and the Rockefeller Memorial.

Parking and trailhead facilities: Newfound Gap has a very large parking lot that rarely fills completely. Rest rooms are available here.

Key points:
- **1.7** Junction with Sweat Heifer Creek Trail.
- **2.7** Junction with The Boulevard Trail.
- **3.0** Icewater Spring Shelter.
- **4.0** Side path to Charlies Bunion.
- **4.4** Junction with Dry Sluice Gap Trail.
- **10.5** Junction with Hughes Ridge Trail.
- **10.9** Pecks Corner Shelter.

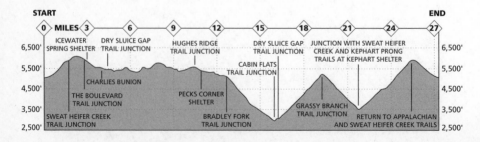

12.7 Junction with Bradley Fork Trail.

16.0 Junction with Cabin Flats Trail.

16.3 Junction with Dry Sluice Gap Trail. Campsite 49 is nearby.

19.2 Junction with Grassy Branch Trail.

21.7 Junction with Sweat Heifer Creek and Kephart Prong Trails at Kephart Shelter.

25.4 Return to junction of Appalachian and Sweat Heifer Creek Trails.

The hike: This is a terrific three-day hike, encompassing much of what the Smokies have to offer. You spend half the time hiking on the high-elevation crest and the other half along headwater streams and through lush forests.

Hike 30: Charlies Bunion describes the first 4.0 miles to Charlies Bunion. From Charlies Bunion continue east on the Appalachian Trail (AT) for 0.4 mile to the junction with Dry Sluice Gap Trail. (If doing the overnight option, you would take this trail southeast.) Continuing east on the AT you pass over the Sawteeth, a fitting name for this series of narrow, jagged ridges. The views through here are good, but nothing like what you experienced at Charlies Bunion. The hiking is typical ridge walking, with ups, downs, and short levels. About 4 miles from Charlies Bunion, and after an arduous ascent, the AT makes a sharp bend to the right (south) and descends along the east side of Laurel Top. Mountain laurel grows densely here, attesting to the mountain's name. Good views of Mounts Chapman, Guyot, and Sequoyah are to the east.

Reach Bradley's View, one of the best of the hike, at 8.9 miles. The view is over the Bradley Fork watershed that you'll traverse tomorrow. At 10.5 miles cut sharply right (south) on Hughes Ridge Trail and hike 0.4 mile farther to Pecks Corner Shelter. At my last visit, the trail sign indicated that the shelter is only 0.2 mile from the AT, but that's not correct.

Pecks Corner Shelter is your first night's stay. The shelter isn't as attractive as some others are, and it's dirty, but there was a pile of lumber nearby at the time of my last visit. Perhaps when you get there you'll have a clean, remodeled shelter in which to stay. Or perhaps that pile of lumber is for a new aerobic outhouse (using oxygen to decompose waste above the ground) like the ones at some other shelters. Water is from a spring about 100 yards in front of the shelter.

From the shelter continue south on Hughes Ridge Trail, pass an old Park Service shack on the left, and reach the junction with Bradley Fork Trail. When you hike this section, notice the change in the forest from dense red spruce at the higher elevations to the more open beech forest.

Now make a right turn (south) onto Bradley Fork Trail, and descend through another forest change, this time to a typical mixed-hardwood forest. The trail is steep and rocky until it meets two joining tributaries of Taywa Creek, and then it becomes a pleasant stroll along an old roadbed lined with abundant spring wildflowers.

At the junction with Bradley Fork and Cabin Flats Trails, turn right (north) onto Cabin Flats Trail and soon cross Bradley Fork on a steel-truss bridge. Just beyond the bridge, you enter an old-growth forest with several big trees. After crossing Tennessee Branch on a picturesque foot log, you come to the junction with Dry Sluice Gap Trail. If it's hot, and you didn't take advantage of dipping in Bradley Fork back at the steel bridge, you might want to take a side trip straight ahead 0.6 mile to Campsite 49, which has a neat shingle beach beside Bradley Fork.

To continue the hike, turn left (west) onto Dry Sluice Gap Trail and head up the drainage of Tennessee Branch. You cross the small branch or one of its feeders seven times in the next mile or so. This mile is a highlight of the trip as it goes through an old-growth forest with many enormous trees. The foliage is lush, and the stream gurgles over and around mossy logs and boulders.

After crossing Tennessee Branch for the last time, the trail begins a series of switchbacks leading to a side ridge that you follow to the east flank of Richland Mountain. After 2.8 miles of climbing, and probably cussing, you reach a gap on Richland Mountain and can now take solace in the thought that all the uphill hiking is over for the day. Grassy Branch Trail heads west from the gap, and Dry Sluice Gap Trail continues north to reach the AT in another 1.3 miles. The gap here is scenic, in a dense stand of rhododendron, but a few open areas look as though they've been used as illegal campsites.

After taking a breather at the gap, follow Grassy Branch Trail down the west flank of Richland Mountain. The trail starts out heavily rutted and soon passes through large, open, grassy areas covered in early spring with spring beauty, trout lily, and mayapple. The steady descent continues under rhododendron tunnels, through open forest, over seeps, and finally follows Kephart Prong downstream to Kephart Shelter. The shelter is your second night's lodging.

Begin the third day by heading north on Sweat Heifer Creek Trail. Sweat Heifer Creek Trail starts right in front of the shelter and crosses Kephart Prong on a scenic foot log. After the crossing, the trail turns left and heads downstream a short distance before switching back right and beginning its ascent to the AT. Pass through an open, grassy area with old railroad rails beside the trail and spring wildflowers carpeting the ground. The ascent is mostly continuous, with a nice level stretch just before crossing Sweat Heifer Creek, 1.6 miles from Kephart Shelter. The creek tumbles over a long series of cascades and makes a good resting spot on a summer day. Around the next ridge you come to another cascade on a side stream, this one smaller but just as pretty.

Around the next bend is a well-laid rock wall just below the trail, looking out of place this far from the nearest road. You also begin noticing the old logging railroad grades below the trail. A steep section brings you to a flat spot where the trail cuts sharply right. There's a trail sign here directing hikers coming from the other direction to go left on the side path instead of straight ahead. It wouldn't matter if they did, because they'd just circle back around to the main trail. This is the site of an old railroad turnaround, and you might notice a few rusty artifacts here from the logging days. You continue to parallel the old grade for a short distance up the trail.

Past the bend, the trail keeps up the steady ascent, crossing a few streams (one surprisingly large for this high up), and as it does the forest changes from hardwood to spruce-fir. There are intermittent views south to Clingmans Dome and east to the Plott Balsams in Nantahala National Forest. Just before reaching the AT, you pass through an eerie stand of dead trees that provides unobstructed vistas south.

At the AT, turn left (west), and retrace your steps to the trailhead.

Options: You can do this trip in one night by dropping off the AT just beyond Charlies Bunion on Dry Sluice Gap Trail. Follow it down the ridge to the junction with Grassy Branch Trail and take it to the right (west). Spend the night at Kephart Shelter. Experienced hikers could also do this route as a strenuous day hike of 13.6 miles.

When I last made this hike, I stayed the first night at Pecks Corner Shelter and finished the rest of the trip the next day, including the side trip to Campsite 49, so that's another possibility for crazy hikers to consider. Just keep in mind that you have to hike 16.2 strenuous miles on the second day.

Hemphill Bald

Highlights: *Views, old-growth forest, wildflowers*

Type of hike: Loop; day hike or overnighter
Total distance: 13.6 miles round-trip
Difficulty: Moderate
Best time of year: April for wildflowers

Maps: Trails Illustrated; USGS Bunches Bald and Dellwood (not all the route is shown, and parts are shown incorrectly)

Special considerations: Heintooga Ridge Road, which you must drive to reach the trailhead, is closed in winter.

Finding the trailhead: At Wolf Laurel Gap (Milepost 458.2) on the Blue Ridge Parkway, turn north onto Heintooga Ridge Road and drive 6.0 miles to Polls (Pauls) Gap on the right. The parking area marks the trailhead for Hemphill Bald, Rough Fork, and Polls Gap Trails. Our hike starts on far right (east) end of the parking lot on the Hemphill Bald Trail.

Parking and trailhead facilities: Parking shouldn't be a problem. Rest rooms are available in season at the picnic area a few miles up Heintooga Ridge Road. (The section of road to the picnic area remains closed until mid-May.)

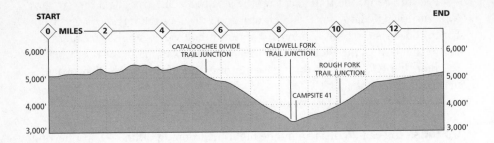

START   END

Key points:

5.5 Junction with Cataloochee Divide Trail.

8.4 Junction with Caldwell Fork Trail.

8.5 Campsite 41.

10.1 Junction with Rough Fork Trail.

The hike: Excellent moderate-length loop hikes are rare in the Smokies. This is one of the best. The only negative is that some of the views encompass more than you probably wish to see on a "wilderness" hike. From the high ridges you can see houses, roads, and, everyone's favorite, Ghost Town in the Sky. Yippee!

The first mile or so is mostly level and rather unattractive. The trail is overgrown, and the surrounding understory is thick and unappealing. This is definitely not old-growth forest. In fact, the course you follow is on an old logging grade. The forest becomes more scenic as you approach Sugar Tree Gap, a small saddle with good spring wildflower displays, and a split-rail fence. You'll see many more fences over the next few miles.

From the gap the trail climbs steadily to Whim Knob and then descends to Garretts Gap. For the next 3 miles or so, the trail follows a similar undulating course along the park boundary. You see fences, pastures, and roads, and at one point there's an open view down to Ghost Town, the popular Maggie Valley tourist trap. A solar-energy collection station marks Hemphill Bald. From the bald you descend less than 0.75 mile to Double Gap and the junction with Cataloochee Divide Trail. (Locals refer to the section of Hemphill Bald Trail you just hiked as part of Cataloochee Divide Trail.)

From the gap turn sharply left (west), remaining on Hemphill Bald Trail. The first mile or so is rocky, muddy, and overgrown in stinging nettle. On the plus side, this section is good for wildflowers. Farther down, at about 2.5 miles from the gap, you cross Double Gap Branch and soon pass a huge oak tree on the right. With a diameter of 6 feet, it's one of the largest northern red oaks I've seen in the park. The forest through here is very scenic, with many nice basswoods, yellow-poplars, and hemlocks.

Reach the junction with Caldwell Fork Trail and turn left (west) onto it. Quickly cross Caldwell Fork on a foot log, and enter Campsite 41 on the other

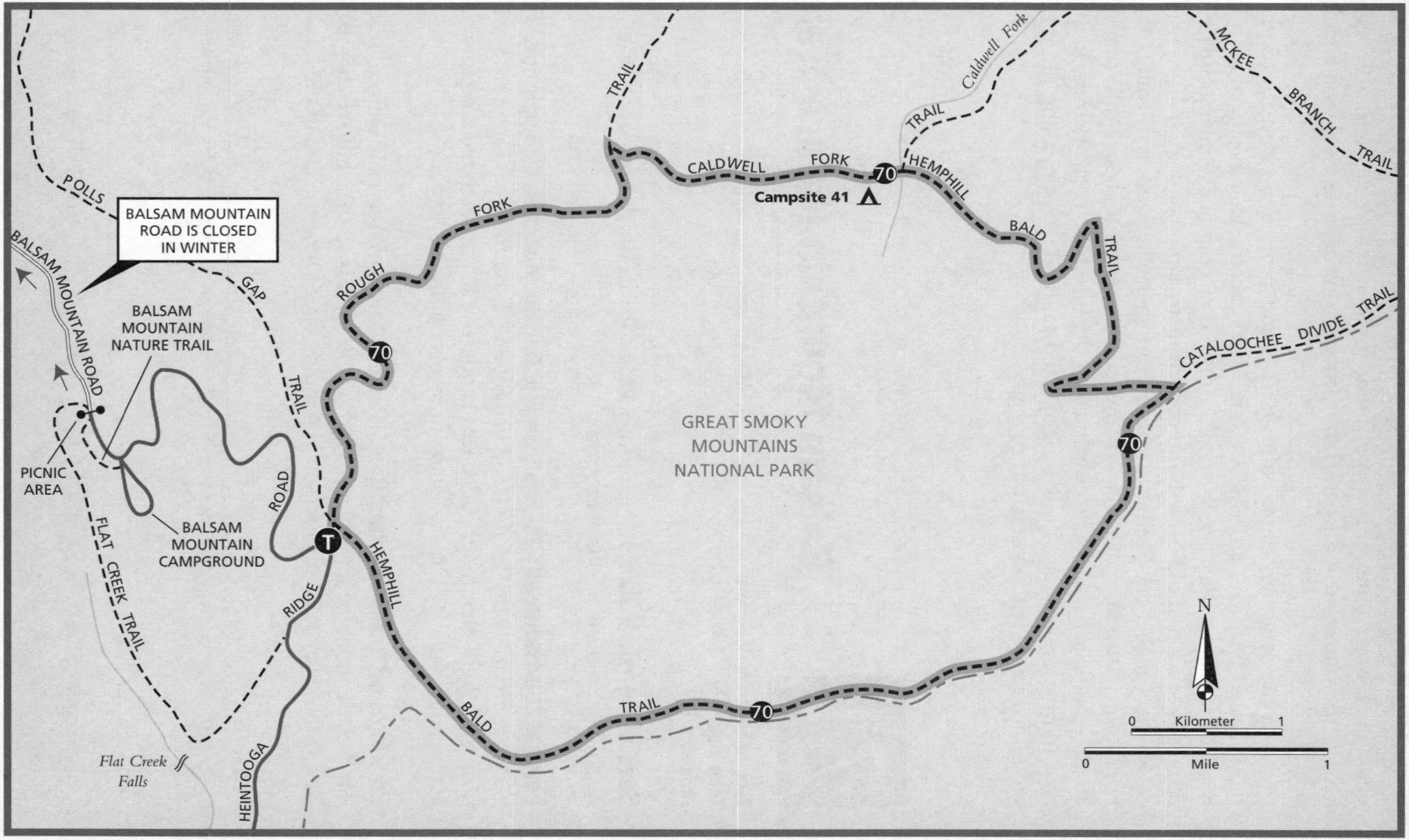

Hemphill Bald

MCKEE BRANCH TRAIL

CATALOOCHEE DIVIDE TRAIL

BALD TRAIL

70

Caldwell Fork

HEMPHILL

FORK

70

CALDWELL

Campsite 41

FORK

TRAIL

GREAT SMOKY MOUNTAINS NATIONAL PARK

ROUGH

70

70

BALD

TRAIL

HEMPHILL

HEMPHILL

T

RIDGE

HEINTOOGA

BALSAM MOUNTAIN ROAD IS CLOSED IN WINTER

GAP TRAIL

BALSAM MOUNTAIN NATURE TRAIL

ROAD

BALSAM MOUNTAIN CAMPGROUND

POLLS

BALSAM MOUNTAIN ROAD

PICNIC AREA

FLAT CREEK TRAIL

Flat Creek Falls

N

Kilometer

Mile

0   1

0   1

side. On an overnighter, this is your home tonight. It isn't the most attractive backcountry campsite in the park, but it's more than adequate for a good night's stay.

From the campsite, climb rather steeply and come to a side path on the right. A sign here says BIG POPLARS, and that's exactly what awaits you a few hundred feet along the path. Back on the main trail, continue climbing and pass through a section of old-growth forest, with many large hemlocks.

Reach Rough Fork Trail at a nondescript spot where the trail climbs Big Fork Ridge. Turn sharply left (south) and climb steeply for about a mile to pick up an old railroad grade. The remainder of the hike follows the railroad grade on a mostly level course. Look for a few old railroad crossties along the way, some with spikes still sticking out of them.

71 Balsam Mountain Nature Trail

Type of hike: Loop; day hike
Total distance: 1.2 miles round-trip
Difficulty: Easy

Maps: Trails Illustrated; USGS Bunches Bald (trail not shown)

Special considerations: Heintooga Ridge Road, which you must drive to reach the trailhead, is closed in winter.

Finding the trailhead: The trail starts at Balsam Mountain Campground. To get there from Wolf Laurel Gap (Milepost 458.2) on the Blue Ridge Parkway, turn north onto Heintooga Ridge Road and drive 8.3 miles to the campground entrance on the left. The trail starts between Campsites 45 and 44.

Parking and trailhead facilities: There is little parking near the trailhead, but that shouldn't be a problem. Most people who hike this trail are campers. Rest rooms are available in season at the picnic area near the end of the hike.

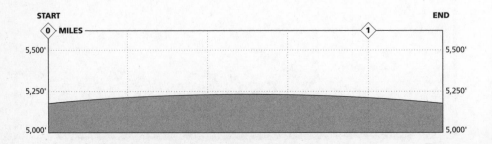

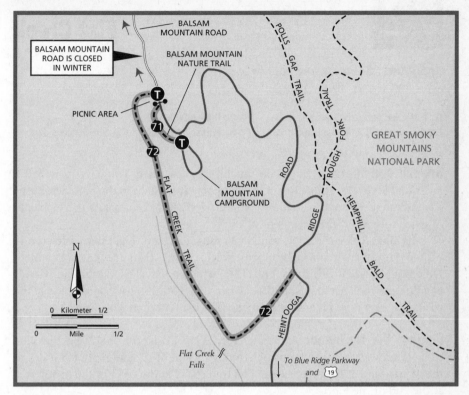

The hike: The theme of this self-guided nature hike is nature's reclamation of a logged Northern hardwood forest. While there's no such thing as a bad walk in the woods, some are better than others. If you are camping at the Balsam Mountain Campground, particularly if you have kids with you, this hike is a good way to spend an hour or so. Otherwise it's not worth the long drive, considering the other options available in the park. At my last visit, the trail was in bad shape—heavily overgrown, many downed trees, and poorly graded.

The trail leads from the campground to Heintooga Ridge Road, just before the picnic area. Walk 0.5 mile down the road to complete the loop.

72

Flat Creek

Highlights: *Scenic overlook, pleasant open forest*

(See map for Hike 71: Balsam Mountain Nature Trail.)

Type of hike: Loop; day hike
Total distance: 6.2 miles round-trip

Difficulty: Moderate
Maps: Trails Illustrated; USGS Bunches Bald

Special considerations: To do this hike as described, you have to walk 3.6 miles on Heintooga Ridge Road. Walking on paved roads in the Smokies is usually discouraged, but this road receives relatively little traffic, and there's plenty of space to step off the pavement.

The Blue Ridge Parkway, which you must drive on to get here, is closed in winter. However, it normally opens much sooner than the last segment of Heintooga Ridge Road, above Polls Gap, which remains closed till mid-May. If you find the road gated, just pull away from the gate and park on the side of the road. This is a loop hike, so it really doesn't matter where you start.

Finding the trailhead: At Wolf Laurel Gap (Milepost 458.2) on the Blue Ridge Parkway, turn north onto Heintooga Ridge Road and drive 8.8 miles to the turnaround at the picnic area. The trail starts to the right of the picnic area at the end of the loop.

Parking and trailhead facilities: Few people come up here, so parking shouldn't be a problem. Rest rooms are available in season at the picnic area.

Key points:

0.1 Scenic overlook.
1.9 Spur to Flat Creek Falls.
2.6 Junction with Heintooga Ridge Road.

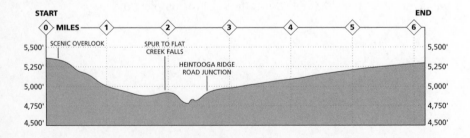

The hike: Flat Creek Trail is an "unknown gem" in the Smokies. Few people know about it, but those who hike it don't soon forget it. Although heavily logged before park establishment, the forest walk is now one of the more scenic higher-elevation hikes in the park.

Begin at the picnic area at the trail sign. A short walk through a spruce forest takes you to Heintooga Overlook, a little-known viewpoint that provides an open vista toward the west—perfect for sunsets. Becks Bald is prominent in the foreground, Clingmans Dome is far to the left, Mount Guyot is on the extreme right, and Mt. LeConte is straight ahead in the distance.

Beyond the overlook, the trail swings to the right and soon descends to cross Flat Creek amidst a tangle of rhododendron. The forest is pleasantly open and the ground carpeted in grass. Although scenic, it isn't natural. Grassy forests are a good sign of former logging activity. Grouse don't care whether it's been logged or not, and you might flush one out through here. On my last hike, I flushed a mom and eight chicks out of the grass.

At 1.9 miles you come to a signed side path on the right that leads a few hundred yards to Flat Creek Falls. There's no good view of the falls, and any attempt to find one is dangerous and damaging to the surrounding soil. In spring, right after the road opens, there's a fair view of the waterfall from Heintooga Ridge Road.

Back on the main trail, you enter a dense forest and descend to cross a fork of Bunches Creek on a foot log. Turn sharply right, climb a small ridge, and descend to another fork crossing on a foot log. Now make a moderate climb of about 0.25 mile to Heintooga Road. Turn left and follow the road 3.6 miles back to the picnic area.

Options: If you have a bicycle, a good option is to leave it at the picnic area (chained, of course), drive back down to the lower trailhead, and hike Flat Creek Trail in reverse. Then you can coast back to your car.

73

Hyatt Ridge

Highlights: *Solitude, great wildflowers, remote hike*

Type of hike: Loop (actually a "reverse lollipop");
day hike or overnighter
Total distance: 9.4 miles round-trip

Difficulty: Moderate
Maps: Trails Illustrated; USGS Bunches Bald and
Luftee Knob

Finding the trailhead: Drive 1.2 miles south from Oconaluftee Visitor Center toward Cherokee and turn left at the sign for Big Cove Road, taking the 0.2-mile connector over Oconaluftee River to the road. Turn left onto Big Cove Road and drive 8.6 miles to a fork, just after crossing Raven Fork. Turn right at the fork onto Straight Fork Road and follow it 0.9 mile to a turnaround at a fish hatchery. Leave the pavement and continue on the gravel road. It's 3.9 miles to a parking area on the right, across from Beech Gap Trail.

Another option is to take Heintooga Ridge Road from the Blue Ridge Parkway to the Balsam Mountain Picnic Area and continue on the one-way Balsam Mountain Road. This gravel road snakes down the mountain, providing good opportunities for viewing forests and wildflowers. The road becomes two-way at the start of this hike. (Blue Ridge Parkway, Heintooga Ridge Road, and Balsam Mountain Road are all closed in winter. The segment of Heintooga Ridge Road above Polls Gap remains closed till mid-May.)

Parking and trailhead facilities: You might have to share parking with a few fishers, but there should be plenty of room. The closest facilities are back in Cherokee.

Key points:
2.8 Junction with Hyatt Ridge Trail.
3.7 Campsite 44 at McGee Spring.
4.6 Return to junction of Beech Gap and Hyatt Ridge Trails.
6.3 Junction with Enloe Creek Trail.
8.1 Straight Fork Road.

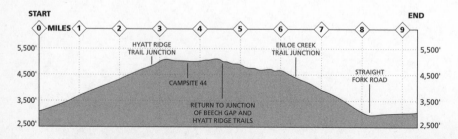

Hyatt Ridge

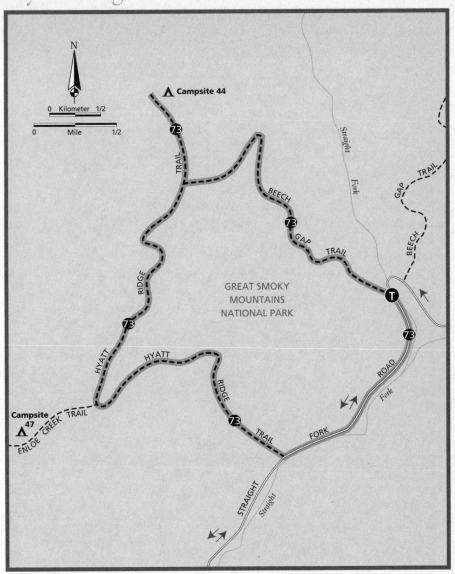

The hike: The trail climbs steeply through lush spring wildflowers to a point high above Straight Fork, then swings west and continues a moderate climb in and out of the broad ridges. On the "ins" you cross several branches. Wildflowers abound in the wet spots throughout the year. Later in summer you can see jewelweed, coneflower, and joe-pye weed.

After a little more than 2 miles, you swing around a spur extending from Hyatt Bald and then go on a short level stretch before climbing the spur flank to the junction with Hyatt Ridge Trail on the ridgetop.

Hyatt Bald.

Turn right (north) and ascend the flank of Hyatt Bald to the summit. On the bald is an open stand of beech trees that prohibit good views, but the carpet of grass, ferns, and various wildflowers throughout the season makes the bald a scenic spot. Norway spruce grows here, too. Lumber companies introduced this nonnative tree after they logged the native red spruce and Fraser fir.

From here follow the narrow ridge from the bald and reach an open, heavily overgrown stretch. Soon reenter the forest and come to Campsite 44, one of the most delightful sites in the park. It lies in a dark stand of old-growth trees at the head of a small, wet glade. McGee Spring, said to be one of the coldest springs in the Smokies, gurgles out of the bank about 200 feet in front of the camp. Lush foliage covers the ground from spring through fall. There's false hellebore, coneflower, bee balm, and many other wildflowers.

Backtrack from the campsite to the junction with Beech Gap Trail and continue on the Hyatt Ridge Trail. Descend steeply to a saddle, then climb gradually a short distance before descending again to begin a narrow ridge walk through mountain laurel, flame azalea, blueberries, and, at one point, lichen-covered trees. This is an eerie sight in the fog.

A steep descent takes you to a gap and the junction with Enloe Creek Trail, which comes up the right side of the ridge. You want to turn left (northeast) and continue on the Hyatt Ridge Trail. The trail leaves the ridge and makes a steady, steep descent to Straight Fork Road. This segment is an ankle-turner. It's muddy and covered in loose rocks that twist under your feet. It also has wonderful wildflower displays—foliage literally carpets the slopes.

Once you reach the road, turn left and follow it 1.3 miles back to your vehicle.

74

Boogerman

Highlights: *Old-growth forest, Caldwell Fork foot logs*

Type of hike: A "lollipop" loop; day hike
Total distance: 7.4 miles round-trip
Difficulty: Moderate

Maps: Trails Illustrated; USGS Cove Creek Gap and Dellwood (most of trail not shown)

Special considerations: During summer you can expect to see many other people on this hike. If you want solitude, try hiking it in winter. You'll probably have it all to yourself—especially on weekdays.

Finding the trailhead: This hike is in remote Cataloochee Cove, in the extreme southeastern section of the park. From exit 20 on Interstate 40, go 0.1 mile south on U.S. 276 and turn right onto Cove Creek Road. Follow this road 5.7 miles to the park boundary (it changes to gravel along the way), and continue 1.7 miles to an intersection with a paved road on the left. Turn left onto this road and drive 3.1 miles to the Caldwell Fork trailhead on the left, just past the Cataloochee Campground.

Parking and trailhead facilities: There's room for only a few vehicles at the trailhead. On weekends you may have to continue on the road a short distance to find a place to pull off. Rest rooms are available at the campground.

Key points:
- **0.8** Junction with Boogerman Trail.
- **4.7** Junction with Caldwell Fork Trail.
- **6.6** Return to junction of Caldwell Fork and Boogerman Trails.

The hike: You might be a little wary of hiking a trail called "Boogerman," but there's no cause for alarm. Robert "Boogerman" Palmer, the former owner of much of the woodland you hike through, supposedly received this nickname in school when he told his teacher he wanted to be the Boogerman when he grew

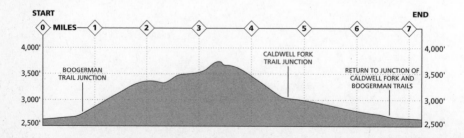

Young hikers pose in the hollowed base of a yellow-poplar tree on the Boogerman Trail.

up. (Another version says he told his teacher that his name was Boogerman.)

The hike begins with the crossing of Palmer Creek on a long, bouncy foot log, just upstream of its junction with Caldwell Fork to create Cataloochee Creek. The next 0.8 mile follows Caldwell Fork upstream. Cross the creek and in a few yards come to the lower junction with Boogerman Trail.

Turn left onto the trail and begin ascending moderately. As you climb, you pass some big yellow-poplars and hemlocks. Upon rounding a ridge, the trail levels a bit, then begins descending through a white pine grove before crossing a small stream branch and ascending again through excellent spring wildflower habitat. On the climb you pass an old metal wheel leaning against a small maple tree, and just ahead on the left is a huge poplar. Now a quick moderate ascent takes you over a ridge and into a mostly level stretch that crosses several springs, a small branch, and a scenic stand of second-growth yellow-poplar.

Now the trail makes a short, steep push up a ridge. As you level out, look to the right to see a huge oak tree, and as you pass through the cove forest, you see many large poplars. At this point you make a short ridgeline walk and begin descending to pick up a small stream. Signs of human settlement start to appear, including a fine rock wall beside the trail. Farther down stands a big poplar on the right that has a hollowed-out base big enough for several people to stand in. If you hike with kids and they run ahead of you like kids do, you can expect to find them standing inside the tree when you get there.

Continue descending along the stream, crossing it several times and passing several more rock walls. Off the trail to the right you might spot a chunk of metal that seems very out of place. It looks like some sort of lift-gate mechanism, or perhaps an apparatus used in a sawmill. Now pass through a small clearing with walnut trees and yucca, both good indicators of a former homesite. On the left in a depression is the nearly decayed Carson Messer Cabin. A short distance farther you come to the upper junction with Caldwell Fork Trail.

Turn right onto Caldwell Fork Trail, cross Snake Branch (the stream you've been following) on a foot log, and shortly cross Caldwell Fork on a sturdy foot log. Before you get back to the lower Boogerman Trail junction, you have to cross Caldwell Fork seven more times, each time on a hefty foot log, and each crossing offers a wonderful view of the creek. The grade is easy but rocky in places, and the trail is very muddy from horse traffic. Once back at the lower junction, retrace your steps to the trailhead.

Options: Once you finish the hike, continue driving through scenic Cataloochee Cove to the road's end a few miles ahead. The cove features an old church, schoolhouse, frame house, barn, and pastures. White-tailed deer browse the pastures, and now the big attraction is elk. The Park Service began reintroducing elk in 2001, and they seem to be doing well. The cove also is the starting point for two more hikes in this guidebook: Rough Fork and Caldwell Fork (Hike 75), and Little Cataloochee (Hike 76).

Boogerman; Rough Fork and Caldwell Fork

Highlights: *Steve Woody Place, old-growth forest, Caldwell Fork scenes*
(See map for Hike 74: Boogerman.)

Type of hike: Shuttle, or loop if combined with road walking; day hike or overnighter
Total distance: 9.2 miles one-way (shuttle); 11.6 miles round-trip (loop)

Difficulty: Moderate
Maps: Trails Illustrated; USGS Dellwood and Bunches Bald

Special considerations: Cataloochee Cove, where this hike begins, is gated at night.

Finding the trailhead: This hike starts in remote Cataloochee Cove, in the extreme southeastern section of the park. From exit 20 on Interstate 40, go 0.1 mile south on U.S. 276 and turn right onto Cove Creek Road. Follow this road 5.7 miles to the park boundary (it changes to gravel along the way), and continue 1.7 miles to an intersection with a paved road on the left. Turn left onto this road and drive 5.5 miles to the parking area at the road's end, passing through Cataloochee Cove (the road changes to dirt) on the way. The trail is a continuation of the dirt road beyond the gate.

If not doing this hike as a loop, you need to leave a second vehicle or arrange for a shuttle to pick you up at the Caldwell Fork trailhead, just west of Cataloochee Campground on the same side of the road.

Parking and trailhead facilities: There's plenty of room to park. Rest rooms are available at the campground.

Key points:
- **1.0** Steve Woody Place.
- **1.5** Campsite 40.
- **2.9** Junction with Caldwell Fork Trail.
- **4.4** Campsite 41.

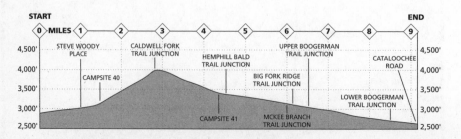

244

4.5 Junction with Hemphill Bald Trail.

6.0 Junction with McKee Branch Trail.

6.1 Junction with Big Fork Ridge Trail.

6.5 Upper junction with Boogerman Trail.

8.4 Lower junction with Boogerman Trail.

9.2 Cataloochee Road.

The hike: The first mile follows the old roadbed along Rough Fork, crossing it three times on narrow foot logs and arriving at a clearing. Here stands Steve Woody Place, a well-preserved homesite open for exploration. The house and springhouse are all that remain from several structures that once stood here.

After exploring the house, continue along the roadbed, which narrows and starts to act more like a trail. You probably are alone now, too, since most people turn around at Steve Woody Place. Pass through a scenic forest with big hemlocks and cross Hurricane Creek on a foot log. Just past the crossing, situated in the fork between Hurricane Creek and Rough Fork, is Campsite 40. This is a neat site, nestled among hemlock, birch, and a tangle of rhododendron. Although the campsite's close to the trail, the dense vegetation provides seclusion.

Now the trail climbs moderately around ridge after ridge and doesn't stop until it reaches Caldwell Fork Trail, 1.4 miles from the campsite. At the junction take Caldwell Fork Trail to the left and head downhill (Rough Fork Trail continues climbing). Soon you begin passing through a splendid old-growth forest with many tree species. Farther down, in a stand of younger yellow-poplar, a side path on the left leads several hundred feet to a few huge poplars known as the "Big Poplars." A short distance down from here is Campsite 41, your home tonight if doing this trip as an overnighter.

Campsite 41 isn't the most attractive site in the park, and it receives a considerable amount of horse use. But it's the only logical choice for camping on this hike. Campsite 40 is too close to the beginning, making for a long second day.

Upon leaving the campsite, cross Caldwell Fork on a foot log and climb a few hundred yards to the junction with Hemphill Bald Trail. Stay left on Caldwell Fork Trail and descend to an easy rock-hop of Double Gap Branch.

At this point you go on an easy, undulating course, passing through a hemlock and then a white pine forest, and then coming to the junction with McKee Branch Trail, forking off to the right in a clearing. Continue on Caldwell Fork Trail and in 100 yards come to Big Fork Ridge trail on the left. From here the Big Fork Ridge Trail crosses Big Fork Ridge and descends to Cataloochee Cove, very near the Rough Fork trailhead. Before 2001 this made an excellent loop hike of 9.3 miles, but in that year the Park Service reintroduced elk into Cataloochee Cove and located the acclimation pens on the Big Fork Ridge Trail. The park expects to close the trail from approximately January 15 to June 30 in 2002 and 2003, but you should check ahead before making specific plans. It sure is nice to know that elk once again inhabit the Smokies.

Steve Woody Place.

Continuing on Caldwell Fork Trail, you cross McKee Branch on a foot log and soon climb slightly to pass the upper junction with Boogerman Trail on the right (see Hike 74). Cross Snake Branch on a foot log and then Caldwell Fork on a hefty foot log. You make eight more crossings of the creek, each time on a sturdy foot log, with each crossing offering a wonderful view of the creek. The grade is easy but rocky in places, and the trail is very muddy from horse traffic.

Reach the lower junction with Boogerman Trail just before the final crossing. From here it's an easy 0.8-mile walk to Cataloochee Road. Just before reaching the road, you have to make one more creek crossing, this one of Palmer Creek on a long, bouncy foot log.

If you didn't leave a vehicle here, you need to turn left and walk 2.4 miles through Cataloochee Cove to get back to your car.

Highlights: *Cultural history*

Type of hike: Shuttle or out-and-back; day hike   **Difficulty:** Moderate
Total distance: 6.0 miles one-way   **Maps:** Trails Illustrated; USGS Cove Creek Gap

Special considerations: Cataloochee Cove, where this hike begins, is gated at night.

Finding the trailhead: This hike starts in remote Cataloochee Cove, in the extreme southeastern section of the park. From exit 20 on Interstate 40, go 0.1 mile south on U.S. 276 and turn right onto Cove Creek Road. Follow this road 5.7 miles to the park boundary (it changes to gravel along the way), and continue 1.7 miles to an intersection with a paved road onto the left. Turn left onto this road and drive 4.6 miles to a parking area on the right, just before the road crosses Palmer Creek. Pretty Hollow Gap Trail begins here as a dirt road.

If doing this hike as a shuttle, you need to leave a second vehicle at the Little Cataloochee trailhead on NC 284. From the entrance to Cataloochee (1.8 miles before reaching the Pretty Hollow Gap trailhead), turn north onto the gravel road. Drive 1.0 mile, passing the Palmer House on the way, and turn right to cross Cataloochee Creek on a steel bridge. Continue 0.7 mile (rough) and turn left. (Straight ahead reconnects to the paved road that goes to Cataloochee.) Now drive 1.5 miles to another crossing of Cataloochee Creek and from there another 2.0 miles to the trailhead on the left.

Parking and trailhead facilities: The starting trailhead has room for several vehicles, but it fills quickly on summer weekends, particularly when horse trailers are here. The ending trailhead has room on the side of the road for only a few vehicles. Rest rooms are available at the Cataloochee Campground.

Key points:
0.8 Junction with Little Cataloochee Trail.
4.9 Junction with Long Bunk Trail.

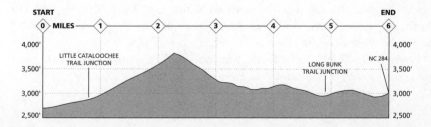

The hike: Few hikes in the Smokies offer a cultural experience like this one. Early in the twentieth century some 1,200 people lived in Little Cataloochee Cove. Few standing structures remain, but you can see two cabins and a church, plus rock walls, old metal and ceramic artifacts, fences, and rock foundations.

Begin on an easy grade along Palmer Creek. At 0.2 mile you pass a horse camp on the right, and at 0.8 mile Little Cataloochee Trail turns to the right (northeast). Take Little Cataloochee Trail and climb moderately, soon picking up Davidson Branch and walking in the creekbed for a short distance. The trail now becomes very muddy in places and continues to be rocky. Continue climbing alongside the creek and then swing away to the right, leaving the Davidson Branch drainage but quickly picking up the drainage of a side stream.

Continue climbing along this side stream and soon pass the rotten remains of a cabin on the left. The logs are American chestnut—most other woods would have decayed long ago. After passing a rock wall on the left, the trail becomes very steep and very muddy. Climbing this section in a heavy rain is a miserable experience. You soon reach Davidson Gap and can take a breather on the fallen tree.

Descend from the gap rather steeply through an overgrown section, and pass a couple of rock walls on the right. Heavy settlement occurred in the area you pass through over the next few miles. Old homesites are now overgrown with trees, but you can still distinguish many of them.

The steep trail soon moderates and joins an old roadbed for an easy walk. Come to the Dan Cook Place on the left at 3.3 miles. This fine cabin is a reconstructed version of an original cabin that was destroyed by vandals in the 1970s. It is one of the most picturesque cabins in the park. Across from the cabin is the rock foundation of an apple house.

Continue the gentle descent and then make an easy climb to reach Little Cataloochee Baptist Church on the right. The church, built in the late 1800s, still stands in its original condition and is still the site of occasional services. From the church the road descends rather steeply and passes a spring on the left, then goes through the old community of Ola. Ola once boasted several structures, including the finest house in Little Cataloochee. In winter you can find scattered artifacts of the community, but the area is now nearly overgrown.

Cross Little Cataloochee Creek and begin ascending. You soon come to a sharp right swing in the road, where a side path on the left leads in a few hundred feet to the John Jackson Hannah Cabin. The cabin is open for exploration. Shortly beyond the cabin is the junction with Long Bunk Trail on the left (northeast). Long Bunk Trail goes 3.6 miles to Mt. Sterling Trail. About 0.2 mile along the trail is the Hannah Cemetery—a nice side trip.

From Long Bunk Trail, Little Cataloochee Trail continues another 1.1 miles on a moderate course to NC 284 and the end of the hike.

Little Cataloochee

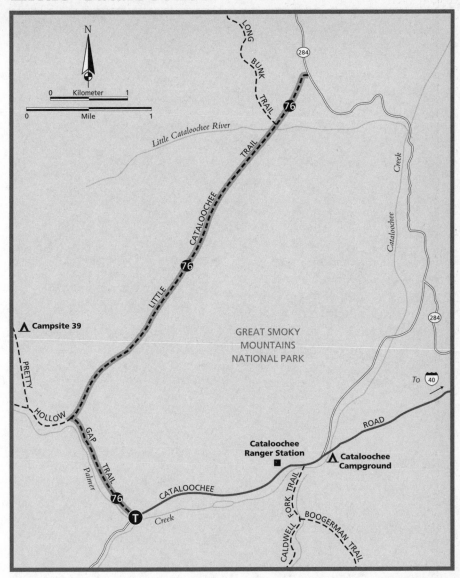

Options: At the start of the hike you can cross over Palmer Creek on the bridge and take the path on the right to the old Beech Grove School for a quick side trip. Actually, if you're interested in old schools, churches, and cabins, plan to spend a day exploring all of Cataloochee in addition to the hike through Little Cataloochee.

Little Cataloochee Baptist Church and cemetery.

77

Mt. Sterling

Highlights: *Spectacular views*

Type of hike: Out-and-back; day hike or overnighter
Total distance: 5.4 miles round-trip
Difficulty: Difficult

Best time of year: Mid- to late October for fall foliage views from the summit and less smog
Maps: Trails Illustrated; USGS Cove Creek Gap and Luftee Knob

Special considerations: Your vehicle may not be safe at the trailhead. It's best to drive a clunker, and don't leave any valuables in it. If you plan to overnight at Campsite 38 (highly recommended), don't forget two things: a reservation (site 38 is rationed) and warm clothes at any time of year. Even in summer it can get chilly on the windy summit of Mt. Sterling. In winter it's frigid.

Finding the trailhead: Getting to the trailhead is as much a part of this adventure as the hike itself. The easiest route is to take exit 457 off Interstate 40 and cross the Pigeon River. Stay to the left after the crossing and follow this road 2.0 miles to an intersection, passing the Walters Power Plant and Mountain Mama's on the way. The intersection marks the community of Mount Sterling. Turn left onto Mt. Sterling Road, and drive 6.7 curvy miles to Mt. Sterling Gap. Pull off the road here; the trail starts on the right.

Parking and trailhead facilities: There's no parking to speak of, just a wide spot at the gap. You might have to park a little closer to the roadway than you'd prefer on summer weekends. Facilities? You're kidding, right? Actually, back in the community of Mount Sterling is Mountain Mama's, a store that has a sort of cult following among Appalachian Trail thru-hikers. You can get just about anything you need there, except on Monday and Tuesday in winter, when it's closed.

Key points:

0.5 Junction with Long Bunk Trail.

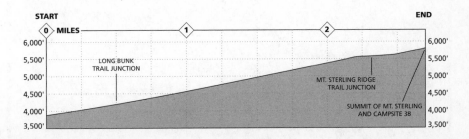

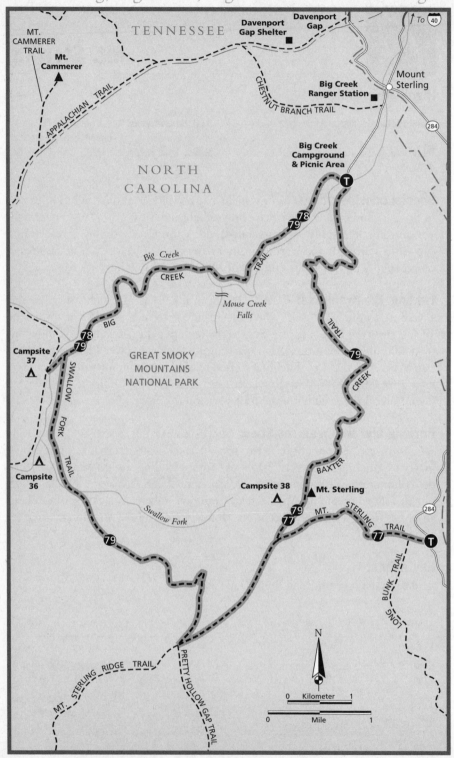

TENNESSEE

MT. CAMMERER TRAIL

Mt. Cammerer

APPALACHIAN TRAIL

Davenport Gap Shelter

Davenport Gap

CHESTNUT BRANCH TRAIL

Big Creek Ranger Station

To 40

Mount Sterling

284

Big Creek Campground & Picnic Area

T

NORTH CAROLINA

78
79

Big Creek

CREEK

Mouse Creek Falls

BIG

78
79

Campsite 37

SWALLOW FORK TRAIL

GREAT SMOKY MOUNTAINS NATIONAL PARK

TRAIL

TRAIL

79

CREEK

Campsite 36

Swallow Fork

Campsite 38

Mt. Sterling

BAXTER

79
77

MT. STERLING

TRAIL

284

T

79

MT. STERLING RIDGE TRAIL

PRETTY HOLLOW GAP TRAIL

77

LONG BUNK TRAIL

N

0   Kilometer   1

0   Mile   1

2.3 Junction with Mt. Sterling Ridge Trail.

2.7 Summit of Mt. Sterling and Campsite 38.

The hike: Of the three hikes in this guidebook that take you to Mt. Sterling, this one is the shortest and the only one suitable for a day hike. It's steep but short enough that you can take all the time you need. Although the trailhead is on the other side (and just to the left) of nowhere, a surprising number of people make this steep trek. Expect company, maybe more than you'd like on summer weekends.

The elevation of Mt. Sterling Gap is 3,888 feet; at the summit of Mt. Sterling, it's 5,842 feet. That makes 1,954 feet you have to climb in less than 3 miles, but it's a continuous, steady climb, without any severely steep sections. At 0.5 mile you pass Long Bunk Trail on the left, which ascends from Little Cataloochee. Continue climbing the old jeep road and notice how the forest changes from an oak association to spruce at the higher elevations, turning into a true red spruce–Fraser fir forest on Sterling's summit.

Reach the junction with Mt. Sterling Ridge Trail 0.4 mile below the summit. Turn sharply to the right (northeast) and pass the horse-hitching rack just before reaching the summit.

Mt. Sterling certainly is not pristine. There's the 60-foot steel tower, the storage building, the power line swath, and the clearings for the campsites. However, something about this place makes you feel as though you're in the middle of an enormous wilderness. Maybe that's because the first three trips I made here were in frigidly cold weather, and the wind howled all night long. It does that a lot up here.

If overnighting, you have three choices for tent sites, each with its own food cable. Look around—they are well hidden from one another. Water is from a good spring on the north side of the mountain. Hike down Baxter Creek Trail (it starts at the tower) about 0.25 mile to the signed side path on the left. Walk a couple hundred yards along this path to the spring.

The view from the tower ranks among the finest in the park. In fact, I don't know any other view that surpasses it for sunrises.

Options: Two other hikes in this guidebook take you to Sterling's summit: Big Creek and Mt. Sterling (Hike 79) and Big Creek Perimeter Loop (Hike 80).

Mouse Creek Falls.

Big Creek

Highlights: *Mouse Creek Falls, Big Creek cascades, geology; ideal hike for inexperienced backpackers*

(See map for Hike 77: Mt. Sterling.)

Type of hike: Out-and-back; day hike, overnighter, or two-night backpack
Total distance: 10.6 miles round-trip

Difficulty: Easy
Maps: Trails Illustrated; USGS Waterville, Cove Creek Gap, and Luftee Knob

Special considerations: If planning to camp at site 37, make reservations as early as possible. This is one of the most popular rationed sites in the park.

Finding the trailhead: Take the Waterville exit (exit 457) off Interstate 40 and cross the Pigeon River. Stay to the left after the crossing and follow the road 2.0 miles to an intersection, passing the Walters Power Plant and Mountain Mama's on the way. The intersection marks the community of Mount Sterling. Go straight, and enter the Big Creek section of the park. Follow the road 0.8 mile to where it ends at the picnic area and walk-in campground entrance. The trail begins to the right, just before the parking area.

Parking and trailhead facilities: Parking space is rarely a problem. A new rest room building is by the parking area, but it is closed in winter. Portable toilets are available when the rest rooms are closed. Mountain Mama's, which you passed on the way here, has just about anything you need in the way of supplies, plus a short-order grill. It's open daily except for Monday and Tuesday in winter.

Key points:
2.0 Mouse Creek Falls.
5.1 Junction with Swallow Fork Trail.
5.3 Campsite 37.

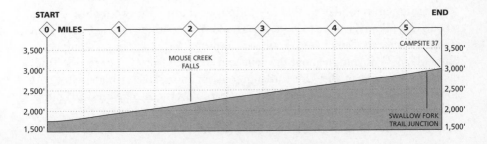

The hike: This may be the perfect hike for inexperienced or first-time back-packers. It's an easy walk but long enough to make you feel as though you've done something. It provides wonderful scenery, and the campsite is among the finest in the park. But just because the walk to the campsite is easy doesn't mean this hike is for weenies. Several options make it as demanding as you want it to be. Actually, this hike is for everyone.

Begin by walking back up the road a few feet and turning left at the gate. The hike is on an old motor road built by the Civilian Conservation Corps (CCC) in the 1930s. It's wide, well graded, and nowhere very steep. Much of it follows the old logging railroad grade. Logging occurred in nearly all of the Big Creek watershed prior to park establishment.

At about 1.0 mile, look to the right to see Rock House, a towering rock cliff a few hundred feet off the trail. Supposedly the rock overhang served as tem-porary shelter for loggers and settlers. Four-tenths of a mile beyond Rock House is Midnight Hole on Big Creek. The entire flow of the creek squeezes through a narrow chute and drops 6 feet into a deep—dark as midnight—pool.

At 2.0 miles you come to Mouse Creek Falls on the left, indicated by a horse-hitching rack. The 35-foot cascade drops directly into Big Creek, creat-ing a grand scene for hikers and photographers. Shortly beyond the falls you cross Big Creek on a bridge and keep steady company with the creek for the remainder of the hike.

At 2.8 miles you pass, on the left, a well-known landmark. Back during the logging days, a logging train engineer placed a brake shoe on the dripping bank to collect the water, similar to the function of pipes you see at many backcoun-try campsite springs. Brakeshoe Spring, as it became known, was a regular stop-ping point for hikers for more than fifty years until some bonehead stole the brakeshoe in the early 1970s.

From Brakeshoe Spring, you have an enjoyable creekside walk of 2.5 miles to Walnut Bottoms at Campsite 37. The campsite is one of the best, with secluded tent sites among hemlocks and beside Big Creek. If the creekside sites are taken, you can camp on the other side of the trail under a stand of buckeyes.

Campsite 37 marks the end of the hike if doing it as a day trip. You backtrack from here.

Options: Many people hike to Walnut Bottoms as a day hike, and many others camp at site 37, but few take full advantage of the opportunities available.

A great plan is to hike to Walnut Bottoms and camp for two nights. On the second day, take a day hike to a scenic cascade. You continue on Big Creek Trail about 0.5 mile to Camel Gap Trail at Campsite 36 (horse campers only). On Camel Gap Trail you go about 0.6 mile and turn left onto Gunter Fork Trail, making a crossing of Big Creek (dangerous or impassable in high water). At about 1.5 miles on Gunter Fork Trail, you pass a pretty cascade on the right; at 1.8 miles you reach a long, sliding cascade known as Gunter Fork Falls. Back-track to Walnut Bottoms from here for a day hike of about 5.8 miles.

A more ambitious plan is to make a day-hike loop that takes you over Cosby Knob on the Appalachian Trail (AT). For this hike you climb Low Gap Trail, which leads from Campsite 37, to the Appalachian Trail in 2.5 miles. Turn left onto the AT, and hike about 2.4 miles to Camel Gap, skirting the summit of Cosby Knob along the way. At Camel Gap turn left onto Camel Gap Trail and follow it 4.7 miles down to Big Creek Trail, 0.5 mile above your campsite. Total round-trip for the hike is 10.1 miles, making for a good workout considering the grade.

Another option is to use Campsite 37 as only the first night's stay on a longer backpacking trip. Hike 79: Big Creek and Mt. Sterling outlines that option.

Big Creek and Mt. Sterling

Highlights: *Waterfall, Big Creek cascades, wildflowers, spectacular views, moss, old-growth forest*
(See map for Hike 77: Mt. Sterling.)

Type of hike: Loop; two-night backpack or strenuous overnighter
Total distance: 17.4 miles round-trip

Difficulty: Difficult
Maps: Trails Illustrated; USGS Luftee Knob and Cove Creek Gap

Special considerations: The two campsites on this hike are popular. Make your reservation as early as possible, and be prepared with alternative dates when you call.

Finding the trailhead: Take the Waterville exit (exit 457) off Interstate 40 and cross the Pigeon River. Stay to the left after the crossing and follow the road 2.0 miles to an intersection, passing the Walters Power Plant and Mountain Mama's on the way. The intersection marks the community of Mount Sterling. Go straight, and enter the Big Creek section of the park. Follow the road 0.8 mile to where it ends at the picnic area and walk-in campground. The trail begins to the right, just before you reach the parking area.

Parking and trailhead facilities: Parking space is rarely a problem. A new rest room building is at the parking area, but it is closed in winter. Portable toilets are available when the rest rooms are closed. Mountain Mama's, which you passed on the way, has just about anything you need in the way of supplies, plus a short-order grill. It's open daily except for Monday and Tuesday during winter.

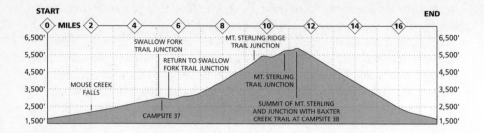

Key points:

2.0 Mouse Creek Falls.

5.1 Junction with Swallow Fork Trail.

5.3 Campsite 37.

5.5 Return to junction with Swallow Fork Trail.

9.5 Junction with Mt. Sterling Ridge Trail.

10.9 Junction with Mt. Sterling Trail.

11.3 Campsite 38 and junction with Baxter Creek Trail on the summit of Mt. Sterling.

The hike: Remember that commercial where those guys are sitting around the campfire drinking beer and one of them says, "You know, it just doesn't get any better than this"? Well, he could have been talking about this hike. It may be the best two-night backpacking trip in the park, even without the beer. It offers everything the Smokies are famous for except historical structures, and while it's popular among backpackers, the summer crowds thin out after the first few miles. On winter weekdays—my favorite time to take this trip—it's possible to hike the entire loop without seeing another person.

Two other hikes in this guidebook cover sections of the hike described here, and you need to read both of them in conjunction with this one: Big Creek (Hike 78) and Mount Sterling (Hike 77).

The first 5.3 miles are easy, following an old roadbed along Big Creek to Campsite 37 at Walnut Bottom, the site of a prepark logging operation. Today it's one of the most appealing backcountry campsites in the park, and it's your first night's stay unless you decide to go for Mt. Sterling in a day. Two-tenths of a mile before reaching Campsite 37, you pass Swallow Fork Trail on the left.

Take the Swallow Fork Trail and climb gradually, crossing a couple of tributaries on the way to Swallow Fork. Cross the fork at 1.0 mile on a foot log over a particularly scenic section. Soon after this crossing, you cross McGinty Creek and pass several old artifacts on the left. There are steel hoops and cables and a metal drum that once served as a belt drive for something (probably a sawmill).

Now climb alongside the tumbling Swallow Fork. In April this is a great wildflower walk. About a mile above McGinty Creek, you make the final stream

Water source for campers on Mt. Sterling.

crossing and begin a fairly steep push to Pretty Hollow Gap. At the gap Mt. Sterling Ridge Trail goes right and left, and Pretty Hollow Gap Trail goes straight ahead, descending to Cataloochee Cove.

Pretty Hollow Gap, like many similar areas in the Smokies, suffers from heavy wild hog damage. The nonnative hogs cause severe damage in the park because they root up the ground. If you see an area that looks as though a rototiller has gone through it, that's the mark of a wild hog. The animals are descendants from true European wild boars that escaped from a game preserve outside the park in the early 1920s. The boars interbred with domestic feral pigs, and the resulting offspring have been causing trouble ever since.

Turn left (east) onto Mt. Sterling Ridge Trail. The first 0.5 mile ascends steeply to cross a knoll in a particularly beautiful forest of spruce, birch, and beech. You soon begin ascending again and merge into Mt. Sterling Trail, coming in from the right. It's 0.4 mile to the summit of Mt. Sterling and Campsite 38. This is your second night's stay, and if the weather is typical, this will be a memorable camping experience. It's often very cold and very windy up here.

The steel fire tower at the summit is open for climbing and is a highlight of the hike. When the wind howls, it's a little frightening climbing to the top, but you need to get above the trees at least. The panoramic view is among the finest in the park.

Baxter Creek Trail starts on the summit of Mt. Sterling by the base of the tower. The trail descends steadily (sometimes steeply) to the Big Creek Picnic Area in 6.1 miles. Take this trail, but don't be in a hurry—the scenery is superb. About 0.25 mile down, you come to a signed side path on the left that leads in several hundred feet to a reliable spring. On the main trail, hike along a ridge and through switchbacks in a boulder field. Lush, thick moss covers every ground surface you see. This stretch—like no other place in the park—reminds me of a southeast Alaska rain forest.

About 2 miles from Mt. Sterling, you make an extreme left switchback off the ridgeline and enter an enchanted old-growth forest with several species of trees. Look all around through here but especially above the trail toward the ridge, where some gigantic gnarly maples grow. A little ways down, you pass several large American chestnut trunks and a huge stump on the right.

Farther down you cross a tributary and soon begin paralleling Baxter Creek. A number of large hemlocks and yellow-poplars grow in this scenic, open forest. After crossing Baxter Creek, you pass through a dense stand of second-growth yellow-poplar and soon reach the bridge over Big Creek. The picnic area is on the far side.

Options: Experienced hikers can make it to Mt. Sterling in a day, but it's a killer hike that I don't recommend. It's better to take your time and enjoy the scenery.

80 Big Creek Perimeter Loop

Highlights: *Grand views, high-elevation forest, old-growth forest, fire tower and lookout*

Type of hike: Loop; three- or four-night backpack
Total distance: 34.0 miles round-trip
Difficulty: Difficult
Best time of year: Winter

Maps: Trails Illustrated; USGS Waterville, Hartford, Luftee Knob, Mt. Guyot, and Cove Creek Gap (parts of the route not shown)

Special considerations: The shelters and campsite on this hike are popular. Make your reservation as early as possible, and be prepared with alternative dates when you call. Although the first night's stay on this hike is only 8.4 miles from the trailhead, it's a tough climb. Experienced hikers can make it in four or five hours without pushing themselves, but inexperienced hikers need to head out early in the morning and plan on an all-day hike.

Finding the trailhead: Take the Waterville exit (exit 457) off Interstate 40 and cross the Pigeon River. Stay to the left after the crossing and follow the road 2.0 miles to an intersection, passing the Walters Power Plant and Mountain Mama's on the way. The intersection marks the community of Mount Sterling. Go straight, and enter the Big Creek section of the park. Follow the road 0.2 mile to the ranger station and parking area on the right. The Chestnut Branch Trail begins about 200 feet farther up the road, on the right.

Parking and trailhead facilities: Parking space is never a problem here. The picnic area that is 0.6 mile farther along the road has a new rest room building. In winter portable toilets are available, including one at this parking area. Mountain Mama's, which you passed on the way, has just about anything you need in the way of supplies, plus a short-order grill. It's open daily except for Monday and Tuesday during winter.

Key points:
- **2.1** Junction with Appalachian Trail.
- **3.0** Junction with Lower Mt. Cammerer Trail.
- **5.3** Junction with Mt. Cammerer Trail.
- **7.4** Junction with Low Gap Trail at Low Gap.
- **8.2** Side path to Cosby Knob Shelter.
- **9.8** Junction with Camel Gap Trail.
- **12.1** Junction with Snake Den Ridge Trail.
- **15.8** Tricorner Knob Shelter and junction with Balsam Mountain Trail.

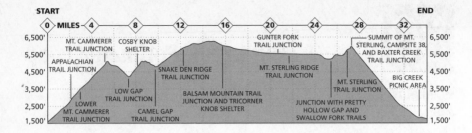

20.7   Junction with Gunter Fork Trail.

21.6   Junction with Mt. Sterling Ridge Trail. Laurel Gap Shelter is 0.2 mile off route.

25.5   Junction with Pretty Hollow Gap and Swallow Fork Trails.

26.9   Junction with Mt. Sterling Trail.

27.3   Campsite 38 and junction with Baxter Creek Trail on the summit of Mt. Sterling.

33.4   Big Creek Picnic Area and campground entrance.

The hike: Hike 79: Big Creek and Mt. Sterling is one of the best two-night backpacks in the park. The hike outlined here, which follows a portion of that hike's route, is among the finest *three*-night backpacks in the park. It follows high mountain crests as it loops around the entire Big Creek drainage. The high-elevation forests are dark and mysterious, even with the disheartening death of trees from introduced pests and acid rain.

The best time to make this hike is in winter and during the week. It can be frigid and even frightening, but you will have an experience that few people do—one you will never forget. If you do choose a winter hike, you need to make a frank assessment of your backpacking abilities and prepare for polar conditions. The last time I made this trek, I left the trailhead with temperatures in the upper 50s. By the time I got to Tricorner Knob Shelter the next day, I was wading through 6 inches of snow in single-digit temperatures.

Begin ascending Chestnut Branch Trail alongside Chestnut Branch on an old logging grade. You pass a huge oak tree on the left that somehow escaped the logger's ax. Several families once lived along Chestnut Branch; perhaps this tree was part of their holdings. You can see signs of settlement along the lower portion of the hike. Except for one decent stretch, it's a steady climb all the way to the Appalachian Trail (AT).

Reach the AT at a small gap. To the right it's only 1.9 miles to Davenport Gap and the eastern trailhead for the Smokies portion of the Appalachian Trail. If you had started there, you would have added considerably more than the 0.6 mile of road walking that's included in the route outlined here. This hike is much more "loop friendly."

Turn left (southwest) onto the AT and make a continuous ascent to Lower Mt. Cammerer Trail on the right. Continue climbing on the AT and pass through a boulder field on switchbacks. Ferns and mosses cover the rocks, and varieties of wildflowers grow among them. At an outside switchback around a ridge, you have the first open view, this one toward the northeast. Now the trail becomes even more interesting as it climbs the steep slope of Cammerer Ridge through rhododendron and by rock walls. You soon come to another outside turn at a rock outcrop. From this outcrop are commanding views into the Pigeon River Valley and the Big Creek watershed. As good as this view is, it's just a tease for what's ahead.

Continue climbing and reach a tiny gap where the Mt. Cammerer Trail cuts sharply back to the right (north). If you think you can add 1.2 miles to your hike and still make it to Cosby Knob Shelter before dark, you definitely should take this side trip. The trail leads 0.6 mile along the ridge to the Mt. Cammerer Lookout. (The term "lookout" typically refers to observation structures that are at or near ground level, while "tower," as in Mt. Sterling Tower, refers to structures built to rise above the trees.) The Civilian Conservation Corps built the fire lookout in the 1930s, using the same design as the lookouts on the treeless and rocky mountains of the western states. After falling in disrepair, the lookout was restored in 1995 and is now open for day hikers to enjoy.

The view from the lookout is outstanding, but study carefully the view from the southwest to the southeast. That ridgeline you see is the one you will follow on the third day of the hike. Look southeast across the Big Creek watershed to the tower rising above the trees. That's the Mt. Sterling Fire Tower. At its base is Campsite 38, your third night's home. Yep, you've got a haul ahead of you.

Back on the AT, continue heading south on a mostly downhill stretch to Low Gap and the junction with Low Gap Trail. Low Gap Trail crosses here, having climbed from Cosby Campground to the right and Walnut Bottoms to the left. Continue straight on the AT and climb steadily 0.8 mile to a side path on the left leading in a few hundred feet to Cosby Knob Shelter. The shelter is your first night's stay.

Pressing on from the shelter, climb through a particularly scenic forest of spruce, hemlock, and rhododendron as you skirt the summit of Cosby Knob. Soon begin a long descent to Camel Gap and the junction with Camel Gap Trail, forking off to the left. Continue to the right on the AT, and begin a long steady ascent of 2.3 miles to another fork. Snake Den Ridge Trail goes to the right here, while our trail goes left and (you guessed it) continues climbing.

As you climb from the junction with Snake Den Ridge Trail, you might spot pieces of wreckage from an Air Force jet that crashed into Inadu Knob on the evening of January 4, 1984. According to the book *Mayday! Mayday!* by Jeff Wadley and Dwight McCarter, the jet was flying 450 miles per hour when it hit the mountain just 80 feet short of the summit. The impact created the largest crash site in the Smokies, at nearly twenty acres. Pieces of the plane are supposedly clearly visible to hikers along this stretch, but when I hiked it snow covered everything. I did see a heavy chunk of an airplane leaning against the

Pigeon River

40

Mount Sterling

284

284

LONG BUNK TRAIL

284

T

Mount Sterling

80

BAXTER

Mt. Sterling

MT. STERLING TRAIL

PRETTY HOLLOW GAP TRAIL

Davenport Gap Shelter

80

Big Creek Ranger Station

CHESTNUT BRANCH TRAIL

TRAIL

CREEK

Campsite 38

Big Creek Campground & Picnic Area

Mouse Creek Falls

Big Creek

CREEK

Swallow Fork

RIDGE

Mt. Cammerer

BIG

SWALLOW FORK TRAIL

MT. STERLING

LOWER MT. CAMMERER TRAIL

MT. CAMMERER TRAIL

SWALLOW

FORK

Cosby Knob Shelter

Campsite 37

Campsite 36

GREAT SMOKY MOUNTAINS NATIONAL PARK

GAP

TRAIL

FORK TRAIL

COSBY NATURE TRAIL

LOW

CAMEL GAP TRAIL

Gunter Fork

GUNTHER

80

Laurel Gap Shelter

To 321

TRAIL

APPALACHIAN

Big Creek

Gunter Fork Cascade

Cosby Campground

TENNESSEE

RIDGE

NORTH CAROLINA

BALSAM MOUNTAIN TRAIL

Hen Wallow Falls

Campsite 34

SNAKE

DEN

TRAIL

Mt. Guyot

80

N

Tricorner Knob Shelter

321

GABES MOUNTAIN TRAIL

Campsite 29

APPALACHIAN TRAIL

MADDRON

ALBRIGHT GROVE LOOP TRAIL

BALD

TRAIL

APPALACHIAN

Kilometer 0 2

Mile 0 2

Cosby Knob Shelter, but if it's from this crash site, the person who lugged it that far has my sympathy.

Finally you top out on a grassy ridge with a great view ahead of Mt. Guyot and Old Black. Continue though an open area and pass over a helicopter landing pad before entering the forest again. The AT skirts the summit of Old Black (6,370 feet) and then crosses a couple of good springs as it skirts the summit of Mt. Guyot—at 6,621 feet, the second-highest mountain in the park. As you skirt some 300 feet below the summit, you pass through a tangle of dead and fallen Fraser fir.

After you reach Balsam Mountain Trail on the left, continue on the AT a short distance to the side path on the left that leads to Tricorner Knob Shelter, one of the most remote shelters in the park. This is where you will sleep tonight. The next morning, walk back up to the Balsam Mountain Trail and turn right onto it.

After the hike you just made on the AT, you're going to enjoy the next 9.7 miles. Except for a few short spurts, it's nearly level the entire distance. The first 5.8 miles take you on a heavily overgrown course to Mt. Sterling Ridge Trail, on the left. (You pass Gunter Fork Trail at 4.9 miles; go right (southeast) to stay on Balsam Mountain Trail.) At the Mt. Sterling Ridge Trail junction, Balsam Mountain Trail continues 0.2 mile to Laurel Gap Shelter. If you planned this trip as a four-nighter, the shelter is your third night's stay. Most hikers will want to hike straight through from Tricorner Knob to Mt. Sterling in a day, a distance of 11.5 miles.

Now on the Mt. Sterling Ridge Trail, the level hiking continues. For some 3.0 miles you hardly leave the contour line as you pass through a rather uneventful forest. You cross a number of headwater branches in this segment, a few of them surprisingly large for this elevation. Leaving the contour line, you enter a scenic, open birch forest and begin an undulating course before descending to Pretty Hollow Gap. The gap marks the junction with Swallow Fork and Pretty Hollow Gap Trails.

The next part of the hike that takes you to Mt. Sterling and back down the mountain is covered in detail in Hike 79: Big Creek and Mt. Sterling and Hike 77: Mt. Sterling. Refer to those narratives for the remainder of this trip. Once you arrive at the Big Creek Picnic Area, walk along the gravel road 0.6 mile to the ranger station and parking area.

Options: Combining the hikes and trails described in the Big Creek and Cosby section of the park—and utilizing shuttles—affords unlimited backpacking possibilities. A number of additional loop hikes exist if you want to make an extended hike. Study a trail map for possibilities.

The Appalachian TRAIL

The Appalachian Trail (AT) needs no introduction to most people in the East. The more than 2,100-mile trail stretches from Springer Mountain, Georgia, to Mt. Katahdin, Maine, passing through myriad natural and modern communities and, in the process, touching on many people's lives. The 71-some miles of the trail that pass through the Smokies are considered by some to be a major highlight of the trail. The Smokies portion has the highest single elevation (Clingmans Dome, at 6,642 feet) on the trail, and most of the trail follows high on the Smokies crest, along the state-line divide between North Carolina and Tennessee, where views abound.

I suppose it's no wonder that the AT is immensely popular in the park, but it's a shame that more people don't seek out other hiking opportunities. Certain portions of the AT are very crowded. Many people who plan trips to the park start out with the idea that they want to hike the Appalachian Trail, no matter what. If they did a little more research, they might find that another trail suited their desires a little better. I don't mean to discourage you from hiking the AT—far from it. I just want to remind you that of the more than 800 miles of trail in the park, the AT accounts for less than 10 percent.

If you do decide to hike the AT, you need to consider a few things. First, although spring is a great time to hike the trail, it's not a good time to overnight at an Appalachian Trail shelter because of all the thru-hikers (people who attempt to hike the entire trail from Georgia to Maine). On any given night from March through May, AT shelters in the park could be crammed with backpackers. On some nights the motley gathering could be dubbed *The Great Smoky Mountains National Park Philharmonic Snorechestra*, and the shelter might be called a "Backcountry Snoratorium." And that's not even getting to the issue of trying to crawl over a dozen hikers to make a nature call, or the fact that none of them has had a bath in a while. If the park was located farther north, it wouldn't be as big a problem. As it is, the park is so close to the southern terminus of the AT that most of the people who attempt a thru-hike haven't yet given up.

Reservations, which you must obtain to camp at any park shelter, don't help during this time of year. AT thru-hikers aren't required to make reservations because it's so difficult to determine exact schedules. Park rules state that thru-hikers must give up bunk space to reservation holders, but who is going to wave a little piece of paper at a group of exhausted backpackers and tell them they have to get out? Your best bet is to plan overnight hikes on the AT for another season.

Another consideration for hiking the AT in the Smokies is the weather. Many parts of the trail are above 5,000 feet in elevation. You can leave warm, sunny skies in Cherokee or Gatlinburg and arrive at Newfound Gap in a snowstorm. Winter hiking on the AT requires a lot of planning—and a frank evaluation of your abilities.

This guidebook doesn't follow the route that thru-hikers use. Spring thru-hikers start at Fontana Dam and hike straight through to Davenport Gap. Rather than beginning at the low elevations outside the park and hiking in, the AT hikes in this guidebook start at Newfound Gap, at 5,046 feet, and head east and west to the park borders. You still have a lot of climbing to do, but not nearly as much.

81

Appalachian Trail West

Highlights: *Incomparable views, old-growth forests, wildflowers*

Type of hike: Shuttle; two- to four-night backpack
Total distance: 38.9 miles one-way
Difficulty: Difficult
Best time of year: October or November

Maps: Trails Illustrated; USGS Clingmans Dome, Silers Bald, Thunderhead Mountain, Cades Cove, and Fontana Dam

Special considerations: Read the introduction to this chapter for general considerations. In very dry periods, the springs at Russell Field and Mollies Ridge Shelters can dry up. It's a good idea to talk with the hikers you meet about the water situation so that you know whether to fill up when you have the chance rather than wait and find a dry spring. For information on spring status, call the backcountry reservation office (865–436–1231), although they don't always have the latest update.

Finding the trailhead: Drive to Newfound Gap on the Smokies crest, and park in the large parking lot. The trail begins at the entrance to the parking area and crosses Newfound Gap Road at the painted crosswalk, heading northwest.

You need to leave a second vehicle or arrange for a shuttle to pick you up at Fontana Dam. From the junction of U.S. 19/74 and North Carolina Highway 28 in the southwestern portion of the park, turn west onto NC 28 and go 21.1 miles to the stop sign at the entrance road for Fontana Dam. Turn right and follow the road 1.1 miles to the dam. Drive over the dam and turn right at the fork. Continue 0.7 mile to the road's end at a trail information board.

Parking and trailhead facilities: Newfound Gap has a large parking area, but it can fill up on summer weekends. Rest rooms are available here.

The Fontana Dam Visitor Center, near where you end this hike, has free hot showers that are open twenty-four hours a day. That's something to think about as you sweat along the trail.

Key points:
1.7 Junction with Road Prong Trail at Indian Gap.
4.2 Side trail on left leads to Clingmans Dome Road and Fork Ridge trailhead.
4.5 Junction with Sugarland Mountain Trail on right. Mt. Collins Shelter is 0.4 mile on Sugarland Mountain Trail.
8.0 Summit of Clingmans Dome. Short spur leads to observation tower.
8.3 Junction with Clingmans Dome Bypass Trail.

Appalachian Trail West

10.2 Junction with Goshen Prong Trail.

10.8 Double Spring Gap Shelter.

12.1 Junction with Welch Ridge Trail.

12.3 Silers Bald.

12.5 Silers Bald Shelter.

15.3 Junction with Miry Ridge Trail.

17.7 Junction with Greenbrier Ridge Trail.

18.1 Derrick Knob Shelter.

22.5 Summit of Thunderhead Mountain.

23.2 Rocky Top.

23.9 Junction with Jenkins Ridge Trail.

24.3 Junction with Bote Mountain Trail.

24.4 Junction with Eagle Creek Trail. Spence Field Shelter is 0.2 mile on Eagle Creek Trail.

26.9 Junction with Russell Field Trail at Russell Field Shelter.

29.5 Mollies Ridge Shelter.

32.0 Junction with Gregory Bald Trail.

34.2 Birch Spring Backcountry Campsite (the shelter no longer stands).

35.1 Junction with Lost Cove and Twentymile Trails at Sassafras Gap.

35.5 Side trail to Shuckstack Tower.

38.9 Parking at end of road from Fontana Dam. Lakeshore Trail starts here.

The hike: Sections of this hike are covered in other hikes in this guidebook (indicated in the text), and there is no shortage of literature about the Appalachian Trail (AT). What I've tried to do here is provide a concise outline of key points and alert you to any potential concerns along the way.

A good time to make this trip is in October or November, when the crowds have thinned. In October there will be crowds from Clingmans Dome to Silers Bald and in the Spence Field area, but most of the "leaf peepers" don't get out of their car. This time of year has another advantage in that there is less smog affecting the views. You also miss the heat of summer, which is good on a hike that has no streams to dip into, but you have to be prepared for cold weather. Snow is common in November, and you should expect it in October.

Cross Newfound Gap Road (if the traffic slows down enough to let you) and enter a different world. The last time I hiked this stretch was on a Sunday, the

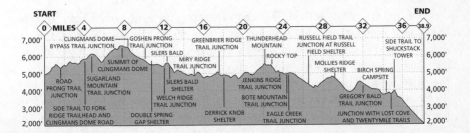

271

week before July 4. I left scads of people at Newfound Gap and met only four people over the next 8 miles of trail.

The 8 miles from Newfound Gap to Clingmans Dome follow the road closely; the grumbling of loud mufflers is rarely out of earshot. The first part of the hike is relatively easy. Come to a hog exclosure with a unique ramp system allowing hikers to pass through. Hog hoofs can't make it up the ramp; hiking boots have no trouble unless it's icy. Descend to Indian Gap and the junction with Road Prong Trail and a parking area. The USGS Clingmans Dome map does not give a name for this gap and names the previous gap you hiked through "Indian Gap." The Trails Illustrated map calls the gap here "Little Indian Gap." However, every other reference I've seen refers to this gap as Indian Gap.

Continue straight from the gap and climb steeply. Crest out in a dark forest of young spruce and fir. This spot provides a hint of what the great spruce-fir forests must have looked like before the advent of the balsam woolly adelgid and acid rain. Imagine what this forest would look like with all the trees being 2 to 3 feet in diameter.

Now go on a long and very scenic stretch where the trail passes through a dense, lush, closed-in forest. There are ups and downs typical of the AT, but the grade is not too bad. A spur path on the left leads in a short distance to Clingmans Dome Road and the Fork Ridge trailhead. Notice the uprooted trees here. Life is hard in the cold and wind of these elevations—hard enough without the extra burden of introduced pests and air pollution.

From the spur path, continue southwest on the AT and reach the junction with Sugarland Mountain Trail, on the right. A 0.4-mile easy walk on this trail takes you to the Mt. Collins Shelter. The AT continues south on a typical undulating course. In summer look for Turk's cap lily growing in patches beside the trail. A long, steady ascent heralds the approach to Clingmans Dome. The trail passes within a few yards of the lookout tower. On a clear day, a side trip up the tower is a must. Fortunately, you don't have to walk on the paved path that leads from the Forney Ridge parking area to the tower. Scoot up the tower, soak in the views, and get back to your dirt and rocks.

Just beyond the tower, you come to another spur on the left, this one connecting with the paved path. Stay to the right (west) on the AT and soon reach the junction with Clingmans Dome Bypass Trail. The next 4.2 miles from this point to Silers Bald Shelter are covered in Hike 54: Silers Bald and Forney Creek. Refer to it for this section.

The trail from Silers Bald Shelter to the junction with Miry Ridge Trail is the typical undulating ridge walking characteristic of the AT. By now you've surely noticed that you left the spruce and fir trees back at the higher elevations and are in a mixed-hardwood forest, with maple, silverbell, and black cherry. At the Miry Ridge Trail junction, continue straight on the AT and climb steeply up Cold Spring Knob. After topping out, it's a mostly easy hike to the Greenbrier Ridge Trail junction. The 2.4-mile segment from Miry Ridge Trail to

Looking toward Thunderhead Mountain from Clingmans Dome.

Greenbrier Ridge Trail is detailed in Hike 16: Lynn Camp Prong and Appalachian Trail.

From Greenbrier Ridge Trail continue straight (as usual) on the AT and climb Big Chestnut Bald before leveling out to Derrick Knob Shelter. This shelter has one of the most scenic settings of any in the park. In summer, coneflower and snakeroot cover the open field in front of the shelter. From the shelter it's a short and easy climb over a knoll, then a nearly continuous descent to Sugartree Gap, marked by sugar maples and an American chestnut log that makes a great seat. From Sugartree Gap climb steeply and then descend to Starkey Gap, also featuring a chestnut sitting log.

From Starkey Gap you make a brutal ascent up Brier Knob, perhaps the most strenuous segment on the Smokies portion of the AT. The elevation of Starkey Gap is 4,527 feet. On the peak of Brier Knob, a little more than 0.5 mile farther, it's 5,215 feet. Beyond Brier Knob you soon come to an open area with views and then descend dangerously over rocks. From here you go on a fairly easy stretch, a steep descent, a short climb, and then an easy ridgeline walk to a gap. A small sign on a cherry tree says WATER, indicating that a small spring lies a short distance down the north side of the gap.

From the gap you proceed on a long (but not too steep) climb to the summit of Thunderhead Mountain (5,527 feet). Thunderhead is the highest peak in the western portion of the park and dominates views from all directions. Unfortunately there are no views from the mountain itself. From the top of a small pile of rocks, there is a fair view to the south and west, but that's it.

A short distance from the summit of Thunderhead, the trail opens into a grassy clearing with great views to the south and west. A good portion of Cades Cove is plainly visible. After a quick descent, you climb on a rocky knoll and enjoy more great views. The view straight down is of graffiti-covered rocks. The graffiti does have historical value in that some of the markings were made by early livestock herders in the late nineteenth and early twentieth centuries. It's a shame that modern hikers sometimes add their mark as well. Continuing along the rocky ridge, you reach the official Rocky Top (according to the USGS map) and its nearly panoramic views. What a special place this is!

From Rocky Top descend steeply to a gap and then climb steeply over a knoll and to the junction with Jenkins Ridge Trail, cutting sharply to the left. You're in Spence Field now, and you will be for the next 0.75 mile or so. Cross a small knoll and descend a short distance to the junction with Bote Mountain Trail on the right and, a few hundred feet farther, Eagle Creek Trail on the left. A 0.2-mile hike down Eagle Creek Trail takes you to Spence Field Shelter. Spence Field, and the segment of the AT from Bote Mountain Trail to Russell Field Trail, is covered in Hike 20: Spence Field via Cades Cove. Refer to that hike for more details.

From Spence Field it's an easy 2.5-mile walk to Russell Field Trail at the Russell Field Shelter. On leaving Russell Field Shelter, the AT goes through rerouted sections that take a lot of the steepness out of the old route (the Cades Cove topo map is outdated). The trail makes an easy descent to Little Abrams Gap, then it begins a long climb before making a short descent to Mollies Ridge Shelter. The shelter sits on a ridge (where else?) in a pleasant open forest of maple, buckeye, and black cherry.

From Mollies Ridge Shelter you go on a long descent to Ekaneetlee Gap. A side path leads off the right (north) side of the gap to a small spring. From the gap you make a long, moderate ascent up Doe Knob, skirting just short of the summit. A quick dip leads to the junction with Gregory Bald Trail. This time you don't continue straight. Gregory Bald Trail does that, continuing to follow the state-line ridge, as did the Appalachian Trail at one time before a reroute took it across Fontana Dam. You need to turn left (south) to stay on the AT.

The 2.2-mile segment from Doe Knob to Birch Spring Gap is downhill, with just enough bumps to keep you from getting lazy. At the gap a sign directs you to Birch Spring Campsite 113, off the right side of the trail. Walk 0.1 mile down the path to the most unique backcountry campsite in the Smokies. At other campsites you find a place for your tent in the clearings wherever you can. At Birch Spring the spots are carefully chosen for you. Scattered along the paths that lead on both sides of the drainage are level tent pads carved into the slope, with timbers from the old shelter (no longer standing) used as retaining walls. Each site is far enough away from the others to offer privacy but close to the central spring and campfire ring. Individual campfires are prohibited. Most of the stone from the old shelter now creates a network of terraces. If you want a souvenir from the shelter, grab a chunk of concrete from the pile, but leave the stones.

From Birch Spring Gap you follow a typical undulating course to reach Sassafras Gap and the junction with Lost Cove and Twentymile Trails. The segment of the AT from here to the trailhead is covered in detail in Hike 61: Shuckstack. Refer to it in reverse for the remainder of the hike.

Options: Most people will want to do this hike as a three-nighter. You can stretch it out as far as you want, but four nights is the most that you can take and not start feeling lazy. Of course, if a lazy outing is what you want, go for it. A two-nighter is certainly doable. When I made this hike I left Newfound Gap at noon on a Sunday and hiked to Double Spring Gap Shelter for the first night. The second night I stayed at Spence Field Shelter, and on Tuesday I made it to the truck around 3:00 P.M. I was cramming hikes in, though, and I'd recommend adding a third night.

Experienced, hard-core hikers can make the trip as an overnighter if they leave early in the morning from Newfound Gap. Some AT thru-hikers do this stretch as an overnighter, having rested and fattened up in Fontana Village before entering the park.

Study a trail map for possibilities. The shelters are spaced well enough that you should have no trouble planning a trip to suit your needs.

Appalachian Trail East

Highlights: *Incomparable views, old-growth forests, wildflowers*

Type of hike: Shuttle; two- to four-night backpack
Total distance: 31.5 miles one-way
Difficulty: Difficult
Best time of year: October or November

Maps: Trails Illustrated; USGS Clingmans Dome, Mt. LeConte, Mt. Guyot, Luftee Knob, Hartford, and Waterville

Special considerations: Read the introduction to this chapter for general considerations. This hike outlines the entire eastern stretch of the Appalachian Trail (AT) from Newfound Gap to Davenport Gap, but if you plan to hike all of it, you may want to consider ending at the Big Creek Ranger Station instead of Davenport Gap. Your vehicle will be safer at the ranger station than at the gap. Dropping off the AT 1.9 miles short of the gap and hiking 2.1 miles down Chestnut Branch Trail adds only 0.2 mile to the total distance. If you're determined to hike all this section of the AT, you could still leave your car at the ranger station and walk an extra 1.3 miles along the road.

Finding the trailhead: Drive to Newfound Gap on the Smokies crest, and park in the large parking lot. The trail begins at the northeastern end of the parking area, between the path leading to the rest rooms and the Rockefeller Memorial.

You need to leave a second vehicle or arrange for a shuttle to pick you up at either Davenport Gap or Big Creek Ranger Station. Take the Waterville exit (exit 457) off Interstate 40 and cross the Pigeon River. Stay to the left after the crossing and follow the road 2.0 miles to an intersection, passing the Walters Power Plant and Mountain Mama's on the way. The intersection marks the community of Mount Sterling. For the ranger station, go straight and enter the Big Creek section of the park. Follow the road 0.2 mile to the ranger station and parking area on the right. For Davenport Gap, turn right at the intersection and drive 1.1 miles. There is no parking lot here, just a wide spot beside the road.

Parking and trailhead facilities: Newfound Gap has a large parking area, but it can fill up on summer weekends. Rest rooms are available here.

Key points:
- **1.7** Junction with Sweat Heifer Creek Trail.
- **2.7** Junction with The Boulevard Trail.
- **3.0** Icewater Spring Shelter.
- **4.0** Side path to Charlies Bunion.
- **4.4** Junction with Dry Sluice Gap Trail.
- **10.5** Junction with Hughes Ridge Trail. Pecks Corner Shelter is 0.4 on Hughes Ridge Trail.
- **15.8** Tricorner Knob Shelter and junction with Balsam Mountain Trail.
- **19.6** Junction with Snake Den Ridge Trail.
- **21.9** Junction with Camel Gap Trail.
- **23.5** Side path to Cosby Knob Shelter.
- **24.3** Junction with Low Gap Trail.
- **26.4** Junction with Mt. Cammerer Trail.
- **28.7** Junction with Lower Mt. Cammerer Trail.
- **29.6** Junction with Chestnut Branch Trail.
- **30.6** Side path to Davenport Gap Shelter.
- **31.5** Davenport Gap.

The hike: Sections of this hike are covered in other hikes in this guidebook (indicated in the text), and there is no shortage of literature about the Appalachian Trail in the Smokies. What I've tried to do here is provide a listing of key points and alert you to any potential concerns along the way.

A good time to make this trip is in October or November, when the crowds have thinned. In October there will be heavy crowds from Newfound Gap to

Appalachian Trail East

Map showing the Appalachian Trail East through Great Smoky Mountains National Park, spanning Tennessee and North Carolina.

Labeled features include:

To Asheville, To Knoxville, 40, 32, 321, 284, 441, Clingmans Dome Road, To Gatlinburg, To Cherokee

Davenport Gap, Davenport Gap Shelter, Mt. Sterling, Big Creek Ranger Station, Big Creek Campground & Picnic Area, Chestnut Branch Trail, Big Creek Trail, Mt. Sterling, Baxter Creek Trail, Pretty Hollow Gap Trail, Mt. Sterling Ridge Trail

Cammerer Mt. Trail, Lower Mt. Cammerer Trail, Mt. Cammerer, Cosby Knob Shelter, Low Gap Trail, Snake Den Ridge Trail, Gabes Mountain Trail, Camel Gap Trail, Appalachian Trail, Maddron Bald Trail, Mt. Guyot, Balsam Mountain Trail, Tricorner Knob Shelter, Mt. Sterling Ridge Trail

Old Settlers Trail, Ramsay Cascades Trail, Great Smoky Mountains National Park, Mt. Chapman, Eagle Rocks, Pecks Corner Shelter, Hughes Ridge Trail

Greybard Ridge Trail, Brushy Mountain Trail, Grapeyard Ridge Trail, Trillium Gap Trail, The Boulevard Trail, Laurel Top, Appalachian Trail, Dry Sluice Gap Trail, Kephart Prong Trail, Sweat Heifer Creek Trail

Mt. LeConte, Alum Cave Trail, Appalachian Trail West, Charlies Bunion, Icewater Spring Shelter, Newfound Gap, Newfound Gap Road, Road Prong Trail, Mt. Collins Shelter

TENNESSEE, NORTH CAROLINA, GREAT SMOKY MOUNTAINS NATIONAL PARK

N

0 Kilometer 3
0 Mile 3

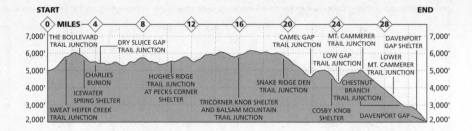

7,000' THE BOULEVARD
TRAIL JUNCTION

DRY SLUICE GAP
TRAIL JUNCTION

CAMEL GAP
TRAIL JUNCTION

MT. CAMMERER
TRAIL JUNCTION

DAVENPORT
GAP SHELTER 7,000'

6,000' 6,000'

LOW GAP
TRAIL JUNCTION

LOWER
MT. CAMMERER
TRAIL JUNCTION

5,000' CHARLIES
BUNION

HUGHES RIDGE
TRAIL JUNCTION
AT PECKS CORNER
SHELTER

SNAKE RIDGE DEN
TRAIL JUNCTION 5,000'

4,000' ICEWATER
SPRING SHELTER

CHESTNUT
BRANCH
TRAIL JUNCTION 4,000'

3,000' SWEAT HEIFER CREEK
TRAIL JUNCTION

TRICORNER KNOB SHELTER
AND BALSAM MOUNTAIN
TRAIL JUNCTION

COSBY KNOB
SHELTER

DAVENPORT GAP 3,000'

2,000' 2,000'

Charlies Bunion, but most of the "leaf peepers" don't get out of their car. This time of year has another advantage in that there is less smog affecting the views. You also miss the heat of summer, which is good on a hike that has no streams to dip into, but you have to be prepared for cold weather. Snow is common in November, and you should expect it in October.

The first 10.5 miles of the hike to Hughes Ridge Trail are covered in detail in Hike 30: Charlies Bunion and Hike 69: Charlies Bunion and Bradley Fork. Refer to the narratives for those hikes for this segment. From the junction of Hughes Ridge Trail to Tricorner Knob Shelter, the hike is on perhaps the least traveled and most remote stretch of the AT in the park. That doesn't mean you won't see other hikers; just that you might see fewer here than elsewhere on the trail. Less than a mile from Hughes Ridge Trail you come to a rock outcrop called Eagle Rocks. The view from here into the Middle Prong watershed is spectacular. Descend from Eagle Rocks to a gap and climb again to cross over Mt. Sequoyah, just below the summit. Now make a long, gradual descent before climbing again to swing around Mt. Chapman. Top out a good distance below the summit of Mt. Chapman and descend to a gap. A short climb from the gap takes you to Tricorner Knob Shelter.

The 13.8 miles from Tricorner Knob Shelter to the junction with Chestnut Branch Trail are detailed in Hike 80: Big Creek Perimeter Loop. Refer to it in reverse for this segment. If you left your vehicle at the Big Creek Ranger Station, at the junction with Chestnut Branch Trail you would turn right onto Chestnut Branch Trail and hike 2.1 miles to the ranger station. If you left your vehicle at Davenport Gap, continue on the AT. The AT is level for a short distance, then descends steeply to a side path leading to Davenport Gap Shelter. The Great Smoky Mountains Hiking Club renovated the shelter in 1998, making it (at the time) one of the finest shelters in the park. Other shelter renovations have occurred since.

From the shelter continue descending nearly a mile to Davenport Gap. If you left your vehicle at the ranger station, turn right onto North Carolina Highway 284 and walk 1.1 miles to the intersection in the community of Mount Sterling. Turn right to reenter the park, and walk 0.2 mile to the ranger station.

Options: If you're doing this hike as a two-nighter, a good plan is to leave early in the morning from Newfound Gap and hike to Pecks Corner Shelter for the first night's stay. The next day you'd hike to Cosby Knob Shelter and stay there. This is certainly doable for experienced hikers, but if you haven't been on a trail in a while, I'd recommend making it a three-nighter and staying at Icewater Spring, Pecks Corner, and Cosby Knob Shelters. On a four-nighter, you'd add Tricorner Knob Shelter.

Icewater Spring Shelter.

Appendix A: For More Information

The best source for books, maps, and miscellaneous Smokies-related items is the Great Smoky Mountains Natural History Association. As noted in Planning Your Trip, the association publishes *Smokies Guide*, a great summary of basic facts on the park. The newspaper contains information about visitor services, trip planning, updates on road and campground closures, emergency numbers, ranger-led activities, general park features, plus lots more useful information. The guide is free and available at park visitor centers and by calling the main park number at (865) 436–1200.

Membership in the association entitles you to a 15 percent discount on books and other items at park visitor centers and a subscription to three publications: *Smokies Guide;* the association's newsletter, *The Bearpaw;* and the park science bulletin, *Sightline*. Memberships start at only $25 per year. To join call (865) 436–7318.

You don't have to be a member to order publications from the association. They sell practically any book or map you could possibly want about the Smokies, including every USGS map covering the park. To receive a copy of their catalog or to place an order, call (865) 436–0120, or visit www.smokiesstore.org.

Appendix B: Further Reading

The following recommended publications are available through the Great Smoky Mountains Natural History Association (GSMNHA).

Alsop, Fred. *Birds of the Smokies*. Gatlinburg, Tenn.: GSMNHA, 1991.

Coggins, Allen R. *Place Names of the Smokies*. Gatlinburg, Tenn.: GSMNHA, 1999.

DeFoe, Don, Beth Giddens, Steve Kemp, and Kent Cave, eds. *Hiking Trails of the Smokies*. Gatlinburg, Tenn.: GSMNHA, 2001.

Dunn, Durwood. *Cades Cove, The Life and Death of a Southern Appalachian Community*. Knoxville: University of Tennessee Press, 1997.

Edgar, Kevin, ed. *Appalachian Trail Guide to Tennessee–North Carolina*. Harpers Ferry, WV: Appalachian Trail Conference, 2001.

Frome, Michael. *Strangers in High Places, The Story of the Great Smoky Mountains*. Knoxville: University of Tennessee Press, 1994.

Holland, Lance. *Fontana, A Pocket History of Appalachia*. Robbinsville, N.C.: Appalachian History Series, 2001.

Houk, Rose. *A Natural History Guide, Great Smoky Mountains National Park*. Boston: Houghton Mifflin Co., 1993.

Hubbs, Hal, Charles Maynard, and David Morris. *Waterfalls & Cascades of the Great Smoky Mountains*. Seymor, Tenn.: Panther Press, 1992.

Kemp, Steve. *Trees of the Smokies*. Gatlinburg, Tenn.: GSMNHA, 1993.

Kephart, Horace. *Our Southern Highlanders*. Knoxville: University of Tennessee Press, 1995.

Lawrence, H. Lea. *The Fly Fisherman's Guide to the Great Smoky Mountains National Park*. Nashville: Cumberland House, 1998.

Linzey, Donald W. *Mammals of Great Smoky Mountains National Park*. Granville, Ohio: McDonald & Woodward, 1995.

McCarter, Dwight and Ronald Schmidt. *Lost! A Ranger's Journal of Search and Rescue*. Yellow Springs, Ohio: Graphicom Press, 1998.

Moore, Harry L. *A Roadside Guide to the Geology of the Great Smoky Mountains National Park*. Knoxville: University of Tennessee Press, 1988.

Oliver, Duane. *Hazel Creek from Then till Now*. Maryville, Tenn.: Self-published, 1989.

Powell, Emilie Ervin. *Gracie and the Mountain*. Johnson City, Tenn.: The Overmountain Press, 1996.

Shields, A. Randolph. *The Cades Cove Story*. Gatlinburg, Tenn.: GSMNHA, 1981.

Tilley, Stephen G., and James E. Huheey. *Reptiles & Amphibians of the Smokies*. Gatlinburg, Tenn.: GSMNHA, 2001

Trout, Ed. *Historic Buildings of the Smokies*. Gatlinburg, Tenn.: GSMNHA, 1995.

White, Peter. *Wildflowers of the Smokies*. Gatlinburg, Tenn.: GSMNHA, 1996.

The following books are available through The Globe Pequot Press (888–249–7596; www.globe-pequot.com).

Blouin, Nicole, Victoria Logue, and Frank Logue. *Guide to the Blue Ridge Parkway*. Birmingham, Ala.: Menasha Ridge Press, 1998.

Blouin, Nicole, Steve Bordonaro, and Marilou Bordonaro. *Waterfalls of the Blue Ridge, Second Edition*. Birmingham, Ala.: Menasha Ridge Press, 1996.

Kirk, Don. *Fly-Fishing Guide to the Great Smoky Mountains*. Birmingham, Ala.: Menasha Ridge Press, 1997.

Kirk, Don. *Smoky Mountain Trout Fishing Guide*. Birmingham, Ala.: Menasha Ridge Press, 1995.

Logue, Victoria Steele. *Backpacking: Essential Skills to Advanced Techniques*. Birmingham, Ala.: Menasha Ridge Press, 2000.

Lord, William G. *Blue Ridge Parkway Guide—Grandfather Mountain to Great Smoky Mountains National Park*. Birmingham, Ala.: Menasha Ridge Press, 1981.

McHugh, Dick, and Mitch Moore. *Insiders' Guide to Great Smoky Mountains, Second Edition*. Guilford, Conn.: The Globe Pequot Press/Insiders, 2001.

Medina, Barbara. *Southern Appalachian Wildflowers*. Guilford, Conn.: The Globe Pequot Press/Falcon, 2002.

Molloy, Johnny. *Day and Overnight Hikes in the Great Smoky Mountains National Park, Second Edition*. Birmingham, Ala.: Menasha Ridge Press, 2001.

Molloy, Johnny. *The Best in Tent Camping—The Southern Appalachian & Smoky Mountains, Third Edition*, Birmingham, Ala.: Menasha Ridge Press, 2001.

Roark, Kelley. *Hiking Tennessee*. Guilford, Conn.: The Globe Pequot Press/Falcon, 1996.

Scott, David L., and Kay W. Scott. *Guide to the National Parks Areas Eastern States, Seventh Edition*. Guilford, Conn.: The Globe Pequot Press, 2002.

Appendix C: Hiker's Checklist

Hiking Equipment: Equipment does not have to be new or fancy (or expensive), but make sure you test everything before you leave home.

Equipment Checklist for Day Hiking:
(* = optional).

- ☐ Day pack or fanny pack
- ☐ Water bottle
- ☐ First-aid kit
- ☐ Survival kit
- ☐ Compass
- ☐ Maps
- ☐ Toilet trowel
- ☐ Toilet paper
- ☐ Sunscreen and lip lotion
- ☐ Binoculars*
- ☐ Camera and extra film*
- ☐ Flashlight and extra batteries
- ☐ Pocket knife
- ☐ Sunglasses

Added Equipment for Overnight Trips:
- ☐ Tent and waterproof fly
- ☐ Sleeping bag (20 degrees F or warmer) and stuff sack
- ☐ Sleeping pad
- ☐ Cooking pots and pot holder
- ☐ Extra water bottles
- ☐ Full-size backpack
- ☐ Cup, bowl, and eating utensils
- ☐ Lightweight camp stove and adequate fuel
- ☐ Trash compactor sacks
- ☐ Zip-locked bags
- ☐ Stuff sacks*
- ☐ Paper towels*

- ☐ Nylon cord (50 ft.)
- ☐ Small towel
- ☐ Personal toilet kit
- ☐ Notebook and pencil*

Clothing: In general, strive for natural fibers such as cotton and wool and "earth tones" instead of bright colors. Dig around in the closet for something "dull." Your wilderness partners will appreciate it. Try out the clothing before leaving home to make sure everything fits loosely without chafing. In particular, make sure your boots are broken in, lest they break you on the first day of the hike.

Clothing for Day Hiking:
- ☐ Large-brimmed hat or cap
- ☐ Sturdy hiking boots
- ☐ Light, natural-fiber or natural-synthetic blend socks (not cotton)
- ☐ Lightweight hiking shorts or long pants
- ☐ Long-sleeve or short-sleeve shirt
- ☐ Lightweight, windproof coat
- ☐ Rain gear
- ☐ Mittens or gloves

Additional Clothing for Overnight Trips:
- ☐ Warm hat (e.g., stocking cap)
- ☐ Long underwear
- ☐ Lightweight, windproof coat
- ☐ Sweater and/or insulated vest
- ☐ Long pants
- ☐ One pair of socks for each day, plus one extra pair
- ☐ Underwear
- ☐ Extra shirts
- ☐ Sandals or lightweight shoes for wearing in camp and fording streams

Food: For day hiking bring high-energy snacks for munching along the way. For overnight trips bring enough food, including high-energy snacks for munching during the day, but don't overburden yourself with too much food. Plan meals carefully, bringing just enough food, plus some emergency rations. Freeze-dried foods are the lightest and safest in bear country but expensive and not really necessary. Don't forget hot and cold drinks.

About the Author

Kevin Adams has had a lifelong love affair with nature, particularly in his home state of North Carolina. In the late 1980s he was given a camera as a birthday present. That gift set the stage for Kevin's total immersion into the outdoors and for his extensive traveling across the Southeast to photograph it. Kevin is author of three other books: *North Carolina Waterfalls*, *Wildflowers of the Southern Appalachians*, and *Waterfalls of Virginia and West Virginia*. He is an accomplished photography instructor and teaches numerous workshops and seminars throughout the year.

When he can get out of the office, Kevin enjoys hiking, of course, but also kayaking, bicycling, camping, and just gazing at the Milky Way. At home he enjoys watching reruns of the *Andy Griffith Show* with his wife, Patricia.